THE SECRETS WE HIDE

BALANCE OF POWER
BOOK 1

BERLIN WICK

This is a work of fiction. Names, characters, places, and incidents either are the product of the author's imagination or are used fictitiously. Any resemblance to actual persons, living or dead, events or locales, is entirely coincidental.

Text Copyright 2024 by Berlin Wick.

All rights reserved.

No part of this book may be reproduced, or stored in a retrieval system, or transmitted in any form or by any means, electronic, mechanical, photocopying, recording, or otherwise, without express written consent of the publisher.

A note to the reader:

The book explores themes around an open marriage, threesomes, sexual exploration, voyeurism, blindfolds and handcuffs, an obsessive husband who's madly in love with his very loyal hotwife, and a sexy billionaire side dish.

Trigger Warnings: Open marriage, consensual sharing between spouses, sexual harassment and exploitation, unwanted sexual advances, blackmail and bribery.

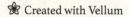 Created with Vellum

DEDICATION

To my husband, my biggest supporter and number one fan.

And to you ladies.
To those who suffer in silence out of fear and judgment.
Fuck 'em.

CONTENTS

Chapter 1 *Jake*	1
Chapter 2 *Elena*	11
Chapter 3 *Jake*	17
Chapter 4 *Elena*	23
Chapter 5 *Jake*	34
Chapter 6 *Jake*	38
Chapter 7 *Elena*	53
Chapter 8 *Elena*	64
Chapter 9 *Jake*	70
Chapter 10 *Elena*	80
Chapter 11 *Elena*	88
Chapter 12 *Jake*	102
Chapter 13 *Elena*	111
Chapter 14 *Elena*	121
Chapter 15 *Jake*	133
Chapter 16 *Elena*	141
Chapter 17 *Christian*	148
Chapter 18 *Jake*	155

Chapter 19 *Elena*	164
Chapter 20 *Elena*	169
Chapter 21 *Elena*	182
Chapter 22 *Jake*	190
Chapter 23 *Elena*	196
Chapter 24 *Christian*	204
Chapter 25 *Elena*	212
Chapter 26 *Elena*	222
Chapter 27 *Jake*	235
Chapter 28 *Elena*	242
Chapter 29 *Elena*	254
Chapter 30 *Christian*	263
Chapter 31 *Jake*	268
Chapter 32 *Elena*	273
Epilogue *Christian*	284
Extended Epilogue *Elena*	296
Thank you	299
Afterword	301
About the Author	303

1

JAKE

"Baby, what time do you want to head out?" I ask softly. I've been ready for the past hour, but my wife, on the other hand, has changed her outfit roughly seventeen times and is now circling back to the first one she tried on. We should have left an hour ago, so I know the answer will be something like "*five more minutes*" or "*I'm almost ready*", but I ask curiously because I don't have a death wish.

"Just a few more minutes. I just need to figure out what shoes I'm wearing." She paces back towards the closet, pulling her top over her head to change again.

"Sounds good. I'll just be downstairs."

If I have learned anything in the three years we've been married, it's patience. I'd wait for her forever, happily. But patience is more than a virtue in marriage. It's essential.

We met the night of my brother's bachelor party. She was getting harassed by the bartender, and I pretended to be her boyfriend to save her from his incessant pestering. The moment I laid eyes on her, I knew I wasn't leaving the bar without her in my arms. I lost myself in her that night and bailed on my brother's party, but nothing mattered from that moment on. We left the bar together, and I proposed to her on his wedding day a month later.

So needless to say, things went fast.

The first couple years of marriage were bliss. We couldn't keep our hands off each other, talked about everything easily, and the most dramatic arguments we had were over where to go to dinner on our date nights. After the second year, we fell into a bit of a rut and suddenly, there was a shift in our desires for each other. When I look back on it, I realize it wasn't an overnight change, but something that happened over the course of a few months. Life had gotten busier for both of us. She got promoted, and I started my own company. Our marriage suffered, and where she needs more intimacy, I need a physical connection. She was feeling the distance in our marriage and felt unloved, and I was feeling sexually frustrated. I started watching more porn, finding my eye wandering and pleasing myself more than necessary.

But nothing filled the void.

No one in this world does what she does to me—mentally, physically, or emotionally. She is stunning, truly breathtaking, and the most visible woman in any room. She's not your typical blue-eyed, blonde-haired bombshell. Her plump, luscious lips pair flawlessly with her high cheekbones and a perfect button nose. The girl next door with a humbled Hollywood star confidence. She's classy and sexy, and truly breathtaking.

One night, a few months back, we had a fight about her schedule and how she was too busy to make time for anyone but herself. I called her selfish, even though she's the most selfless person I know. She slapped me, grabbed her keys, and left the house. I paced around the house, knowing I had fucked up. She was doing well at work, climbing the corporate ladder, and I just hadn't been effectively communicating what I needed in our marriage. Neither one of us had been. I picked up my phone and tracked her location and decided I wasn't going to wait until she got back home. I plugged the address into my GPS and followed her to the location blinking on my screen.

She was sitting on one of the barstools by the time I had arrived at the bar. Her thick blonde hair was entangled with the thin straps of her dress that draped over her shoulders, wearing a million-dollar smile with a martini in hand. The overhead lighting that streamed below appeared like a spotlight and she was at the center of the stage.

I couldn't help but notice how the bartender was desperate to keep her attention for more reasons than just taking a drink order. One man was staring at her from his table while another man was hovering next to her like a cub, ready to pounce. The bartender pushed another drink in front of her, courtesy of the tall, dark, and handsome man at the table in the far corner of the room. She took the drink, looked his way, toasted in his direction with a smile, and unwittingly took the sexiest sip I'd ever seen.

I've been out with her, had her on my arm night after night, for years. But that night she never looked sexier. She seemed interested, shy and seductive, but still totally unattainable.

A strange wanton desire burned inside of me. An instant gasoline fed inferno.

The man at the table stood, rolled his shoulders back, popped his neck from side to side to side, buttoned his suit jacket, and then ran his hands through his thick black hair.

I had seen that look before.

I had given that look before.

He was a man with a purpose.

He was going to try to fuck my wife.

I should have walked over to her, grabbed her, and took her home, but my legs disowned my thoughts. I found myself moving further into a dark corner, following where my mind was going. I trust my wife more than I would trust myself in any tempting situation. She is loyal to a fault and always puts everyone else before herself. But as the stranger inched closer to her, my cock inched closer to a full-blown erection, hardening at the thought of his chase and her flirting. And maybe the thought of her doing more than just flirting.

I kept my eyes on them as I shifted my stance in an attempt to hide the uncontrollable growing appendage in my jeans. I should not have been feeling that way, but my desire superseded my guilt, and I couldn't help but visualize so many impure thoughts.

I envisioned him spending time pretending like he cared to get to know her while trying to find an excuse to touch her exposed skin. Trailing his index finger along her arm, over her collarbone, and up her neck. I pictured her enjoying it, giving him a smile that signaled it was okay to keep going. I just couldn't stop my unfiltered imagination from running away from me.

He slams down his drink. The amber liquid sloshing over the sides of the glass landing on the top of the bar, grabbing her as he spins her stool to face him. Her legs part open as he moves himself in between them, minimizing the unwanted space. Running his hands through her hair, he tightens his grip at the base of her neck and pulls her face towards his. He leans in closer to her, his lips a splinter distance away from hers as his other hand caresses her cheek.

"You want me to fuck you," he states as a fact more than a question.

Closing her eyes, her chest rises and falls, reflecting what could only be a roller coaster of uncertain emotions. She opens her eyes and those bright sapphires are pure blue flames; the burning desire outweighs the guilt in her expression as she gives him a simple nod.

He slams his lips into hers, closing the space between their bodies. His hands move with purpose, wrapping themselves around her ass and pulling her into his hips as she lets out a whimper, getting the attention of the man next to her. He watches them as he takes small sips of his whiskey, a lopsided smirk peeking through from behind his glass as he reaches out to slip the strap of her dress off her shoulder. It falls, pooling at her elbow and exposing her breast to the man ravaging her mouth. He pulls away, seeing her unruly display and firm pebbled nipple. He's unable to control himself as he pulls the dress down further, cupping her breast, wrapping his lips around the peak. Flattening his tongue lapping over the hardened bud, he licks and nibbles over her flesh, her moans getting louder and gaining the attention of the bartender.

Mr. Tall, Dark and Handsome is dry humping her so hard on the stool she's losing her balance. One of her hands grips tightly on the bar while trying to use her other hand to catch herself from falling, but the man behind her leans in to act as a backrest for her body. She reaches up and grabs his neck to hold as a base, inviting him to join their party. He reaches around and pinches the free nipple while the other man lifts up her dress to expose her panties, already soaked with her arousal. Too impatient to remove them, he pushes the heavy lace to the side, then feathers his thumb over her glistening lips.

"Fuck."

"Oh... God. Fuck." She groans as his thumb begins to rub circles over her clit.

"I'm going to make you come, and you're going to beg me to fuck you while you suck that mans cock." He points towards the guy she is using as her throne.

The bartender moves around the bar towards the front door and locks it. He takes a seat at one of the tables, perfectly angled to watch her writhing body succumb to the two men.

I watch my gorgeous wife. Her baby blues that are now burning sapphire, glance over at the bartender turned voyeur, as he unzips his pants. His cock springs out, the head pearled with pre-cum. Showing her his impressive cock, he grabs the base and pulls on the length of his shaft, staring straight into my wife's eyes. Tall, dark, and handsome is still circling her clit vigorously, in perfect rhythm. She closes her eyes tightly, leaning her head back. Her moans permeate the empty space as she screams, "Oh God, you're going to make me come."

"Beg me to fuck you," the man says, starting to slow the movement of his thumb over her clit.

"No, don't stop, please..." she begs, opening her eyes to face him.

"Look at me and beg for my cock," he threatens.

The bartender is on the verge of climaxing, grunting and stroking himself.

"Please fuck me," she whispers, ashamed but needy.

"With what? What do you want? I want to hear you say it," he demands as his thumb caresses over her slit.

"Your cock. I need your cock. Please... fuck me," she pleas.

Putting his thumb in her mouth, he moves it around her tongue, then back to the bundle of nerves, disobeying any logical thought she has. He massages her clit, bringing her instantly to her climax. The sound of her orgasm is infectious, the bartender's need for his own release imminent as he begins groaning and grunting uncontrollably, spilling all over himself.

As she comes down from her high, Mr. Tall, Dark and Handsome unbuttons his pants and they fall easily to his ankles, the hefty buckle clanking on the hardwood floor.

"Pull out your cock," he says to the man behind her as he pulls her forward into an upright position.

Leaning forward, he takes a nipple into his mouth as he pulls down her wet panties, heavy from her arousal. Gripping her arms, he whips her around and bends her over the bar stool. Her face is a mere few inches away from the other man's cock. He grabs her wrists and pulls them behind her back to help hold her up, in line with the barstool. Her spine is parallel with the seat and her face and ass are in perfect alignment with both men.

He moves forward and thrusts into her without a second thought or a warning. He releases a loud grunt as her mouth falls open and available for the hard cock in front of her.

"You're so fucking tight. Holy shit." His head falls back as he hisses through his teeth.

Pulling her wrists further behind her body, he aligns her face at the perfect angle as she opens her mouth for man number two. Their movements become erratic and sloppy, losing control due to the instant pleasure that barrels through their bodies. Both men in perfect rhythm together, taking as much of their own pleasure as giving it to her. She is closing in on another orgasm, and in a matter of minutes, after the continuous thrusting and face fucking, she lets out a muffled scream. Her words are unclear but loud, echoing off the walls. The sounds fading with her orgasm.

"Swallow my cum," breaks the silence, as man number two grabs the back of her head. He thrusts himself further down her throat, holding himself there through a shaky orgasm and guttural moans, sending man number one over the edge. He pulls out, strokes his cock, and the first jolt of his release reaches the middle of her back. Groaning through the rest of his orgasm, it spills over his hand as he falls over her spent body.

I HAD ONLY BEEN STANDING in the corner for a few minutes while I envisioned this entire scene. When I come back to reality, I see she is still sitting at the bar, nursing her martini, with multiple men still just watching from afar.

Whatever vision I had was more than a simple fantasy. It was a scorching desire that couldn't lie dormant. I knew I had to explore more of whatever that was, but how am I going to share this with my wife? She'll think I've lost my fucking mind, or am just a pervert who wants to share his wife with strange men.

The thing about the fantasy is that I want her to enjoy it, too. That was the best part. Seeing her beg for it. Need it.

I loved watching her beg for it. Witnessing her pleasure and theirs.

I've watched plenty of porn, but nothing compared to the vision of *her*.

My wife.

I didn't even know how to decipher the thoughts I was having without feeling an overwhelming amount of shame. My mind was racing, and I just kept thinking to myself that it couldn't be something that I really wanted. I just needed to let the feeling pass. It can't be something anyone would truly want.

THAT WAS the day that something changed in me. That vision kept coming back, which morphed into more indecent thoughts over time. These thoughts bounced back and forth between desire and guilt, but I couldn't think of anything else. Nothing else would turn me on like the thoughts of my wife.

It led me to share the vision I had with her when I had followed her to the bar. She was initially surprised, as was I, but unusually intrigued and aroused when I told her the fantasy. I retold the story while I was fucking her, like it was something I witnessed firsthand, telling her how she was begging for it and how he was teasing her with an orgasm.

It was the best sex we had in years, if not ever.

A short time after that, we were out at one of the local sports bars to watch the hockey game. Before I left to go use the restroom, we made a bet on her getting approached by another man. She's one of those women that people are drawn to easily. She's friendly, gorgeous, and could stop a runaway train with her million-dollar smile.

"If any man talks to you before I come back, you're drawing from the jar. *MY* jar." I wiggled my eyebrows at her. And because she's completely unaware of the natural magnet she is, she took my bet. She's the smartest woman I know, but a complete fool taking that bet.

So, naturally, I high five myself when I start to head back to my seat and look up to see a man standing next to her, pining over her attention. As they carried on easy conversation, he just smiled and was completely wrapped up in all things Elena. She glanced my way, her lip turned up with a squint in her eye.

I came to a halt.

That unspoken command told me that she wanted me to pull back and observe.

He was definitely interested, but she had her ring on, and you can't miss that Goliath of a rock. Somehow, that didn't seem to stop him from nonchalantly touching her forearm or placing a hand on her shoulder when they would laugh.

Watching her converse with another man in this way made me feral. Literally just talking, which was ridiculous. After observing for a few minutes, I walked up to the table and the man. Friendly enough, he reached out to shake my hand, talked about the game, and then politely excused himself. Elena silently gave me the take-me-home-and-fuck-the-shit-out-of-me look. So, I placed my hand on her lower back and led her out of the bar because I'm not one to not do what my wife says.

That night, after what arguably could have been the best sex of our life, I couldn't help but remind her of the foolish decision she made to take my bet and how terribly she lost. That man wasted no time trying to go in for the kill. I should win twice. Once for the win itself and twice for the speed in which it happened.

So, needless to say, I presented her with my fantasy jar. A jar full of written notes of my fantasies, kinks, desires–anything that I want to experiment with. We both have one and pull from it when the other is *owed*. This is something we created to spice things up and help her communicate things she wanted, since that's always been difficult for her.

She reached in and pulled out a folded note.

As she peeled open the delicate paper, her breath seized in

her throat. Her lips parted before she nibbled on the corner of her lips and looked up at me with a tsunami in her ocean blues.

She turned the note to face me, and a tornado fluttered through my stomach.

To watch my wife

So, here we are a month later, and she told me she's ready.

And seventeen outfit changes, or however many more it will take, I'm still waiting patiently for my wife for as long as she needs.

Tonight, my ultimate fantasy is coming to life.

2

ELENA

I should feel nervous, but I don't. I feel excited, anxious even. But the lack of nervousness is flooding me with an overwhelming amount of guilt, more than anything else.

How can I be a happily married woman, enjoy everything about my marriage, and not feel guilty about what we're planning to do tonight? I wonder if he's feeling the same, or if he's worried. I can't say that I would be thrilled if the roles were reversed, and I was going to watch him flirt with another woman, potentially taking her to bed. I wouldn't consider myself a jealous woman. I've always been confident in myself and in our relationship. In fact, I've never doubted our love or loyalty, or even considered sex with another person. So, this is all new territory for us both.

After our blow out fight, I ended up at a bar by myself, attempting to drink the thoughts of our argument away. That night, I remember feeling desired. I reveled in strangers taking an interest in me. There were multiple men in the bar that night who stole glances my way, and normally, I wouldn't pay any attention to them, but after the fight we had, I was just looking for something to *feel* other than my irritable emotions and bitterness. So, when I narrowed in on the men watching me, the hunger they had in their eyes, I had felt it.

It felt good.

It felt sinful and wrong.

Yet so... enticing.

When I sense men appraising me, I don't shy away in meeting their gaze. In doing so, they typically dart their eyes in the opposite direction the moment my head turns towards theirs. But the men at the bar that night were different. They couldn't seem to control the look in their eyes, as if some primal instinct began to override any attempt their logical brain made to look away. I felt defenseless, as if my stares did nothing more than provide them with the consent that they were seeking to completely undress me in their minds. My poker face was not as strong as I thought it was, or maybe they saw in my eyes that my primal instincts for lust were betraying the will to defend myself.

Perhaps that is exactly what Jake saw, as well.

The desire in my eyes and the sexual appetite in theirs.

Regardless, no matter how deep the urge is, I would never cheat. It's against everything I stand for. The attention just felt good, and all I wanted to do was run home so I could get ravaged by my husband. Even though my intentions were pure, my thoughts were not, and the shame flooded over me.

I was stunned when Jake sat down on the barstool that night. Surprised to see him because I didn't realize he had followed me, but even more surprised by his yearning. His entire body was tense, his fists were clenched, and he was hungry. Hungrier than any man in that room. Something happened between that moment and when I left the house.

His eyes were burning with desire. Ruinous. Intense. Murderous, even.

He downed the rest of my martini, grabbed my hand, and kissed the tips of my fingers, lightly teasing them with his tongue. He took me home and fucked me like he'd never have the chance again. When he started to share the vision he had at the bar of the things those men were doing to me, I felt the shame he was feeling. With the weight of his body on top of me, he used one elbow as a base and his other hand was wrapped in my hair, pulling it back as he nuzzled into my neckline. He was unable to look me in the face, constantly apologizing while telling me everything he witnessed in his daydream. He was remorseful, apologetic, and desperately libidinous.

It was the most erotic sex we'd ever had.

"You look flushed, baby. Are you feeling okay?" His hand leaving the steering wheel, entangling his fingers between mine.

He's worried about me, and his nerves are probably on high alert, unsure if I'm really feeling ready or ready to run for the hills. I have to admit there are moments of both. Fight or flight emotions are fleeting and battling each other, but only because I can't figure out how to navigate through the guilt I feel over the excitement.

"It took me two hours and about twenty outfit changes to get here. I better be feeling pretty damn good right now." I smile, kissing the hand he has entangled with mine.

After all the outfit changes, I eventually went with the first outfit I tried on. *Of course.* A classic black dress that trails into a low V neckline between my breasts. It falls a few inches above my knees with a small slit up the side, exposing even more thigh.

He chuckles. "I haven't been able to keep my eyes off you. But that's nothing new compared to any other day. You are more captivating than the sunrise and more luminous than the stars in the night sky. My celestial beauty." His tone is soft and worried.

He's nervous about tonight.

My gorgeous husband is always complimenting me. But *this*, his words, he needs assurance, just as much as I do.

"You know, you're my one and only spumoni?" I repeat the words he often says to me.

He throws his head back and laughs, because he knows I'm terrible at emotional communication and complimenting other people, even my own damn husband. So I do what I do best, and show him physically.

Releasing his hand, I inch over the center console of the car and rub my hand over his thick, muscular thigh. I rest my palm between his legs and my eyes widen at how hard he is.

"Someone feels ready for tonight," I whisper in his ear, grazing my palm back and forth over his now exceptionally tight pants.

His eyes close slowly as he takes a deep breath, trying to fight for some control. I don't know how he's going to make it through the night.

"Baby, I've been hard for the past two hours." He places his hand over mine, preventing me from creating any more friction as he shakes his head at me. "You should stop unless you want the night to end right now."

I smile, kiss his cheek, and slither back into my seat. I open my legs to cross one leg over the other. My dress rises up over my knee, pooling slightly on the side of the seat. It's impossible to hide the smirk on my face while he grips the steering wheel with white-knuckle force.

It's only a few minutes later when we pull into the parking lot of the bar we decided to go to. We chose a high-end bar across town, about thirty minutes from our house, so that we didn't risk running into someone we know.

"I'll head in first." I lean in to kiss him, then turn for the door handle.

"Elena." Placing his thumb and forefinger between my elbow, caressing the sensitive skin. Goosebumps erupt, sending chills that I feel all the way to my toes. "I love you." His gaze is deep and meaningful.

"I know." I smile, cupping his cheek.

"If you don't feel comfortable, or want to leave at any point in time, we will go. Understand?"

"I know." I lean in to kiss him again. His nerves are filling the small space with thick tension, and less words are more right now. I smile and exit the car, glancing back as I walk towards the front door. His eyes never leave me, not even for a moment.

They're primal.

Desperate, yet protective.

I walk through the parking lot, placing my silver gem-studded clutch under my arm as I near the building. Grabbing the door handle that runs vertically with the robust door, the long twisted brass is cold to the touch due to the crisp, cool temperature outside. The door is large and heavy, but to my surprise, it flies open with ease before I realize someone is exiting. His push and my pull have him stumbling into me.

"Oh my God..." I gasp, as his hands scramble over my body in an attempt to stop his fall; fumbling over my chest, then on my arms before landing on my waist. My hands land on his thick chest, which feels more like a concrete wall than a human body. An aroma of woodsy spice, whiskey, and mint wafts through the air as he looks at me, confused. His slow gaze trails up and down over my body as his eyes frantically take me in. Finally balanced, he releases me, then steps back, instantly chilling the space between us.

"Oh, wow. I'm really sorry about that. That door was deceiving. I went in full force."

"I can tell." I giggle, crouching down to pick up my clutch. I wipe off the invisible dirt, then stand back up, fixing my dress lines. I fondle the fabric as I glance down at myself, fixing my deep neckline, before looking back at him.

His amber-colored eyes eat up the movements of my fingers as I mend the lines of my dress back into place. The depth of his irises is both kind and intense.

"Are you going in alone?" His brows pinch together, like I shouldn't be here.

"I'm meeting my sister here." Looking at my watch, then the parking lot where my husband watches intently. "But she's running late, so it looks like I am coming in alone for the moment."

I turn back to look at my new stranger friend. He's handsome, to say the least. His short, thick, light brown hair is freshly cut, offsetting the roughness of the stubble that lines his jaw. The slight pigment to his skin makes me think he's mixed, Greek or Italian, maybe. Descendant of Sparta, perhaps.

He looks like he's had a long day at the office, with a five o'clock shadow tinting his sharp jawline. His white dress shirt tailored to his body is unbuttoned at the top, yet still tucked in neatly to his charcoal-colored dress pants.

"Well, I think I might owe you an apology drink. Can I join you until your sister arrives?" he says, trying to conceal his smile.

Shit, really? He was just leaving.

That thought paints my face like a canvas which he clearly notices because he puts his hands up in defense and says, "Hey look, no funny business, I just want to make sure no one else uses you as a human airbag in there."

Laughing, I hold out my hand. "I'm Ellie."

Deciding partial anonymity is necessary, I give him my nickname that no one ever calls me.

"Ellie, that's a beautiful name." He reaches for my hand. "I'm Chris."

3

JAKE

"You've got to be kidding me," I whisper to myself as I watch my wife being led through the door being held open by a stranger, who she just shook hands with less than sixty seconds ago. She glances at me from the corner of her eye, then steps through the doorway into the bar. He continues to hold the door as he runs his hands through his perfectly styled hair and down the front of his perfectly tailored shirt, then covers his mouth to smell his own breath. When he appears satisfied, he steps through the door, following closely behind her.

Well, he's not leaving now.

I can't believe that happened so quickly. Actually, I can. Girl, guy, gay or straight, there is something about her beauty and charm that easily commands anyone's attention.

But damn, *that* was fast.

I hope this helps her feel confident about tonight. She seemed okay on the drive here; there wasn't a sense of any nervous energy. But I know my wife well enough to know she'll hide some of the true emotions that she feels if it makes her appear weak or vulnerable. My hope is that she is feeling as excited as I am, and that this is something that is as arousing for her as it is for me.

I step out of the car and take a commanding breath in, holding the crisp air in my lungs for a moment before exhaling through my mouth, bellowing steam into the night air. It's unusually chilly tonight. There are a few clouds rolling in, and in true Pacific Northwest fashion, the scent of the rain has buried itself in the air like a semi-permanent fixture.

I pick up my pace and trot towards the front door. I don't think anything will happen too quickly, but I don't want to miss anything either. Even if nothing happens tonight, just watching her flirt with another man puts me in an entirely new dimension of uncontrollable need.

Entering through the same door they did, I notice the bar is fairly quiet. Busy enough to hear a number of different conversations, but slow enough to still have open high tables and seats at the bar. The overhead lighting is dim, with up-lighting bordering the walls that surround the bar and open seating area. There is an acoustic guitarist playing on a small stage in the corner, singing a pretty slick rendition of *"Red, Red, Wine"* by *UB40*. On each side of the bar, there are deep hallways that lead to another section of the building.

We made a great choice. This place is nice, classy, and it feels sexy.

I immediately spot her voluptuous blonde hair swept over her shoulders, with a glass of wine in her hand, sipping seductively, talking and laughing. She's standing at a high table near the corner at the end of the bar.

God, she's stunning.

I move through the floor, picking a high table at the opposite end of the bar with the perfect view of her and the man wooing her tonight.

I'm not understanding all the emotions going through my body right now. The rush of seeing her like this, sexy and desired, but yet the pull of the possessiveness I feel to claim her at the same time.

"Good evening, sir. Can I get you something to drink?" The waitress places a small napkin on my table.

"Old fashioned, please." Never taking my eyes off my wife.

"You got it." The waitress spins around back towards the bar as I slide back into the seat placed at the table.

I wonder what they are talking about. The weather probably. Basic introduction life questions. The surface level, 'get-to-know-you' questions that are forced and robotic when you first meet someone.

Although he's engaged in her, leaning into her, finding reasons to stand closer to her and touch her. A heaven-filled hour must go by as I watch them continue to laugh, talk, and flirt. He has not turned away to look at anyone or anything else. He is wholly consumed by her and I entirely by them.

Tapping the top of her empty wine glass, he shouts towards the bartender. He's either trying to get her drunk or he's just very attentive to make sure she's taken care of. Either way, I'm sure his reasons are selfish. A whistle back from the bartender finally breaks him out of his trance, and he walks towards the bar to pick up the newly poured glass of rosé. Instead of returning to stand across the table from her, he slithers in behind her, reaching over her shoulder to place the glass down in front of her.

My view is perfect.

I can see her straight on. She dips her head to look at the drink he just placed down, then tilts her eyes up and meets my gaze dead on. He moves his hand over her shoulder, slowly caressing her arm and gently pulls her hair from one side to the other, exposing her soft skin and gorgeous neckline. Turning her head towards him with a smile and I can see her lip the words, 'Thank you'. He nuzzles into her shoulder and places a kiss at the nape of her neck.

"Should I start a tab?" The waitress sets a second drink down.

"Yes." I hand her my credit card, my eyes still laser focused on my wife.

He runs his index finger over the area that he just kissed, then leans in to sprinkle kisses over her body, starting from her shoulder, all the way up to her ear. She leans her head to the side, giving him more access, her chest rising and falling quickly. He cups her face and pulls it towards his. Their lips are so close that, from here, it's hard to tell that they aren't touching. They are staring at each other with so much intent and so many questions, his eyes bouncing between her eyes and her mouth. He's debating. Waiting. Unsure if it's too soon to move in.

To his shock, and mine, she grabs the front of his shirt and tugs him forward, slamming his lips into hers.

Fuck.

He grabs her waist, twisting her towards him and closing all the space between them. His hands run through her hair, gripping the base of her neck.

I can see her fingers slipping through the holes between the buttons of his shirt like she needs more. Her hands seem to have a mind of their own and begin to drift further south. I have a perfect view of one of her hands moving over the front of his pants, then towards his pockets like she's trying not to be obvious, but his face hides nothing. He pulls back from her lips, tilts his head towards the ceiling and blinks quickly. I'm laughing to myself because I know how frustrated she can make me feel, and I know exactly how he feels right at this very moment.

The look on his face is desperate and intense. His brows are pinched together as he stares into her lustful eyes. His jaw is tight and teeth are clenched. The grip he has on her waist is possessive with need. He needs to make love to her and destroy her at the same time.

As he forces his gaze from hers, his eyes bounce around the room, then land on me, kicking me out of my trance. I turn immediately to look for the waitress, the stage, the bar, anything except looking in their direction to avoid looking like a complete creep.

I turn around briefly to look around to the other side of the room and take a sip of my drink. The burn of the cool liquid is a dose of reality, and I'm still in shock that this is all happening.

I take another sip, followed by a deep breath. I shift my weight from side to side and quickly reposition myself to hide my obvious bulge. After a few meditative breaths, I turn back to see the table completely empty.

What the hell.

Frantically, my eyes skim the room, and I jut out from behind my table, walking slowly towards the other side of the room to see him holding her hand and leading her towards one of the hallways on the side of the bar. I really should have scoped out this bar prior to coming, so I knew more about it. I only told Elena the details about this bar from what I read about it online, and neither of us has ever been here.

Trinity Club is just a bar when you walk into it. It has an open space concept, but is deceiving in that it is divided into three separate spaces, the bar and two different clubs. One club always has hip hop, R&B, and pop music DJ's spinning every night. The other side of the bar leads you into another section that themes out its events. It could stretch as far as country music one night to house music another, and sometimes they hold special event nights, depending on the time of year. It's an all-inclusive, can't go wrong with this club, kind of vibe.

I don't want to be obvious, so I'm wandering the area slowly, glancing around like I'm just enjoying the scenery on a leisurely hike around Puget Sound. The music ascends with each step as I make my way down the hallways. I see the silhouette of my wife disappear through the doorway into a vast, loud space, and as I get closer to the threshold, the expansive dance area comes into view.

And just like that, I've completely lost sight of her.

4

ELENA

Chris is intense; a total alpha like my husband, but with a seemingly softer edge. I think he can be more aggressive, but being that we just met, I feel like he might be holding back. At least a little bit. He's walking me through the club side of the bar; the music is much louder back here and there is a large dance floor area with VIP seating that surrounds the floor. There are different levels and areas where you can stand and mingle or drink or dance. The entire room is dark and dim, occasionally being lit by the overhead strobe and party lights that flash to the beat of the music from the DJ's table.

They must use some kind of fog machine or dry ice for effects. The air is damp and feels thick and heavy, or maybe that's just my anxiety weighing on my lungs.

I don't know why, but I'm suddenly worried Jake won't see me and will freak out. I'm panicked thinking he's lost me, and I should probably bail out of here now. The plan was for some flirting, a bit of teasing, and potentially exchanging phone numbers. The possibility of more was only a thought, but I assumed it wouldn't happen on our first night out. We never discussed the details of what to do if this happened, and it's all moving faster than I ever expected it to.

Should I stop, or should I keep going?

We really didn't consider this moving so quickly, but Jake did say this is for me as much as him, and to do whatever makes me feel comfortable.

I'm just not even sure what that is at the moment.

My mind is reeling and my skin feels like it's coming off the side effects of a full body shot of lidocaine.

Chris yanks me forward, spinning me around as my back slams up against the wall. We're in the far corner of the venue, and it's even darker back here. I find myself misstepping in an attempt to avoid falling, but really I look like a newborn giraffe trying to walk in an unknown and uneven space.

My grace has left the building.

As my eyes begin to adjust to the darkness, I can see the vastness of the room from this corner. Even though it's an entirely open space, you'd really have to be searching for someone back here to actually find them.

"Is this okay?" Chris asks, nuzzling into my ear as he places one hand on my hip and using the other to cup my face. The scrub from his day old shave tickles my jawline, forcing my ear down to my shoulder with a giggle.

"You smell so good, Ellie." His thumb and forefinger pinch the bottom of my chin as he inches my mouth closer to his. "Can I taste you?" There's a desperation in his voice. A tone that's asking and demanding at the same time.

At a loss for words, I bite my bottom lip and force myself to pause a moment so I don't look as feral as he sounds, but my head nods quickly and abandons any logic. He presses his mouth urgently into mine, slipping his tongue through my parted lips, swallowing the uncontrollable moan that escapes me.

Bourbon and mint invade my taste buds and the scent lingers around us as his hard body leans into mine.

He feels so different from my husband.

He *smells* different.

It's good, weird good.

My hands are reaching around him, feeling his arms and back and his ridiculously tight chest. The familiar tingling sensation between my legs, that typically only results in my husband touching me, is engaged full force.

I'm aroused, and blanketed with so much guilt, simultaneously.

How do cheaters cheat without feeling remorse?

I should stop this.

God, it's so good.

He releases my hip and places his forearm against the back wall, caging me in. His other hand grazes the outside of my dress when he stops over my hard nipples, slowly making circles over one, then pinches lightly.

"Chris," I gasp into his mouth.

"Jesus, Ellie, I've been so turned on by you since the moment I saw you. But this," caressing his finger over my bottom lip, "my name coming from your mouth, that is indescribable. I want to do so many things to you right now."

What do I say? What would a supposedly single girl say to a terribly attractive guy that's turning her on in so many ways she can't even see straight? She would say 'take me home', but all I need is Jake following us home and getting arrested for peeping through some strange man's window.

Oh, the headlines that would bring.

Man arrested for public masturbation outside a window while spying on his wife in sexual act with her paramour.

So, what does the slightly remorseful, pretending to be single, really horny girl say?

"We should stop. Someone might see us." Unable to hide my heavy breath.

"You sure you want me to stop?" He pinches harder. Hovering his mouth over mine for a moment before his lips trail downward to kiss my collarbone, then he proceeds south, meeting the end of the V neckline of my dress.

"You don't really sound like you want me to stop," he says with a smirk.

Because I don't.

"Chris, I... I..."

"You say my name like that, Ellie, I can't promise to behave myself." He groans as he pulls back the front of my dress, turning that V line into an obtuse angle. My breast bounces out, the cool breeze making my hardened nipple pucker even more. His lips wrap around the peak, his tongue flickers on the tip, and everything inside me is screaming.

I want him to touch every part of my body with that tongue. And it feels like he does. How can his hands be everywhere I want them to be, but nowhere I need them to be at the same time? I don't know if it's the dark corner of a public place or that he's not my husband or that my husband could be watching somewhere. My thoughts are mixed somewhere in the confusion of all that is happening. I just know if he goes anywhere near my pussy, he's going to know exactly what he's done to me.

And just like that, his hand grazes my knee, slowly rubbing the inside of my thigh, all the way up to the apex of my thighs. My breath hitches as he hisses with pleasure.

"Jesus, you are soaked for me, Ellie." He reaches over the top of my panty line and dips his fingers into my thong. "I would ask you if this is okay, but this wet pussy of yours already answered my question."

My mouth drops open, and I let out an uncontrollable gasp as he moves his finger through my slit, making circles around my clit. One hand flies to the back of his head, gripping his hair while the other tries to grip the flat surface of the wall behind me. I am pathetic. This man has me completely undone in the matter of minutes, and I'd literally do anything to come.

This is pure desperation.

"Please…" is all that comes out, in the form of a cry.

"That's it, baby, beg me for it. All you have to do is say my name again."

"Please, J…" Fuck, I almost called him Jake. The loud music plays to my advantage.

My head falls back against the wall, gathering my thoughts as I peek across the room. My eyes are searching the open space to make sure we don't have an audience, with the exception of one sexy voyeur I'm desperate to find. I can't decipher any of the bodies in the room, and no one appears to be paying any attention to this area of the room.

Shit.

I pull my head forward and my hair falls down in front of my face. I'm disheveled, flushed, and so aroused. I shift to turn my gaze at him as he pulls the hair back behind my ear.

"Ellie, I just need to hear you say it." Like he's asking for permission, but he knows damn well he doesn't need it.

"Please, make me come, Chris," I beg, grabbing onto his hair and looking straight into his eyes. His eyes squint, almost painfully, and his hips press into me like what I just said stabbed him in a spare organ he doesn't really need.

His finger slides down towards my entrance. He pushes one finger inside me, followed by another. He fucks me with his hand, placing his palm perfectly at my hardened clit, rubbing in perfect unison with his finger thrusting.

It's so good. So, so good.

I bite my lip, trying to resist the urge to moan and beg for more.

He leans his body into me, pushing me against the wall. His

free hand grabs my chin, squeezing my cheeks, forcing my mouth to fall open. "Don't you stop yourself. I want to hear you scream, and I don't care who can hear us," he breathes into my mouth, nipping at my lip.

Yup, he was totally holding back earlier.

He curves his fingers up towards my belly while pumping in and out of me. I lose complete control. A rush of explosion comes spiraling down my stomach, all the way to where his hand is moving in perfect rhythm. I let out a yelp and scream more profanities in a five second span than I'd care to admit. My head is dizzy, my breathing is labored, and everything is tingling.

Slowly, he pulls out of me and brings his fingers up to our mouths, his still hovering over mine. Pressing his fingers against my mouth, he swipes them across my lips, then kisses me, mixing my arousal on both of our tongues.

I grab his head, nuzzling it further into my neck, and he trails kisses along my pulse point. I can see the entire room and a lone silhouette standing across the dance floor, looking straight in this direction. He can probably only see shadows, but my lip still turns up with a flirtatious smile for my husband while another man explores my body with his tongue. It feels so wrong and so good at the same time. I find myself building up again.

"It's your turn," I whisper in Chris's ear, even though my eyes are still looking across the room.

Pressing his hands against the wall, he pushes himself back and cages me in while I unbutton his pants and pull down his zipper. Our gazes meet and his eyes laser through me, demanding his pleasure without the use of any words.

My back glides down the wall, keeping my eyes on his until I'm crouched directly in front of his hips. I reach into his boxers, having no trouble freeing his enlarged cock as it bounces from the restriction of his pants.

It's huge.

Thick. Veiny. Gorgeous.

He looks down at me with a knowing smile. "Do you still think that's a good idea, Ellie?"

I smile, my tongue darting out to wet my lips.

This man has no idea how much control he just gave me. If I can do anything ten out of ten, it's a blow job. A deep throat, no gag reflex, grade A, BJ. He is a little bigger than Jake, probably the biggest I've had, actually. But a big dick has never intimidated me.

I lick my lips and flatten my tongue out, grazing the base of his cock all the way to the tip. I repeat this, licking the sides from base to tip over his entire length, coating him with my saliva.

His eyes close tightly as I continue to tease. When he opens his eyes, they immediately meet mine. I'm still staring up at him, watching as he tries not to fall apart, forcing himself to hold back.

I wrap my lips around the crown, slick with precum, then grab his hips to pull them closer to my face. His cock slides down over my tongue and hits the back of my throat as I grip his hips to pull him flush against me. My nose is buried deep into his perfectly groomed hair, and I hold it there for a brief moment. A slight bob of my head back and forth in short motions gives my throat just enough space to adjust to his considerable size.

"Oh, fuck..." Drawing out the F sound with a heavy breath.

He pulls back quickly, retreating from my mouth. He's hunched over and panting. "Jesus." Blinking quickly with his eyes widening.

I don't think he often gets that kind of deep throating with his size.

"Where's that confidence now, Chris? Are you questioning your ability to handle my mouth?" I can't help but smile at him.

"Yes, Ellie. Yes. I fucking am." His tone makes me laugh. He grips the base of his cock like he's trying to hold himself back. "Your mouth is unbelievable."

I pull him forward again, moving my lips and tongue up and down the shaft, bringing my lips together at the tip, kissing off the precum that's beading at the top.

"So, are you going to fuck my face now, or should we call it a night?" I say, taunting him.

The look on his face. Priceless.

I can't tell if he wants to kill me or fuck me.

He leans forward, lowering the tip into my mouth, and pushes urgently. His movements are choppy and beastly. Like something in him snapped, and he's not waiting any longer to use me for his pleasure. His moans grow louder as his cock pulls in and out of my mouth, hitting the back of my throat and sinking further down with each thrust.

Still pressing against the wall, he falls onto his forearms, allowing him to cage me in even more. The DJ is playing loud house music, and thank God the bass is turned up high, because the sounds coming from this man are rivaling the speakers blaring through the club. I can feel his orgasm building. His cock is so hard and feels even bigger than it did just seconds ago. I groan and attempt to say anything to push him over, but the vibration of my throat did that instantly. His cock throbs in my mouth as he pushes further into my mouth, holding my head in place while he empties everything he has down my throat.

Throwing his head back, "Fuck, Fuckkk," he grunts out, along with some other inaudible sounds.

After a brief moment of panting, he pulls out and helps me back up, leaning his boneless body into mine.

"That was the best idea anyone has ever had," he breathes out.

I giggle, feeling redeemed with the power that I just held

over him. I look around the club and it's getting crowded. I don't see my husband's shadow any longer, and I wonder if I was just seeing things earlier. Maybe it wasn't him I saw and he wasn't able to witness any of this. Immediate guilt begins to flood over me. I just had a pretty amazing time, and I shouldn't feel this way. I'm instantly conflicted between these mismatched emotions.

Chris lifts his head to look at me. He follows my eyesight around the room then looks back at me. "You good?"

"Yeah," I turn my head towards him, "but we should probably get out of here before someone gets suspicious," I suggest, looking around for the exit.

"You're right." He pushes himself off the wall and zips himself up while I straighten out my dress. Grabbing my hand, he leads us back towards the doorway towards the bar.

We land back at the table we started at, and he calls the bartender for another round of drinks. Whiskey, neat, for him, and another glass of wine for me. I'm feeling anxious to leave, find Jake, and get my thoughts straight. I'm looking around, and consider telling him I need to bail out for the night, but I don't feel right just leaving either. I don't know if Jake is in the car or around here somewhere. I don't want to go to the parking lot and get stuck wandering outside.

"Is your sister here yet?" Chris asks.

"Oh," Shit, I totally forgot about that. "I don't see her. I'm going to shoot her a text."

I pull out my phone and send a quick message to Jake asking where he is, then slip my phone back into my clutch.

"I'm going to go clean myself up. I'll be right back." I place my hand on his arm to squeeze around him and begin to head towards the bathrooms, but he grabs my hand and brings it up to his lips, kissing my fingertips.

"I don't mind you smelling like sex." He tips up a brow and smiles at me.

I lean into him, pushing up onto my tippy toes to reach his jawline. "My sister probably will," I whisper into his ear, placing a soft kiss on his cheek.

Giving him a sweet, seductive smile, I turn around and head towards the bathrooms. There is a small hallway that leads to a few doors in the back. Two bathroom doors, an employee-only door, and what appears to look like an emergency exit.

Suddenly, someone pushes into me from behind and grabs my arm, pulling me in the opposite direction of the bathroom and right through the emergency exit door. The crisp, cool air hits me instantly, and even though it's dark outside, the street lamps provide more light than most areas of the bar. I close my eyes tightly and open to adjust my vision. Jake is pulling me forward towards the car and my feet are shuffling to keep up.

Shit. He looks mad.

Like, really mad.

He opens my car door, and I quickly plop down into the seat. The door closes, and he moves around the front of the car, turning only briefly to look through the front windshield at me. My head looks straight ahead, but my eyes follow his. His eyes are dark and unreadable.

God, he looks sexy. Angry, but damn sexy.

The top buttons of his shirt are undone, exposing the hard lines of chest. His sleeves are rolled up to his elbows and his pants the perfect fit around his ass. His dark champagne hair is wickedly wild, and his usually golden eyes are burning a deeper shade of hazel. Maybe he was just stressed from not being able to find me, but he's definitely on some kind of mission right now.

He gets into the driver's seat, buckles his seatbelt, and drives out of the parking lot as quickly as he pulled me out of that bar.

Reaching for my hand, he entwines his fingers with mine, then brings them close to his mouth. His chest rises and falls as his eyes close like he's trying to calm himself down.

This is total bullshit. He's been talking about doing something like this for months. And now he can't handle it.

I don't fucking get it.

"Did you see?" I ask quietly, still looking forward. I see in my peripheral vision a soft elongated nod and tilt my head to look at him. "Are you pissed?" I ask more aggressively.

He just shakes his head.

"Say something," I insist.

I see his chest rise with a deep inhale, then fall with an even bigger exhale.

What. The. Fuck.

What the hell is his problem right now?

"You can't do this, Jake. Say you want this..." waving my hand between him, me, and the air like it represents everything we've talked about doing, "then be pissed off about the outcome."

5

JAKE

"It's not that, Elena," I snap at her.

How do I explain myself? How do I tell her I'm barely holding myself together? Watching her with another man was the sexiest thing I've ever witnessed. The sexiest I've ever seen her.

Ever. Period. Ever.

Fuck.

"Then what the fuck is it? I can deal with a lot of shit, Jake, but I won't put up with this attitude you're giving me." I pull my hand away from hers, slam on the brakes, and turn into an empty parking lot. Unbuckling my seatbelt, I push myself off my seat and hover over her.

"Tell me what he felt like." I can't explain my thoughts. I don't have any words in my head that make any sense. I just need to hear how she felt. What he felt like to her. Was she turned on? Was it him, or was it maybe because I was watching? I don't even know if she saw me.

I yank down at the material at the top of her dress. Her tits come into full view, which is probably my favorite part of her. I lick and suck exactly where he was. I don't care if he was tonguing her here earlier. I need to remind her so she can tell me how it felt. She gasps and throws her head back. I feel the need to claim all of her again, my mouth moving between her neck, ears, nipples, and my hands are roaming everywhere. I can't get enough of her, and I know he felt the same. I saw it in the way he took her. The way he devoured her as she came. God, watching him completely lose himself in my wife, I swear I could have come in my pants without even touching myself. I'm not even sure if that's possible as a grown adult. I glide my hand under her dress and reach for her panties.

"Fuck, you are soaked." I have to get these off immediately. It's times like this I see no point in any sort of underwear or why they were even invented. I tuck my fingers into the sides and rip them down her long, gorgeous legs. The black heels that tie up her ankle catch the dainty fabric as it hangs lopsided at the knot.

"I need you. I need you now." I lean back into my seat and pull her with me, unbuttoning my pants. "Take my pants off."

I lift my hips as she yanks my pants down past my knees.

We are feral.

Neither one of us is able to get enough of whatever it is we need.

Her legs are straddling my thighs. Her dress is hiked up to her waist, and I pull her straps off, exposing the perfection of her naturally full breasts. Shifting her hips upwards, she comes down easily on my cock and whimpers immediately as I enter.

She smells of wine and sex and lust-filled sin.

Gripping her hips, I thrust to meet her grinding. She's already moaning for need of a release.

Another one since a stranger just gave her a mind-blowing orgasm in public.

"Elena, I won't last long baby. Please tell me what he felt like," I whisper, pulling her face closer to me.

Elena has never been a talker in bed. Don't get me wrong,

she moans and groans and verbally tells me how she is feeling or if something feels good. But the dirty talking has always been something I do. I have a better chance of her sharing the details of her experience if she's not looking at me straight on. I nuzzle into her neck, placing her mouth close to my ear.

"Please, my beautiful wife, tell me. What did it feel like when he touched you?" My tone is vulnerable and desperate. "Please."

I'm grinding into her, pulling her flush to my body in desperate need of more. More of her, more of anything. Just fucking more.

"Everything just happened so fast. He was flirting with me at the bar, touching my arm and back. It felt so sexual and so wrong. Knowing you were watching me... God, it made me so wet." Her moans echoing in my ear.

My cock is throbbing, I feel like a dormant volcano, intrusion incoming and un-fucking-avoidable. "What happened in the club, Elena?"

She remains quiet for a brief moment, only the sound of our heavy breath and rain beating on the windows. "Tell me."

My cock is so goddamn hard and throbbing painfully, trying to hold back.

"He pinned me against the wall, pulled down the top of my dress and sucked on my nipples. It felt so good. I felt desperate for him. I wanted him to have his way with me, any way he wanted. I wanted you to be forced to watch with no control. That's all I kept thinking about. You, confined, trapped, nothing you could do but watch."

My sadistic, fucking sexy, wife.

I groan, uncontrollably. Just hearing her say that is careening me into an orgasm. I swear I'm going to come so hard she's going to rocket off my cock.

"I was dripping, everything was so wet. He was fingering me and rubbing my clit. I lost all control. I didn't even know if you could see, but I couldn't stop it. It was so good, honey, I'm sorry." She whimpers in my ear. "I'm so sorry."

I'll do whatever I need to do to comfort her and wash away the guilt she shouldn't be feeling, but right now, there is no stopping the orgasm that's been edging me all night. I wrap her hair around my hand and pull back so her face is staring straight through the sunroof. The rain now beating down on the car, the sound of large water drops pelting the roof matching the tenacity of both of our moaning.

My hips have a mind of their own and vigorously thrust harder and harder. Nothing in me is controlled. My body, my breath, my roaming hands that can't touch enough of her body, my cock hardening to the point it aches. I reach between us, my thumb finding her hardened clit, putting pressure there as I move my thumb up and down. She screams. The pitch is so loud I swear the windows will crack. Her walls close in and pulse against me, wrapping around my cock, gripping me so tightly that I completely lose it.

Our orgasms rip through each other.

Hard. Violent. Destructive.

I'm done.

Totally fucking destroyed.

6

JAKE

I pull up to the house and shift into park. The rain has stopped, but the lingering scent of the moisture in the air invades my senses as I exit the car. I stall a brief moment to take in the stillness of the night and attempt to brand the memory of what I saw tonight. Absorbing the unruly passion that ran through my veins, igniting a fire that singed me from soul to skin.

I never want to take our relationship for granted, and I would never expect her to do anything that she wasn't comfortable with, but tonight brought something out in me that I never knew I needed. Now that I've had a taste of it, I can't imagine our sex life without it.

But what will she think?

I don't want to share her. I want to experience all of these things *with* her.

I need her to know that she holds the cards. In any way that she is comfortable. But I know I want more of whatever happened tonight. I just don't know if I can say what I desire in a way that doesn't make her feel like I'm tossing her in a cock-full stockade.

Shaking my head to get that image out of my brain, I walk around to the other side of the car to open her door. She fell asleep only minutes after I pulled out of that parking lot. Between the emotional and physical highs, the events tonight must have completely wiped her out.

Wrapping one arm around her back and the other behind her knees, I pick her up like I did the first night we came home after our wedding day, the first time as Mr. and Mrs. Jenkins. I lean down and kiss the temple of her beautiful face. The face I fell in love with instantly that night at the bar when my eyes first met hers. The face I stared at while saying our wedding vows and that same face I saw across the club tonight being pleased by another man.

I don't know where we go from here or how this will incorporate into our lives. All I know is I fell deeper and harder in love with this woman tonight in a way I never thought was possible.

I woke up early this morning. My mind is still spinning from last night. I should have slept in until noon after the stampede of highs last night, but the moment I rolled over and saw the slight bit of sunlight peeking through the blinds, I was up. It is Sunday, typically a non-work day, but I answer a few emails anyway. That way I don't feel so behind come Monday morning, and then make breakfast for Elena.

She's still asleep by the time I finish plating everything, and the decision to bring her breakfast in bed was an easy one. I feel this undying need to spoil her. I'm not sure if it's my guilt that she did something for a fantasy of mine or me trying to ease the shame she expressed last night. Regardless, I need her to feel loved, worshiped, and adored. Because I feel all of those things for her tenfold this morning.

I place the tray on her nightstand and sit down on her side of the bed. I sink into the mattress as her eyes blink open.

"Hey, sleeping beauty." Her hair is splayed over the pillow, with a few strays falling onto her face. I tuck the wild strands behind her ears and caress her earlobe, which grants me a smile and a moan.

"Good morning, handsome." She places her hands down on the mattress and pushes herself up to lean back on the headboard.

Elena in the morning, groggy, and looking like a lioness, is my favorite Elena.

"Breakfast, my lady." I smile, placing the tray on her lap. "Avocado toast with an egg, sunny side up. Fresh berries and, most importantly, your coffee."

"Wow. This is perfect." She grabs the coffee mug, wrapping her dainty hands around the ceramic, and hugs it close to her with a smile the size of Texas.

"So, how do you feel about last night?" I ask.

"You're right to it this morning, aren't ya?" she replies, sipping her coffee.

"I've had some time to think this morning. You've been sleeping for like a year." She chuckles as I steal a kiss.

I've thought of nothing else the entire morning. Even answering some work-related emails, I had to be careful and not type out my practice speech with Elena this morning.

"Good. Really good, actually." Smiling as she pops a blueberry in her mouth. "I think I should feel strange. A part of me felt a little guilty last night right after everything happened, but now that I know you were there the whole time, I feel... good."

"Good. Good?" My eyebrows breach my forehead. "Calling last night good is like saying childbirth is neat," I quip.

She throws her head back with an infectious giggle. "So, I take it you enjoyed yourself?" Staring back at me with those bright eyes I fell in love with. The loyalty behind them shining brighter than any diamond.

Enjoyed myself? That's the understatement of the year.

We have had plenty of sexual experiences together, and I had my fair share of wild nights before I met her, but last night was the most sexually stimulating night of my entire existence. Enjoyable? Yes. It was really fucking enjoyable.

"Elena, last night was unbelievable. Every moment of it. I couldn't dream of something better." I pause to find my words. "I need you to know something. You... me... us. This is something I want to experience together, but I need you to drive this. Watching you last night. God, it was beautiful. Let me just say I don't trust myself to not accidentally push too much for more. So, I need you to know that I trust you to make any choice in this... with or without me." Her brows pinch together.

"With or without you?" she questions.

"I mean, I have no idea how to do this. Do we try to find a partner that we share these details with or not say anything and sneak around? Do we just keep hitting the bars? Do we sign up for some adult matchmaking company? You..." I blow out the remaining air in my lungs and stare down at my hands. "We are in this together, even if there is an opportunity for you to talk to someone for us or even do something without me. You know, that could lead to other things for us. I just need you to know you have that freedom."

She's in deep thought, pushing the berries around her plate. I've thought about this all morning. I know it's a lot to take in first thing, but I didn't want to wait to have this conversation.

"So, you want an open marriage?" She stares at me deadpan.

"What the hell? No," I reply urgently with both my words and a disgusted look on my face. "I want no one other than you,

Elena." I place my palm over her cheek rubbing her gorgeous cheekbones, still flushed pink. "You are my world, my everything. I want you to know I'm open to the idea of whatever this could be for us."

I wipe my hand over the mirror, clearing off the heavy layer of condensation covering it. Elena jumped in the shower after we returned home from a six-mile hike through Snoqualmie Pass. She's an avid hiker. It shows in every inch of her body, but her legs and ass are unprecedented in comparison to all others. Which is why I always trail behind her. I don't actually like hiking. It's watching her hips sway back and forth, more mesmerizing than a grandfather clock, and her ass bouncing perfectly in those skintight leggings that motivates me to hike.

By the time we got back home and she peeled her leggings off, nothing was going to stop me from following her into the shower. She told me about a shower head scene she read in a romance novel once, and I've been feeling compelled to see if it actually works.

Oh, it does.

She fell apart almost immediately, especially when I made her sit on her hands on the marble bench and forced her to keep her legs open as wide as she could spread them. Some of the sounds she made were louder and deeper than I've ever heard, the echo from the wet tiles amplifying them even more. I teased her to the brink of her orgasm, then would stop. I love it when she begs for me to make her come and take her beyond her breaking point. Watching her fall weakness to that kind of desperation is... Well, it's my weakness.

"You love that orgasm torture shit, don't you?" She slides in behind me, wrapping her arms around my waist. Wetness still covers my body as I envelop my hands over hers and intertwine our fingers together. She presses her naked body into mine and rests her cheek on my shoulder.

I smirk, raising my eyebrows as I stare at her through the viewable space in the mirror. "Getting you horny, frustrated, and begging for my cock? Yes. Yes, I do." I wink.

"I was not *begging* for your cock." She swats at me, acting embarrassed, as she pulls away from my grasp. I turn around and pull her hips into mine so she can feel my half hard erection already making its claim for round two.

"You're right, you weren't begging for my cock. You were praying to a bathroom appliance knighting it into sainthood, and it was pretty fucking sexy." I smile, looking down at her, amazed at how beautiful she is in everything that she does. From the way she bites her lip when she's nervous, like she's doing now, to the way she commands a room without even trying.

I remove the towel wrapped around her head and her now damp and darker blonde hair whips out, landing flatly on her shoulders. The coconut mango scent from her conditioner wafts through the air. She has used the same products since we met, and I hope they bury me with this scent when I'm six feet under.

"So, I made a reservation at Magnolia's. It's in an hour." She glances at herself in the mirror, knowing that she doesn't have enough time to get ready the way she would like to for that type of dinner. "But I also called ahead to Rudy's. The Seattle Smashers are playing so they'll have the game on, annnnd it's mystery wheel karaoke night." I hike my brow at her, knowing damn well she's in for the latter.

She takes one step back slowly, then another. Still facing me, walking backwards. "You are going down tonight, lover."

She winks, turning around to skip towards the dresser. I watch her as she gets dressed. Stepping into a light pink lacy thong, she pulls it over her knees and the fabric barely covers, well, anything. Another favorite version of Elena comes to life as she pulls on her leggings and baggy off-the-shoulder t-shirt. She tops her outfit off with a baseball hat and her good old-fashioned Keds. I decide at this moment that this is my favorite Elena. Tomorrow will be my new favorite with whatever she picks out to wear.

"I'll bet you, double or nothing, it will be you picking from the jar after tonight," I shout to her from our closet as I start to get dressed.

She pops into the doorway. "You sure you want to do that? You don't have the best track record against me, you know," she says with a pretentious smile.

"Oh, you're on, baby."

Well, I should have known better than to have bet double or nothing with her on the night of a baseball game. There were far too many men in the crowd that would rather see a beautiful woman karaoke than some guy singing a random song by himself. And by random, it's literal. When you sign up to sing, you don't get to pick your song. Instead, you get a spin on the mystery wheel, and you have to sing *that* song.

It's like gambling for wanna-be performers.

She landed on Alanis Morissette's *'Ironic'*, while I ended up with *'Man, I feel like a woman'* by Shania Twain.

How she got that goddamn lucky blows my fucking mind.

I can't say it wasn't the most humorous thing the crowd has ever seen. I haven't seen Elena laugh that hard, probably ever.

She's gloating in the passenger seat next to me, knowing I am picking, not one, but two items from her fantasy jar. Our fantasy jars contain notes of things we want to try, desires we want to ask for, or just basic requests. Every opportunity we get to bet on something, we do. It ranges from something as simple as a foot massage on the couch while watching a movie to a visit to a sex club. As simple or as wild as we want it to be.

Rudy's isn't far from the house, and I swear I've barely parked the car when she jumps out of the car and skips through the doorway, still gloating.

Brat.

What I don't think she's ever realized is as much as I love for her to pick something from my jar, I'm a pleaser, and since I love watching pretty much anything she does, this is something I never mind losing at.

When I walk into the house, I lock the door behind me and take off my hat. I run my hands through my thick hair, placing my hat upside down on the counter and empty my pockets into the bowl of the hat. Turning around, I see she's already sitting on the couch, jar in hand. A smug-as-hell smile taking permanent residency on her already gorgeous face.

"Someone is ready." I smirk as I walk over to the couch, kneeling in front of her so we're facing each other with the jar between us.

"One tonight, and one I'll save as a *credit* for later." She wiggles her eyebrows at me.

"I think that may be your way of saying you can't handle me twice in one night." I wiggle my eyebrows back at her, challenging her.

"Oh, shut up and pick one." She shakes the jar in my face.

I reach in, which always feels like Christmas morning. The anticipation of not knowing what will come out of it. The last time I picked one out, it said 'Froyo', which entailed me driving to her favorite ice cream spot to get her frozen yogurt. I tried to eat the frozen yogurt off her body, but she actually just wanted to eat it. So I just sat there watching her seductively spoon it into her mouth. She was a total tease.

I pull out one of the notes and unfold it, staring at her the entire time. She's biting her lip, shifting uncomfortably in her seat. She likes the anticipation, too.

I glance down and smile.

"What is it?" She attempts to snatch it from my grip.

"Oh, no, you don't. Don't move, baby." I push myself off my chair and run up the stairs, taking two at a time.

We invested in a massage table years ago, which we've only used a couple times for an actual massage. I've never been happier to have one than at this moment. I pull it out from the storage space in our closet and unfold the legs. Placing it in the middle of our room, I cover it with a sheet and then light a few candles around the room.

I quickly change into gray cotton jogger pants and a white t-shirt that hugs me well, showing off my broad chest and muscular arms so I can play the part of the masseuse.

I head back downstairs and sneak a glance back at her as she is fidgeting with her fingers on the couch, still in the same spot.

Good girl.

I grab my phone from where I left it on the counter and find a spa playlist to connect to our Bluetooth speakers in the room. Sliding my phone into my pocket, I walk over to her, holding out my hand. She quirks her head at me, reluctant but curious, giving me a quick scan at the outfit I'm now wearing, then slips her hand into mine.

Gently, I pull her up and lead us to the stairs and into the room. As she turns into the door and sees the setup, she bites her lip to hide her smile, now knowing which note I grabbed.

"Strip off everything you are wearing and lie on the table, facing down." My voice, low and deep.

"Okay," she whispers as she tucks her thumbs in her leggings and bends forward, pulling them down towards her ankles.

Fuck me, I'm never going to make it through the massage.

She places her clothes on the bench at the end of our bed and grabs a hair tie from the top of the dresser. The flickering glow of the candles light up her body enough to see her smooth skin and gorgeous curves as she strides over to the massage table, pulling her hair up into a messy bun.

Now that she's facing down and can't see what I'm doing, I walk into the bathroom to grab some lavender-scented oil. I also snag some lube and place the bottle on the nightstand near the table.

I walk back around the table and snap open the massage oil, squeezing a generous amount in my palm. I rub my hands together, creating friction to warm them, playing this part to perfection. Some of the oil seeps through, dripping onto her back, making her flinch in anticipation.

I bite back my smile.

Bringing my hands down to the top of her shoulders, I spread the oil down her arms and back up, then down towards the small of her back. Spending time to apply pressure around her shoulder blades and the muscles that hug her spine. I continue massaging her entire posterior. All the way from the nape of her neck, down to the heels of her feet. Ensuring I touch, graze, and oil every centimeter of her luxurious body I so easily get lost in.

Squeezing a small amount of the lubricant in my hand, I stand next to her and place both my palms on the inside of her thighs, putting enough pressure to force her legs a little wider. Using my fingertips, I trail up toward the apex of her thighs, falling just short of her center, then round them up over her ass, spreading her cheeks slightly open. I can hear her breath hitch slightly, and I continue that same movement. Over and over. After another minute of that continuous rhythm, I slow that pace and hover my fingers over her pussy, applying enough pressure for her to moan and jut her hips back.

She wants more. So much more, and I love teasing her like this.

Using my pointer and ring finger, I spread her lips enough for my middle finger to find her swollen clit and circle the pad of my finger around it.

"Oh my god," she gasps.

"Shhhh, we'll get caught. If you can't be quiet, I'll have to stop the massage." I role play with her. I don't know if that is really part of the fantasy for her, but fuck, it is for me.

Her fingers tighten around the headrest, and I see how difficult this is going to be for her. I can't help but smile and wonder why we've never done this before.

My fingers continue circling with one hand while my other rubs her perfectly round cheek, then the other until those fingers are grazing the cleft of her ass.

She keeps her mouth closed to prevent herself from making

noise, but she's unable to refrain, which earns me a throaty groan.

I instantly pull away.

"No, please," she begs in a whisper.

"Turn over." My voice is deep and stern, like I'm upset with her for failing to remain quiet.

Pressing her palm into the table, she lifts her shoulder and hip together, then shifts onto her back. Her breasts are now exposed to me in all their glorious perfection. The glow from the candle highlights the curves of her body, the oil reflecting the light perfectly off her smooth skin.

She is golden perfection and so damn gorgeous.

I replenish the oil in my hands and start at her collarbone, down the middle of her chest to her navel, and to the sides of her torso. Repeating that movement over and over until I can feel her trying to move towards where she wants me to put my hands. The tell-tale signs of her arousal are evident in the way she is pulling her thighs closer together. The way her toes are scrunching down as she presses her feet together. Biting her lip and arching her head and back. She's restless and angsty, and her desperation is feeding mine.

I lean down and grip her chin while I place my lips to hers, pulling down enough to part her lips and caress her tongue with mine. She releases a low moan, and I cover my mouth with hers, our tongues dancing together while my hand descends to her peaked nipples that crave attention. Taking one between my thumb and finger, I roll gently and squeeze. Another deep moan leaves her throat as she bites my bottom lip.

No longer am I able to stop myself. I pull away and quickly squeeze more lubricant into one hand, then press into her inner thighs again, pushing her legs as wide as the table. I gently hover my thumb over her mound, enough for her to feel something is there, but not quite touching. My other hand massages the skin underneath her belly button, forcing her clit to move up just enough to graze my thumb.

"Fuck," she whispers, testing her breath as she forces all the air out of her lungs.

Repeating a few times, until neither one of us can stand it anymore, I spread her lips apart, pushing my thumb onto her clit, moving swiftly back and forth.

"Oh, Jesus," she squeals, attempting to be quiet but fails.

"Is this kind of massage okay, or do you want me to stop?"

"This is fine," she stutters in a breathy whisper.

"Are you sure? I can stop if you like, miss?" Still playing the part.

"Please don't stop." she pleads.

"Can I fuck you if I make you come?" I ask. Acting like I need to earn it from her.

"Yes, anything you want. Just keep going." She throws her head back.

"Good girl. Come for me," I growl in her ear. "But don't forget, you owe me this pussy if you come. So, don't come if you don't want my hard cock moving in and out of this tight cunt."

That does it.

Her release is nothing short of pure magic. She squeezes the sheets in her hands, pulling and groaning through her climax, and it's so goddamn beautiful.

She's barely coming down from her orgasm when I yank my pants down and my cock juts out like an angry python. I'm probably only going to last like half a second when I finally get inside, but I'm so desperate for her I don't even care. I pull her hips down towards the end of the table, which is a perfect height when I'm standing, and slide into her still throbbing pussy.

"Fuck. Your pussy feels so good." My tone is deep and desperate.

She yelps at the quick invasion.

"Oh my God," she squeals in an audible whimper.

I try to grip her hips to keep her in place, but there is so much goddamn oil everywhere my hands are like a slip and slide all over her body. I'm distressed. My hands are frantic to find something to grab as my orgasm pools at the base of my spine.

Her hands are dry and clean, so I grab them and scissor our fingers together with the sheet, then pull them over her head as I lean over her, thrusting deeper. Our movements are fluid, yet sloppy. I don't know if it's the oil or the foreplay or the beautiful chaos of the mess that is all over us, but Jesus Christ, she feels so good.

I squeeze my eyes shut, seeing stars as I erupt into her. Both my cock and my mind completely blown from tonight, and frankly, our entire weekend. I'm still high from everything that's happened, and I have no idea how we're ever going to top it.

"That was unbelievable," she pants.

"There are no words for what that was." I smile, kissing her forehead as I release her hands. I push myself up and walk into the bathroom to grab a towel, using it to clean off my hands. "Should I wipe you down or do you want to shower?"

"Oh, I *need* to shower. No towel will properly wipe off the amount of oil I have on me. Did you use the entire bottle?" She giggles as she leans up with her arms held out to the sides like she's afraid to touch anything.

"I didn't realize oil was so... oily." I shrug, unable to contain a smile. "Go shower, gorgeous. I will clean up downstairs."

She tiptoe bounces into the bathroom. Holding her arms out to her sides like the Stay Puft Marshmallow man, trying to avoid touching anything, and I'm failing at hiding my laughter.

"El, remember that senator from Striptease with Demi Moore? You know, the guy that doused himself with Vaseline and was walking around his hotel room in his...."

"Shut up! I'm so much more graceful than Burt Reynolds!

And this wasn't self-inflicted!" She screams from the bathroom, way too loud, just to get her point across.

I shake my head and laugh. She's fucking adorable.

I slip on boxer shorts and head downstairs to turn off the lights. A shimmering glint from the metal corner of the mason jar shines with the flicker of the light, reminding me of my karaoke loss from earlier tonight. I still have one more to pull for "later", according to Elena.

I reach into the jar, grabbing another folded piece of paper. Unfolding it...

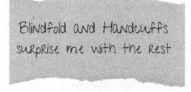

7

ELENA

"Elena!" I hear, pulling me out of my Monday morning daze. I'm nearly hugging the communal office coffee pot while it brews at the pace of a sloth overdosed on muscle relaxers.

"Hey, Cruz," I reply, knowing I don't have nearly enough caffeine to handle him at the moment.

"I knew I was going to find you here. I have too much to tell you about my weekend. How was yours?" He pulls the coffee pot out of the brewer a minute premature, so coffee drips to the bottom of the coffee drain. Luckily for me, he pours straight into my cup first because all he cares about is that I get my morning cup of coffee so he can verbally attack me with the events of his weekend.

Taking that first sip, "Mmmmm, mine was great. You know, same ole' stuff." I shrug. Which is a complete and total lie. Jake and I did nothing "'same ole" this weekend. What we did was sinful in the most amazing way. It has consumed my thoughts all weekend.

Our post-hike sex, mystery karaoke, and the jar. I remember writing that fantasy down months ago, and I'd been dying for that experience. It was far beyond anything I could have ever imagined.

God, the sex. The sex with Jake was always good, but this weekend took our sex life to a completely new universe. And that orgasm that Chris gave me was unforgettable. I do feel guilty about leaving so suddenly, but I'm happy that I didn't have to do the awkward goodbye at the end of the night. Who knows what else could have come out of it. Either way, I'm content because it was exactly what I was looking for. What both Jake and I were looking for.

Thinking about it, I have to hide my smile. Never have I felt stronger or more confident than now.

I used a man.

For what I wanted, and it felt so good. I mean, we both used each other. But to have felt that in control and powerful. It's addicting.

"So, what shenanigans did you find yourself getting into this weekend, Cruz?" I ask, preparing myself for literally anything.

"Girl," he drawls out, "I met this guy on XConnect, you know that friend with benefits dating app I told you about? His profile pic was hot, like fire, baby. He said he was all into the same stuff I was into but when we met up... Elena, Oh Em Gee, he was like forty pounds heavier than his picture! Different hair color, completely unrecognizable. Like seriously. Who does that? I mean, I'm into some teddy bear love, but don't tell me one thing and turn out to be the exact opposite. It's just like those damn *Snapchat* filters. Those fucking things need to be banned from all existence. At least banned from using them on any dating site, like that's some bullshit." He finishes the last word out of breath because I don't think he took one breath in between everything he just said.

"Of course, that happened to you," I say, laughing while pouring my second cup. "So what did you do?"

"I didn't! He took one look at me and said, 'I'm good', threw his hand up at me, and walked off. Can you fucking believe that?"

I am dying of laughter. "He rejected you before you could reject him. Ouch!"

"It's stupid. Dating is stupid. Can't I just find a hot little plaything to get my rocks off? Oh, speaking of, here comes Matthew and all his hotness." He circles the air with his pointer finger and nods in the direction where Matt is walking up to us.

His name is Matt, it's always been Matt, but Cruz likes to call him Matthew to get under his skin. Matt has an average build, and not half bad looking, but his cocky personality is a complete turn off. Regardless, Cruz likes to flirt with pretty much anything that walks. Male or female, he's just a flirt.

"Morning, Matt," I greet him between sips of my much-needed brain juice.

"Matthew, looking fabulous this morning." Cruz gives him a once over with a smile.

"Cruz, I've told you a hundred times, it's Matt, not Matthew. How would you feel if I called you Cruiser or Tom or some other weird variation of your name?" Matt states, his tone dripping with annoyance.

Cruz's full name is Cruz Thomas and Matt likes to give him shit about that fact. Cruz's parents apparently conceived Cruz while watching Top Gun and they love Tom Cruise. With their last name being Thomas, they decided to name him Cruz. Kind of cute. Kind of weird. Cruz seems to be proud of it.

"I told you Matty, you can call me Maverick." He gives him a pat on the shoulder, then stalks off, his hips popping with more drama than the marble pendulum that sits on my desk.

Cruz was hired about a year ago as our team assistant. He can be a handful, but he's the best assistant we've ever had, and Matt knows it, so he puts up with his banter. I personally adore Cruz. He makes me laugh every day and has yet to let me down personally or professionally. He's been loyal and dedicated since day one, and I share almost everything with him.

I'm not sure I'll be sharing the weekend's escapade with anyone, though. I'm feeling more than a little self-conscious about someone finding out and judging me and my marriage or ruining my reputation. When you work for a corporation like mine, they tend to like when your views align with theirs. If they don't, who knows what backlash could happen if they hear I'm in an open marriage or swinging or whatever the hell you call what my husband and I are currently experimenting with.

I can't tell Cruz because I can't risk anything coming out in the open.

"Are you ready for the meeting, Jenkins?" Matt likes to call me by my last name. He was recruited to our marketing team at Ashford and Stephens just after Cruz came on board. He came here from our biggest competition, and we've partnered on a handful of projects that have gained us top recognition within the company. We're both sought out marketing executives in our field. With his background in sports and entertainment and my technology and business background, we make a pretty good team.

Although, it didn't start out that way. The first month he was here, he used his self-proclaimed charm and aggressive sales personality to weasel his way into things. I didn't like his tactics, and at the company holiday party last year, he pinned me in a corner, came on to me, and told me how badly he wanted to see me on my knees. He was extremely aggressive, touching me and pulling at my dress.

My knee jerk response; I punched him in the face.

I threatened him with a sexual harassment lawsuit and not only would I get him fired, but blacklisted from the entire industry. He was taken aback and appeared stunned. Almost like he couldn't even believe his own behavior. I chalked it up to him having far too much to drink that night, and other than the standard male joking banter, he hasn't tried anything since.

I let him off easy, and sometimes I think it was a mistake, because even if it was just the alcohol that sparked that behavior, people are who they are. Since that night, he has not shown that side to me again and I hope he never does.

"I am. I prepared a pitch for that smart water bottle, you know, the one that blinks to remind you when you haven't drunk enough water and sends a reminder notification to your phone. I think they're going to love it," I state proudly.

"The shit companies come up with nowadays." He shakes his head.

"I know, but I love those projects. Promoting these smaller businesses' products helps get them on the map. They are passion projects, and I enjoy them more than the larger accounts." It really does mean more to them and to me.

"I finally nailed down the CEO of Ford Enterprises for an appointment, and if I can get them on board with Ashford and Stephens," he claps his hands rubbing them together and whistles, "Director status, here I come." His face, smug. Annoying. I want to punch it again.

That account would be the pinnacle.

God, he would be my boss.

Kill me, kill me dead, now.

It wouldn't be the worst thing in the world, but he really isn't qualified for that, and well, I just don't trust him.

"Wow, congratulations!" My tone verging on shrill. I need to look away to keep an eyeroll to myself. "I'm going back to my office to get ready for the meeting. See you later."

I walk away, annoyed. Caffeinated, but annoyed. I don't know how he is able to get these appointments with the companies he does. They are exactly what firms like ours want. The big money maker accounts. Is he really just that good? There has to be a bully factor or maybe there is some bribery happening. Regardless, he's gotten some great accounts in the door, but he can't get them hooked in. He's a great salesperson, but his marketing ideas are mediocre at best. I'm the polar opposite.

The meeting goes a little longer than usual. Our Marketing Director and CEO love my pitch and will be moving forward with production on my full advertising plan for them with our creative team.

Towards the end of each meeting, they typically ask for shout outs or 'wins' for the week. Which is a great way to promote teamwork within the group and for us to celebrate the good stuff. I love it, because hey, life is fucking hard, and there is enough crap that when you have a win, you should celebrate it. Revel in it. Boast about it.

Of course, Matt shouts out... himself.

Typical.

He calls it a win, but let's call it what it is. Matt bragging about his appointment with Ford Enterprises. He shares that their CEO is giving him ten minutes this afternoon. He'll have ten minutes to win over a man who already has his company embedded with another advertising firm. That's a feat in an hour, much less ten minutes.

Bryan Ashford, our CEO, is at the head of the table, deep in thought. He puts one finger up, and I have never seen Matt shut up so fast. Bryan floats up from his seat, his face stoic like there was no effort in his movement. The man has literally said nothing, not one facial motion, and Matt looks like he is going to pee himself.

Bryan pauses, looks at Matt, then continues to pace around

the table. He pauses again, glancing towards my side of the table, then continues to pace again. Circling back to his seat, he stands still for a few seconds that feel like hours, then says, "You're taking Elena with you."

My wide eyes snap over at our CEO, who is still expressionless. I look over at Matt and his head is rallying back and forth between me and Bryan like he's watching a tennis match.

"What? But I..." he stammers.

"No buts, Matt. You got the appointment. Excellent job. We need to nail the account, and Elena is the best for that. You guys work together on this and don't muck it up. Report back to me after the meeting and let me know how it goes." Bryan grabs his laptop and exits the conference room.

The glass door barely closes before Matt stands and kicks his chair back against the wall, heading the same way Bryan just left. Not before gritting through his teeth to tell me, "The meeting is at two pm. I'll meet you there."

I look around the table at our other colleagues, giving them an awkward, tight-lipped smile before slipping out of the room. I glance at my watch and it's just after noon. In most cases, I have at least a week to research to find out more about the company we are pitching to. What their vision is. What other companies have used in the past. What kind of advertising they've done and find out what kind of consulting is needed on their products or platforms. I never want to repeat or give them ideas they have already tried. I like to dig into the executives that I'm meeting with so I can see what they are into. Knowing that helps engage easier with them, but I don't have time for any of that.

I feel like I'm going into a gunfight with a squeegee.

"Okay, breathe," I whisper to myself.

What do I know? I know Ford Enterprises is a parent company to a conglomerate of different companies. They specialize in publishing and own a wide range of different mobile applications that dominate the social media and gaming market.

The spread is so wide it is terrifying.

I have to nail a presentation to a room full of executives and attempt to capture the attention of a target audience ranging from eight years old to eighty years old in a multi-industry market in less than ten minutes.

I'd rather herd chickens on crack.

I can't go back to my office. I'll pace and panic. I need to get to my car, drive for a bit, and I'll go to the Ford building early. I can scope out their office and see if I can understand their tone and what they're all about. I'll Google some more information on the executives while I'm there and get a good idea on their likes so I can be more relatable.

After driving around for a short while, I pull into the parking lot of the Ford building and park. Glancing at my Apple watch, I have a little less than an hour until the meeting to explore and do a bit of research.

The skyscraper is pure glass and breathtaking. It's clear they represent class and luxury. Peering up from the entrance doors, I'm daunted by the size but completely engulfed by its beauty. As I step into the building, the sound of my heels echoes off the walls from the marbled tile flooring. There are large glass sculptures posed all along the lobby entrance and mirror displays that confuse your mind, moving from one dimension to 3D as I walk by.

It's magnificent.

I stop and gaze at my reflection in one of the structures. I'm one hundred percent satisfied that I went with my black and white pinstripe blazer and skirt today. I matched it with a white lacy cami and a gorgeous pair of Jimmy Choo's. I'm checking my buttons and straightening my jacket when Matt's reflection appears in the mirror. I turn around to see him walking with purpose through the lobby peering down at his phone.

"Matt," I call out. "You're early?"

He stops moving his feet, but his momentum still pushes him forward, stumbling.

The look on his face.

I know straight away.

"You fucking lied to me. What time is the actual meeting?"

"It's at 1:30pm, so, right now." His shoulders drop in defeat and not the defeat of shame. The kind that's pissed he got caught.

I pause for a moment. I need to gather my thoughts to find the decent professional woman that lives within my soul so the demon woman that wants to rip his tongue from his trachea doesn't rear her ugly head.

"I didn't ask for this, Matt. It's not my fault that our boss lacks confidence in your skills and asked me to be here, but setting me up for failure is not going to do you or the company any favors. This isn't *just* about you." I am pissed.

I walk towards the elevators to avoid listening to anything he has to say. It will be an excuse or something ridiculous and rude. I have no interest.

He follows me into the elevator and punches the penthouse button with his entire palm. Standing on the opposite side of the enclosed space, he's clearly throwing a silent temper tantrum.

I wonder if my heel can accidentally, somehow, oh I don't know, poke him in the eye and blind him for all eternity.

The elevator is smooth and fast, and I have to push out my jaw to pop my ears as we arrive at our floor. Then my eyes pop out of the sockets as we exit the elevator.

If Caesar had a modern-day Pantheon, this would be it. Large pillars line the back wall, forcefully making their appearance known. Marble graces almost every inch of the floor and walls, with exception of the glass doors behind a desk that flows into the room so well I would have missed it if it weren't for a young girl with beautiful brown eyes and brunette hair standing up to greet us.

"Mr. Randall and Ms. Jenkins?" she asks, her tone as quiet as it is formal.

"That's us," Matt replies back with an unreasonable sharp tongue.

"Great to meet you both, my name is Jenny. Please follow me." She waves her arm in the direction we're heading.

I can't help but side eye roll as he slithers his way in front of me with zero manners.

"Here we are." She opens the floor-to-ceiling glass door and holds it open as Matt walks through without so much as a comment to her. I whisper a *thank you* to her as I walk by. Why a whisper, I have no idea. It felt like anything more would echo through the city like a foghorn. She grants me a silent smile and looks down at her feet.

Upon entering the room, I see three men circled around each other talking, and a fourth man, who has his back to us, looking out the window. His phone is pressed to his ear, engulfed in conversation. I work in a male-dominated industry, and I'm constantly choking on testosterone. For some women, this would be intimidating, but for me, it's liberating.

Matt storms past me, taking charge like the bull that he is, holding his slimy hand out for a shake. He must be nervous. His typical cologne invades my senses, but it's mixed with musk, sweat, and lies. It's off-putting. I watch him talk to a couple of the guys that he must have previously spoken to when he made the appointment. It looks like he knows them casually, maybe at least they are acquainted. He steps back and opens up his closed off space to allow me to step in.

"Gentlemen, I'm here today with my partner from Ashford and Stephens. David, Quincy, Bill, may I introduce..."

"Ellie?" someone calls from the corner.

And my heart plummets to the depths of my terrified soul.

In slow motion, my eyes follow my periphery to see the man pulling the phone away from his ear, now walking towards us. His figure is only a silhouette, blinded by the sunlight streaming from the window behind him. I've only ever given my name as Ellie to one man. The man who had his hands and tongue all over my body two nights ago. The man whose touch seared me to my crumbling bones. The same man I left in the bar without a word, number, nothing.

The same man who just came into my full vision.

Standing right in front of me.

8

ELENA

His gaze is fervent, even more so than the other night. It's mixed with confusion and excitement, and his lip turns up into the sexiest slow motion smile I've ever witnessed.

The air in the room has gone. Evaporated. Leaving nothing but his crisp linen scent and gorgeous smile. How is this man even here? I have absolutely no idea what to say, and I'm three seconds away from running out of the building or jumping out of the window for a faster reprieve.

"Christian Ford! Matt Randall, great to meet you, man!" Matt holds out his hand, nearly pushing me out of the way to stand in front of Chris, breaking our gaze. I stumble slightly and Chris reaches for my forearm to provide some balance. His touch brings on a swarm of memories and forces my breath to hitch.

His eyes shift over to Matt, who's looking star-struck and ridiculous. He's talking incessantly about himself, and Chris says nothing. He doesn't need to say anything when his shoulders tense behind his neck and the grinding of his teeth sound like they cracked a crown. He reaches his hand out to shake with Matt, then pulls away, looking down at his open palm before placing it on his hip, wiping it down his pant leg.

Matt is nervous. Chris is annoyed. And my stomach is in my throat.

This combination is deadly. My eyes side-eye between the floor and Chris, and I realize that we have said nothing to each other. I don't think he'll talk about our Saturday night rendezvous, but I can't risk it either. Matt knows I'm married, and if he gets any idea of what's happening here, he will use it to his advantage. Matt's voice is drowned out, and it feels like a daylight savings hour has passed with no words exchanged, just deep stares and inquisitive looks.

"... Appreciate you making the time. Did I hear you call her Ellie?" Matt's question pulls me from my trance.

Chris's eyes bounce between Matt and I, before he begins to speak, I interrupt. "Elena Jenkins, great to meet you, Mr. Ford," I state, wide-eyed with a Kodak smile. His hand reaches for mine, and he places his other hand over our clasp, engulfing one small part of my body but making it feel like he's everywhere.

This is how I'm playing this? Dumb? Like I've never met him.

Smooth, Elena. Smooth.

He cocks his head with a curious squint. "Great to meet you, too, *Elena*. I thought you were someone else. My apologies." He smiles and mine fades into a close-lipped, shy smile.

What are the chances I just tricked him into thinking that I am not *actually* Ellie? I look more professional, less make-up, and my hair is up in a low pony with my bangs side swept. A hard contrast from the night we met. I might need to get down and pray to baby Jesus for that to come true. I am internally punching myself for not giving him some random name. That way I could really play this card.

"Thank you for the opportunity to present today." Matt

breaks the silence and Christian releases my hand. I didn't even realize he was still holding it. "I know you have limited time..."

"About that," Christian cuts in, "I will need to reschedule this meeting. Something urgent has come up that I need to tend to."

Matt glances at me with a look like that of a toddler. Unsure whether to cry or throw a temper tantrum. He cleanses his face before turning back to Christian. "Christian, I assure you..."

Christian interrupts again, establishing his alpha status. "We're not on the golf course, we're in my office. You can call me Mr. Ford until we're on a first name basis."

Damn.

He just shit on Matt and then used a cum rag to clean him up.

"Your company has a stellar reputation, and I'm interested in hearing your presentation on what you can bring to mine, but I do have to reschedule," Christian states factually.

I glance back at Matt, who is about to open his mouth to counter back with Christian again. He has no idea when to back down. It's infuriating. This actually works out in our favor; we will have more time to prepare a proper presentation. It's a win-win. How does he not see that?

"Mr. Ford, we appreciate the opportunity and will reach out to your team to reschedule. I hope your urgent situation isn't too problematic for you." I place my hand on his arm and the déjà vu hits me like a bolt of lightning. Warping us back to the moment I left him in the bar with this exact gesture. Christian feels it, too. When he looks down at my hand, then back at me, he gives me a knowing smirk, and I want to melt into the floor.

Shit.

"Thank you for understanding. I would like to reschedule with you directly. May I get both of your contact numbers?" Christian asks kindly.

Shit, shit. Double shit.

My wide-eyed expression speaks for me as I remain speechless. Considering he is now a potential client, a big one, I don't have a choice but to give him my number, but that was never the plan. I can't say I don't have a twinge of guilt about that night, but we never feel guilty unless we're caught in a circumstance with whatever is causing that guilt. If this were anyone other than *Chris,* I would not feel guilty about my current lifestyle choices.

Jake and I made the choice to open up our life together sexually, to explore each other and our desires. I have felt more alive in the last few months than ever before. I've never felt sexier or more desired. In my entire life. My husband has brought that out with the fantasy he shared with me, and I've enjoyed every moment we've experienced. I want more. I know I want more. I don't want to feel guilty, but I wish discretion was easier.

That's the thing about choices. All choices have consequences, some more than others.

"Actually, Matt is your point of contact and our team lead. It would be best to reschedule directly with him." I gesture over at Matt and take a step back.

Almost as if there is an invisible string attached to us, Christian glides with my step, keeping the distance the same.

"I'm not asking for my team to have your contact number. I am asking for you to give me your contact information so I can reach out to you directly." He's stern and all business.

He has the upper hand, and he knows it. I can't say I don't enjoy that kind of dominating attitude, but the loss of power has me wanting to get on my knees and remind him how he fell apart in my mouth in seconds.

"Of course, no problem." I smile, reaching into my purse to grab my business card. I glance over at Matt, who is shoving his business card in front of Christian. Christian snatches it from his grasp, not taking his eyes off me.

I look up, grazing my teeth over my bottom lip. My nerves are getting the best of me as I hold out my card. "We won't keep you any longer. Have a great day, Mr. Ford."

"I look forward to hearing from you to reschedule. We will make our calendars available for you anytime that is most convenient," Matt says through gritted teeth.

"Thank you both." He nods at us as he exits the conference room. The room feels ten times bigger now, without his large frame and colossal force. His colleagues follow him out of the room without saying anything to us at all.

I don't know if he is just brushing us off, or if he truly has something urgent to tend to. Either way, I can't help but blow out a sigh of relief when I glance over at Matt, who is scowling at me.

"What's your issue?" My question comes out more hostile than I intend.

"What the hell was that?" he asks with an even more aggressive tone.

I have to tread lightly here, like that whole scene wasn't just Chris and me in an awkward silent banter on display for all to watch. Even though it certainly felt like it.

"He had an emergency. He's rescheduling. We now have more time to prepare for a meeting that you were not ready for. This is a miracle. A really, really good one!"

I trudge toward the conference room door, the tension in the air making it more difficult to walk, when Matt grabs my arm. His grip halts my step. I glance down at where his hand is wrapping tightly around my wrist, and I slowly move my eyes up to meet his.

"No, not that. Why did he call you Ellie? And what was with the weird sexual energy? It was like the intro to a fucking porn video." The squint in his eyes and scowl on his face are lethal. "What are you not telling me?"

I'm transported back to the holiday party when he cornered

me in a room. The same empty look in his eyes. Like his soul has vacated his body and all that is left is a shell, a robot, capable of anything in order to get what he wants.

"Let. Me. Go," I demand.

He blinks and steps back, releasing my wrist.

There is a dark side to Matt that I've seen twice now. I can't imagine him doing anything to hurt someone, but the void in his eyes that fill those moments make me question my own judgment.

"Don't ever touch me again." I am not going to give him any excuse or reason to look deeper into the energy between Chris and me. He can overthink it all he wants. I'm professional and will remain that way without a hint of what happened between us. "I'm going to the elevator. You can take the stairs or wait for the next one."

I pull my arm away from him and walk out of the conference room, leaving Matt behind. Pressing the elevator button, I inhale deeply in hopes of relieving my rising blood pressure. It feels like this is the first breath I've taken since Chris, or *Christian*, appeared in front of me.

God, what are the chances?

I step into the empty elevator, hearing the light sound of music coming through the speaker. An acoustic version of *Manic Monday* playing quietly in the background, which couldn't be any more accurate at this very moment.

I shake my head vigorously, like it will wake me from a bad dream. Instead, my phone buzzes three short times, indicating a text message. I pull my phone from my purse and glance down at the notification from an unknown number.

> Unknown Number: See you soon, Ellie. CF

9

JAKE

Today's productivity levels are near zero. I had a couple of meetings, but the hours in between were spent in another world. Elena has always been at the forefront of my mind, always making sure that I try to do things to help relieve her stress or make her feel like the queen that she is. My Aphrodite.

Today is no different, but it's reached another level. My love for her has always been undying and my attraction to her is near obsessive. The new discovery of our sexual exploration has done nothing but ascend my appreciation, love, and need for her into an uncontrollable hunger.

The memories from that night are just a boomerang in my mind on a continuous loop. Everything about her was captivating. Her dress, her smile, her energy. She was pure desire. He was a moth to a flame, and we all felt the burn.

I finish my workout in our home gym and head upstairs to shower. I'm anxious to see how Elena feels today. That's been one of my favorite things about opening our sex life the way we have. It's unlocked these hidden desires that neither one of us knew existed. They were camouflaged behind embarrassment and uncertainty. Now that we've washed that away, the floodgates have opened and talking about it is one of my favorite things.

Not more than the act itself. It's more so the talk about the act. The anticipation of what *could* happen. The knowledge that it turns her on just as much as it turns me on.

Yesterday when we were at karaoke, she shared with me how Chris made her feel desired in a way she hadn't felt in a long time. That should have made me jealous, but it didn't. It made me realize as much as I try to cater to her needs, it might not speak to her the way I intend it to. I need to do better, for her, in ways that she feels it to her core.

Earlier that day, I gave her permission to "play around", even if I wasn't *around*, and she hated the idea, but told me she knew where I was coming from. She just didn't like that it made her feel like she was doing something unfaithful.

I told her I don't feel that way, especially if the end result is finding a partner for us, for her to play with–hell–even if I joined in for a threesome. We've never done that before or even talked about it, so when I mentioned it last night, during the most inopportune time, she almost snorted her wine out of her nose. I'll never forget that blush.

My sexy wife can stop a freight train with her sexual energy, but will blush at the thought of a threesome. *Adorable.*

The thought of her with two men makes all the blood rush to my cock, and I'm hard as a rock by the time I hit the shower. I have tried to hold off touching myself all day, knowing I am planning to take my wife in every position I could tonight, but I just can't wait any longer. The thought of her on her knees and watching her orgasm in the corner of that bar. It's too much.

I wrap my hand around the base of my cock and slowly stroke myself under the running water. The steam rising around me, and the sounds of the water beating over the tile, muffle the groans coming from deep in my core. She conquers me. Even when she's not here with me. The fact that most men need to watch porn with random women, but all I need is the memory of my wife with me, with any man, leaves me defenseless.

I place my left hand on the tile and lean forward. My body feels heavy as it climbs toward a release. My cock hardens to the point it aches, and my grip tightens as I stroke faster and faster. Remembering how wet she was when I fucked her in the car. When I pulled down her thong and it was soaked with her arousal from the orgasm she received by another man. Kissing her with the taste of his whiskey on her tongue, mixed with his release and her desperation.

Fuck, that does it.

I feel my orgasm climbing when the shower door opens. I turn around and my wife stands before me in nothing but a tiny white tank and a thong. But not before I release a squeal somewhere near that of a pre-teen schoolgirl.

"What are you doing home so early?" I question. " You scared the hell out of me."

Unable to hide her laugh from her words, "I could tell you were getting close. I couldn't even get all my clothes off." She steps into the stream of water that acts like glue to the shirt that now clings to her body. The water makes the cloth suction to her like a second skin. The distance between us is the length of my jutting cock that presses firmly against her belly button. Her hands trail up to my chest and the water is splashing wildly in every direction, including on her white tank top, now soaked and completely see through.

"God, Elena, you are so perfect." I run my hand through her hair. The tips are now partially wet, laying over the tops of her shoulders.

"Do you know how much I crave you? How much my body needs you? You are the sole purpose for my beating heart. The nucleus of my dreams and the salvation of all my nightmares. Every part of me is addicted to you."

I lean down, taking her clothed nipple between my teeth, which earns me a long moan. I close my mouth, sucking on the tight peak, getting a mist of water that coats my tongue. With my free hand, I pull down her panties, and sopping wet, they plop to the ground. Her legs move effortlessly to step out of them, her upper body unwavering, so I can remain attentive to her nipples.

"Did you miss me today, my queen?" Sliding my finger down her center, the distinct feeling of slickness from her pussy defies the moisture from the water.

"You have no idea." Her statement ends with a gasp as my finger enters her swiftly. A second quickly joins the first in perfect rhythm. "You're going to make me come so fast," she whines.

I love it when she's desperate for me.

"So, then I only have one question for you." My lips are feather light against her ear. "Do you want to come on my fingers, my mouth, or on my cock?" I continue to move my fingers in and out of her at a steady pace, curling them just enough to graze her g-spot as her moans grow louder.

Her head is tilted back against the tile, her mouth wide and eyes squeezed shut. She's so close already, and I'm ready to explode. I release her nipple and meet her face to face. "Elena, look at me. Look at me and tell me where you want to come."

She opens her eyes, a storm of ocean waves locked directly on mine. "I need your cock."

I teasingly withdraw my fingers out of her and wrap my hands around her perfectly round ass. I lift her easily as she wraps both her legs around my waist. Her wet pussy aligns with the length of my hard cock, and she circles her hips, rubbing her clit against the pulsing vein that feeds my erection.

Jesus, she's so ready.

I need to fuck her. Hard.

I palm down the shower faucet with force and push open the glass door. Both her legs and arms are wrapped around me, her small frame engulfing me entirely. I step out of the shower. Droplets of water fall to the floor as I walk straight to the edge of our bed and place her down on it. Her white top is completely spackled to her gorgeous curves, and I remain paused, hovering over her and caging her in. I peer into her gorgeous sapphire eyes I fell in love with, and I need her, I just need her so goddamn much.

The height of the bed aligns perfectly with my hips as I pull back and position myself at her entrance. Slowly, I inch in the tip to her wet heat, teasing us both as I pinch her nipple between my fingers.

I hear her gasp and whisper to herself, begging for my cock. She squeezes her eyes shut and I fucking hate that.

I pull my hand away from her nipple, grab her hands in mine and yank them over her hand. Gripping her wrists, I press my weight into my hold.

"Open your eyes." Her eyes snap open as she bucks her hips, silently begging for more. "Eyes on me."

I thrust fully into her until there is no room between us. "Oh, God," she screams as I hiss almost painfully to hold back my need for release.

"Don't fucking move." My free hand pressing into her hip to hold her steady. When I look at her, she's smirking at me, knowing she has me in a chokehold. A literal fucking chokehold with her cunt.

"Someone is ready for me," she states proudly, wiggling her hips just enough to make my breath falter.

"I was ready for you before you rudely interrupted my shower." I smirk at her, as we both try to maintain power.

Still holding her wrists in place, my other hand trails down to her clit, which is easily exposed to me with her legs spread wide around my waist. I place my thumb on the hardened bud with little pressure and rub back and forth, knowing this is her downfall. She gasps and loosens her grip on my waist enough for me to pull back and pump in and out of her.

I continue at a perfect tempo, in and out, my cock getting thicker with each thrust. I keep my thumb on her clit with the same pressure and tenacity that I know she loves. It doesn't take long for our moans to become deeper and more desperate, knowing we are on the precipice, ready to fall.

Her walls start to clench around me, her moans and pleas getting louder, which is now my downfall.

"Don't stop, Jake... Oh, God, I'm going to come," she screams, her words and groans mixing with the slapping of my skin on hers. I can't hold back any longer. My cock hardens like that of platinum steel, exploding into her with the force of a hundred exploding stars.

"Fuck, Elena," is all I can muster when I fall on top of her. Our breathing is heavy and labored, and I have to find the energy to roll over onto the bed next to her.

God, I needed that. I think she needed that, too. The euphoric sensation of the post release is overwhelming, a high I never want to come down from.

"So, how was your day?" My question causes her to giggle. She's clearly still high on her orgasm, too.

"It was interesting," she states, leaning up to kiss my cheek, her demeanor coy.

"Well, that's an *interesting* answer. How so?" I inquire.

"A meeting popped up that I was told I had to do. I wasn't prepared or ready for it at all, so I had no information on the client or their business."

"Well, that happens sometimes. Nothing you couldn't handle, I'm sure," I reply with confidence, knowing my wife and how she hates to be unprepared, but also knows how to wing it.

"When I walked into the conference room for the meeting, it was him." Her head turns to face mine. "Chris."

I press up on my elbows in shock. "Chris. The same Chris?"

"Yup." She pops the P.

I finish plating dinner that we have just cooked together. Neither one of us typically have any meetings on Monday nights, so we decided that we would cook dinner together. I'm a horrible cook, but she bosses me around well in the kitchen. She has a few signature dishes but loves to explore and try new things.

Which is her personality in almost all things in life. One of my favorite things about her. She never shies away from a new experience or challenge.

Tonight is an Italian Sausage and Kale pasta dish with a spring salad and champagne dressing on the side. As I fork into my pasta, I finally ask, "So, how did it happen that you ended up in a conference room with the same stranger that made you orgasm two nights ago?"

Perfectly timed on my part, she was taking a sip of her wine and snorted, almost earning her a nasal enema.

She tells me that Matt, who I have never liked, was able to get a meeting with Ford Enterprises and her CEO demanded she attend the meeting. I sit up straighter, proud of the reputation she has built for herself in that company, and I'm happy to know they see her value. Matt is like a used car salesman and doesn't represent the class that her company portrays. It's like putting a ferret in the same den as dogs. Ferrets are mischievous and frantic compared to the loyalty and intelligence of dogs, and he sticks out like a bull in a china shop.

She finishes telling me the details of the meeting and I'm speechless. I have no idea what the chances of that are, but I would imagine it's somewhere close to getting hit by lightning.

Twice.

"I'm not trying to steal his account, but Bryan asked for me to partner with him and I had no choice. It's good for the company that we team up on this one, being that it's such a big account, but I had no idea that Christian Ford was *the* Chris. I want to try to find a way out of this, but I don't think there is one. It's too big of an account and there is no way Bryan will let me bow out." She takes another sip of wine.

"I thought *maybe* I was able to get away with him thinking I was someone else, but then he texted me," lowering her voice to mock the male tenor, "'See you soon, Ellie,' after I left the office. I knew my jig was up." Her hands are animated as they move around with her words, so I can tell this has her a bit on the edge.

I can't say I'm not feeling the same. A tad bit edgy, perhaps a little inadequate and there's a tinge of jealousy spreading through my veins. The feeling is foreign and I'm not quite sure how to process it.

The stranger that gave her a mind-blowing orgasm is the CEO of one of the biggest media companies in the world. Why couldn't it be some low life punk with no job and minimal ambition? Not that I'm worried about it changing her feelings about me or affecting our relationship, but it would help if he wasn't a goddamn billionaire.

I need to limit my words to let her work through this situation. It can't be easy being in the position she is in. She doesn't want her company to find out about her extracurricular activities, understandably. She's married, which her colleagues are aware of, but her client is not. I'm starting to feel a bit guilty that we didn't try a bar further away or try harder to be discreet.

"What do you think you'll do?" I ask. Letting her know that I am supporting whatever decision she feels is best.

"I'm not sure. But Matt cannot find out. I don't trust him."

Oh, don't I fucking know it. I hate that guy.

She takes another sip of wine. "I don't think Chris paid attention to my hand today, so I doubt he saw my wedding ring, but I think I need to find a way to tell him because it can't continue. He's a client now and it's too risky. I have to wear my ring to work. It would look weird if I took it off now or just for those meetings. I just don't know if he'll keep that kind of secret or use it against me. Plus, what do I say? *'Oh, by the way, I'm in an open marriage and my husband watched you and I in that club.'* No one can find out. I just..." She takes a deep inhale while shaking her head... "No one can find out." The stress radiating from her face is like the sun on a July day in Florida.

She only rambles like this when she overthinks situations. I don't blame her. This is quite the predicament. I can't even imagine the thoughts that are going through her head right now. I know it's ten times more volatile than what she is saying with her words.

"I know this is going to cause you additional stress, and that was the furthest thing from our goal in doing this." I place my hand on her back and spin her stool towards me so we are facing each other. "I don't give a shit what anyone thinks about whatever they find out about our marriage. I care about how you feel and your comfort level." I tuck a loose strand of hair behind her ear, taking in her stunning features. "You are beautiful and strong, and we will work through this like we do with everything, baby. You can tell him or not. You can cut it off with him for any reason you want. You don't owe your co-workers or anyone an excuse for anything. And bottom line, if you want to stop, we stop. Point being, you are in full control, Elena." She leans her forehead into mine, granting me that beautiful smile of hers.

"You are always so calm. How is that?" she asks.

"I am the calm to your storm, baby. I always will be."

10

ELENA

"Cruz, what are you not telling me that you are trying to tell me?"

He's been wandering in and out of my office. Placing documents on my desk, leaving, then coming back to move them to a different spot on my desk and pacing around the office, alternating between humming and whistling. "I know something is up with you," I say as I type on my computer, not glancing his way.

I've been focused on planning for the presentation with Ford Enterprises, even though I don't know when it will be yet. It's only been three days since my run in with Chris, or I should say Christian, and I haven't heard anything from him since. My anxiety about the whole situation is still there, but faded a little. Although the moment I have to meet with him again, I'm certain the stress will barrel through me like a bullet train.

"Who, me?" Placing his hand on his chest, like I just accused him of the assassination of the President.

"Cruz, you forget how well I know you." I smile at him, stepping away from my computer to give him my full attention. "What's up?"

"Finally, jeez. All you've been doing is work, work, work, since this Ford meeting came up. You aren't very fun when you are in serious *work* mode. Do you know that?"

Yes. Because I think everyone can see right through me and judge me for my sexual activities.

"What! I am always fun. You are delusional," I say, stunned, placing my hand on my chest.

"Well, no. But you can keep telling yourself that." He sits down on my chaise lounge, expertly located next to the floor to ceiling bookshelf in the corner of my office. I don't have much space in here, but I did utilize the space to make a comfortable place to relax when I have time.

Which is never.

"You've been in your own world the last couple of days, so I haven't been able to tell you. I have another date this weekend." He smirks, picking at his cuticles.

"How is it that one person can get so many dates?" When I was single, I swear I had a date every other month. Cruz seems to have a date every other day. It's mind blowing and so impressive.

"Gay dating is so different than straight dating. Girls never accept a date. Gay males will go out with anyone at least once and we're not afraid to ask like those boring straight males."

Cruz's openness about dating and his sexuality is so inspiring to me. It makes me wonder why I'm so worried about everything with Christian.

Because you didn't tell him you were married and he's a potential client.

Cruz tells me all about the date he has this weekend, and he sounds excited. His usual tone is uninterested and nonchalant. Like none of it is a big deal, but he's clearly worried about where to go and what to wear on this date, which makes me think he's into this guy already.

"So, why have you become a recluse this week?" he asks, the

sudden change of subject causing my head to snap in his direction.

"I knew it. Something is up, and it's not just the presentation. Talk to me, Goose." He giggles anytime he gets to make a Top Gun reference.

I know I could tell him. He would keep it secret. I trust him, through and through. I just feel uncomfortable. Maybe a little ashamed. Even though there is no reason to, not in front of Cruz. And there's the fact that I'm a grown woman in a consensual open relationship with her husband. Who the fuck cares what anyone else thinks?

"So... I—" My phone pings, interrupting my confession. I glance down the screen, lighting up brighter than a helicopter spotlight with the name, *Christian Ford.*

Fuck.

I look around the room guiltily, wondering if the whole building now knows that Christian Ford is texting me. I feel like a rebellious teenager who just got busted dating the bad boy, the *off-limits* guy that everyone tells you not to date.

Technically, you shouldn't be.

But I'm not.

Jesus, Elena, get yourself together.

I reach for my phone to tap the message and view it. The *FaceID* popup appears just as my office door flies open, thundering against the wall and forcing me to look in that direction.

"Matthew, what in the dickens is wrong with you?" Cruz yelps, holding his hand to his chest.

"Matt. It's still Matt. Always Matt," he scolds Cruz with both his tone and a physical eye roll.

"Have you heard from him?" Matt asks, shifting his gaze towards me.

Placing my phone back on my desk, I grab my coffee cup to keep my hands busy and turn to face him.

"Who?" I ask, my face saying more than my words.

"Who? You know who." He stares at me with his hands displayed out like he just asked me what one plus one is. "Christian Ford, Elena." His words laced with anger and drenched in annoyance.

I am a horrible liar.

The fact that I have technically not seen his text message grants me the ability to say, "No," without remorse. It's been three days since that meeting and I'm surprised Matt hasn't reached out to reschedule the meeting. It's not his personality to wait for anything that he wants or hold off on calling a client like Christian Ford to immediately reschedule. If I had to guess Christian and his team are ignoring Matt.

Matt stalks towards my desk, stopping directly in front of me. "I don't believe you," he accuses, as easily as ordering his morning latte. "I know what a man in need looks like. He wanted you like he's already had you. Has he?" He smirks, and his eyes trail over my body in a way that makes me want to vomit.

"Why don't you eye fuck me like that, Matthew?" Thankful for Cruz's interruption since I'm currently left speechless.

"This doesn't involve you," he spits at Cruz, not tearing his gaze away from me.

I hate confrontation. My blood pressure spikes, my pulse races, which I can start to feel everywhere, and anything I had in mind to say flies out of my brain into an abyss of nothing, so if any words come out of my mouth, they are never the ones I had envisioned saying. It's like all my knowledge of the English language evaporates and I'm left with the vocabulary of a pigeon. I even do the weird neck thing they do.

But he is fucking pissing me off, and I'm going to say exactly what I want to say.

Professionalism, gone.

"Matt..." I'm interrupted again by my phone, ringing this time. Not only does it sound loud enough for the entire block to hear, but it's also buzzing on my desk, shrieking for attention.

I don't need to turn to look at it to know who it is. I can tell by the look on Matt's face as he studies my phone, and his eyesight returns to mine.

The smile that creeps on Matt's face is like that of Satan.

"Your *friend* is calling." Sinister smile on full display.

If I don't answer it, it's obvious something is going on. But, if I do, I have no idea what Christian might say.

I can't risk either.

I am totally fucked.

I reach for the phone, matching the speed of a sloth. Matt is clearly uneasy and panicking, but all Cruz needs is a bowl of popcorn as he watches us, reveling in the drama.

With my phone in my hand, I glance back up at Matt. "The presentation isn't ready, and I don't want to take his call if he asks us to rush down there right now. I have no idea why he would call me, but I can only assume it's because he knows you're a pompous prick with inapt ideas that are total shit."

Cruz coughs once, then again, and chokes on what appears to be his own spit.

Paying too much attention to Cruz, I didn't sense Matt step forward. He quickly swipes my phone to answer the call. It was so fast, when I look down, I realize he also pressed the speaker button.

"Ms. Jenkins?" How his deep gravelly voice radiates through the room even though it's out of a tiny ass speaker is magic, Merlin business I'll never understand.

"... Hello?"

I have never wanted to pretend to be an auto-attendant voice message more than at this moment.

"Hi, it's me, hi..." *Jesus Christ, who am I Taylor Swift?* "Mr. Ford, my apologies. I've been having some... technical issues with my phone this morning." I shoot daggers with my eyes at Matt and circle around back to my desk chair.

"It would appear so, considering you read my text message I sent earlier, but did not respond back." I can't read his tone. Not angry, not playful. Just factual.

Matt's face. Red. Steaming. Readable.

Shit.

"I'm glad you called. We've been working on a few ideas to present to you and your team whenever you're available to reschedule our meeting." I am a professional deflector today.

My anxiety is boiling over as I wait for the shoe to drop.

There's a pause that feels like a lifetime as I steal glances at both Cruz and Matt, then look back down at my phone. I'm internally praying to any higher being that nothing sexual or anything that references my sins from Saturday night is exposed.

After the pause of the century, "My morning opened up tomorrow. If you could come by around 11am, I have about half an hour before a lunch appointment."

Releasing my stalled breath, "That sounds great, Mr. Ford. We will be punctual and prompt." Matt mouths *yes* with a dramatic fist pump to himself.

"I wouldn't mind if you left Mr. Randall behind. His presence annoys me, in more ways than one." Matt's face drops.

Cruz's hand flies over his mouth as he falls back onto himself, trying his best not to burst out in laughter.

What the hell do I say to that?

"*I agree.*"

"*You're telling me.*"

"*We have something in common.*"

"I'm sorry you feel that way, Mr. Ford. I assure you Matt is one of the best marketing consultants that we have. It would be a detriment to your company to not give him the opportunity to present with me. If, after the presentation, you feel the same way, we can absolutely assign another consultant to work with you on this project." My praise for Matt tastes like a moldy sour patch kid.

"I think I might prefer just to hire you for my team. You can sell ice to an Eskimo." You can practically hear his smile. "I'll see you both tomorrow at 11am." He abruptly ends the call, and I toss my phone on my desk and fall back into my chair.

I'm relieved. We got a meeting, and I wasn't outed. I need to go buy myself a lottery ticket because I've never felt so lucky in my entire life. Matt doesn't hide his scowl. I think I actually see his eye twitch and he's sweating, but I don't care. I look at my office door and hold my hand out towards it, inviting him to see himself through it.

"I'm not leaving until you tell me what the fuck is going on," he blurts out.

"Nothing, Matt. You just can't stand it that he doesn't like you. Now, get the hell out of my office." Cruz is still trying to hide his giggling. "You, too, Cruz."

I swear if I don't get a minute alone to get my shit together, I'm gonna lose it.

"What did I do?" he squeals.

"I have work to do. Both of you. Go."

Cruz stands up. "This was priceless. I couldn't pay for this kind of entertainment." He blows a kiss to me and saunters out.

Matt leans forward, placing his palms flat down on the opposite side of my desk, trying his best to intimidate me. "I don't know what you're up to, Elena, but I'm going to find out, and when I do..."

"Get. Out." I rise. Thankful I wore my extra high heels today to rival his height.

He pushes himself off my desk and leaves my office, slamming the door hard enough one of my picture frames sways and shifts unevenly against the wall.

Dick.

My phone buzzes in front of me.

> Christian Ford: Between our encounter Saturday night and putting me on speaker today, you are making me believe you like to have an audience, Ellie.

11

ELENA

"So by changing the algorithms to bring forward some of the features that were most prominent on our survey, you'll not only increase user engagement but create more value for each individual user. The goal—" Matt interrupts me for what must be the tenth time. I stare up at the ceiling and close my eyes to conceal my eye roll.

"The goal is making a more addictive platform. More use, more ads, more clicks, more money for you." Matt smiles at the Ford team as he slaps his hands together in a praying motion, like he's presenting the Holy Grail that will make them an ungodly amount of money.

And, no, that is definitely not the goal.

I've spent countless hours putting together this presentation, more than any other account. It helped that I had quite a bit of background, being that Cruz was, well, still is, an avid user of XConnect. He was able to fill me in on the details from a user's perspective. The detail that went into the planning, the census polls I created on the platform to get an idea of what the existing users were feeling and would want to see to make it better.

I created my own profile with a fake name, of course, and realized how it might actually help Jake and me in our newfound sexual adventures. XConnect is not like any other online or application-based matchmaking service. It's a matchmaking platform, yes, but for specific needs.

Currently, you can choose from a few different options for what you are looking for when you create your account. It can be as simple as someone looking for a hiking partner or a friend to play sports with. Pet parent options to find friends for their fur babies. Book lovers looking to connect, all the way to no strings attached, friends with benefits, profile options for people just looking for a quick hookup. It even dives further into different types of sexual pleasures. The options were vast and overwhelming.

According to the Ford team, the original concept of XConnect was that "X" was the unknown variable and "Connect" was to connect people with endless options for specific needs. Great concept–amazing actually–but too widely loose from a user's perspective. I incorporated all of these things into presenting the best plan for the next steps for XConnect. This was far more than just a standard marketing plan; it crosses over into consulting to make their product better.

And this is a tiny portion of their entire company's portfolio. Just one of their social media platforms that we may get contracted on. If this succeeds, they have so much more to offer.

But so do I.

I know I'm the best person for this. After my research, I'm not only intrigued, but fully invested, more than I probably should be.

Now, in the middle of the meeting I've spent the entire week preparing for, Matt has consistently interrupted me. Taking over, bullying me silently, and frankly, I'm getting fucking tired of it.

I don't know if Christian and his team have realized it. They might just think that it's part of our presentation. Me speaking eloquently on the facts, then Matt "coming in for the kill", so to speak, in some aggressive and sleazy way. Like it's the Matt and Elena roadshow and we've planned our scene.

I'm disgusted. And I've never felt like this before.

I did see Christian shift in his seat and whisper something to someone on his team, but that could have been totally unrelated.

Not only have I had to see him, I've *felt* him, too. His attention is laser-focused when I'm speaking, and even when Matt takes over, his focus remains on me. I can't say it's not stirring something inside me. It's the same attention I felt from him at the club that night. Like when he wants something, he goes after it and isn't afraid to show it. Standing in front of him presenting this today, I feel like I'm naked on a platter, serving myself to him. My body is all for that, based on the incessant throbbing between my legs.

I still struggle with the feeling of being so attracted to another man, but whenever Jake and I talk about it, the openness of the possibilities are actually bringing us closer together. Plus, I'm talking to him more about my needs and desires, and I can feel myself letting loose, wanting to explore more.

I wouldn't mind doing more with Christian.

Focus, Elena.

I bring myself back into the conference room that we're presenting in. It's different from the one that we came to last week. This one is set up specifically for presentations. An old-fashioned whiteboard at the front, along with a projection screen backdrop and monitor displays that are remote controlled that can move down from the ceiling to meet some additional monitors that come up from the wall to wall credenza to make one ginormous screen.

It caters to all styles of presenting.

It's impressive.

Jesus, he is still talking, and they are getting bored. It's time to end it before they call it.

I interrupt Matt. "To summarize, we feel this approach will not only gain more traction for you but, also—" annnnnd he interrupts me again. This time my neck cranks over to him so fast I almost pull a muscle. I won't say anything unprofessional in front of them, but I can't say I won't punch him in the elevator in private.

Although, I realize I won't need to do that when Christian stands up so abruptly, his chair flies into the back wall and the arm handle breaks off upon impact, making a loud cracking sound. Matt looks over at him in shock. Christian leans forward, placing his palms on the table he was just sitting at, his hazel eyes turning to a dark shade of amber that could be mistaken for fire. It's the scariest death stare I think I've ever seen in real life.

"Get. Out," Christian grits between his teeth.

"Excuse me?" Matt shifts in place, putting his hands in his pockets, probably to hide his clenched fists.

"You heard me. Get. Out." Christian pushes himself off the desk, standing upright as to assert domination and walks around the desk to meet Matt, face to face.

Oh, shit.

"Mr. Ford." I step forward to try to stand between them. All we need is a full on brawl inside the Ford Enterprises building to make headlines with my company.

Christian says nothing, but holds his palm in my direction as to tell me to shut the hell up and stop moving.

And I listen.

"I'd like to hear what your partner would like to say. What she has said has been substantially more entertaining and valuable than anything that has come out of your mouth, and I'm tired of seeing you interrupt her because you can't get your ego under control. Get out of my building. You're not welcome back here."

Chris tilts his head to make eye contact with someone standing outside the glass conference room doors and holds up two fingers, beckoning him into the room. He barely has one foot through the door when Christian tells him to escort Matt out of the building.

Matt's glare scrutinizes me as he steps backwards, then turns on his heel to walk out of the door the man is holding open for him.

When the door shuts, Christian walks back over to his team, who are completely unfazed, like this is a daily event. "Thank you, Ms. Jenkins. Your presentation was excellent. I'd like to hire Ashford and Stephens for this project with you taking the lead on it. I will only do this under the condition that Matt Randall is not a part of this project. I don't like his vision or his attitude, and I don't want that associated with my company." Christian is all business now.

"Absolutely. I completely understand, and I'm honored to be part of this project with you and your team," I say, graciously. Although, my inner goddess is screaming. Not just screaming, but the high-pitched, rolling over myself, squealing, kind of screaming. It's amazing that I'm able to contain my excitement.

"We will draft up the contract and send it over to you before the end of the week. I'd like you to start immediately and expect a full commitment until we've finished this project. I have off-site teams that I would like to introduce you to, so that may require some travel. Starting next Wednesday, with the meetings already scheduled in Arizona and California." He ends it there, as a statement.

"That's not an issue, Mr. Ford. Thank you for choosing Ashford and Stephens for this project," I say, matching his professionalism.

"You can call me Chris, and I didn't choose your company. I

chose you." His eyes meet mine, and I think all my insides just evaporated into tiny pin needles. My lips turn up slowly into a smile, and I'm trying to find words–any words to make this moment less awkward. "Will you excuse us?" he says.

"Oh, of course." I jolt. Shit, I missed my exit queue. That definitely did not make this any less awkward. Shaking my head out of the trance of his gaze to gather my belongings.

"Not you, Elena. Guys, will you excuse us? I'd like to have a word with Ms. Jenkins in private." He motions his team to exit.

Shutting their folders and laptops, they quickly exit the room. I've never seen such a militant exit before.

Leaving just the two of us in a space alone, which has not happened since our night in the club. I suddenly feel the nerves and anxiety I was able to suppress earlier come back full force. The doors close as his team leaves the room, and apparently, they take all the air with them, because it feels like there is nothing but a thick fog of tension.

"Ellie, you are one impressive and mysterious woman." He walks towards the middle of the table and grabs one of the controllers, hitting a couple of buttons, then glances towards the door everyone just left through. A low buzzing sound fills the room, and I peer around the room as a black out shades roll over to cover every single glass surface in the room. A soft click on the door, and I assume we're locked in *and* everyone else is locked out.

Shit. Shit. Shit.

I'm not sure what my response should be to his comment. It's really a half compliment so a *thank you* would sound weird. My nerves are on display and I have no idea how to control them. This man was dominating in the sexiest way when we met, but here, in his territory, he's more intimidating than a brown bear coming out of hibernation desperate for his next meal. He prowls around the same as he crosses the room toward me. Naturally, I ease a few steps back until my ass bumps into the wall, mirroring the same position I was in that first night.

"I like you in this position," he whispers, leaning into my neck.

"I think I like it, too." My eyes widen at my words. Jesus, why did I say that out loud?

I feel his warm breath on my skin. Frozen in place, he wraps his hand around my waist and pulls me flush against him, feeling how hard he already is through his pants. Every ounce of sensation I can feel pulses down between my legs and I know he can sense it.

"Do you see what you do to me, what you have done to me since the moment we met?" Pulling me closer to him, which seems impossible, yet he manages to squeeze more air out of the space between us. "I feel the need to remind you how great Saturday night was so you don't disappear on me again."

He unbuttons the top two buttons of my silk blouse, allowing it to fall open, exposing my red satin bra. Leaning his upper body back, he scans me up and down, then hisses, clenching his teeth like the view is painful.

"You are impossible to resist." He slams his mouth to mine. A moan escapes my mouth as his tongue strokes my lips, sending electric heatwaves to my core. I reach for his buckle as he reaches for my top. He's unmatched in speed and my blouse is now fully open. Already pulling up my skirt to my waist, reaching underneath, exposing my matching red thong.

He pulls back again, giving me a once over again. "Fuck," he growls.

Spinning me around, "Put your hands on the wall," he demands in a deep growl.

Like a robot with no mind of its own, I do as he says. My heartbeat matches the throbbing coming from that small bundle of nerves at the apex of my thighs. He grabs my hips, rubbing his rock hard erection on my ass. His pants are still on, but I can feel everything, everywhere. He reaches around, inching his fingers towards my clit, and the moment the pad of his finger meets the hard bud, I almost collapse and groan in unexplainable pleasure.

"Oh, God." I throw my head back as he wraps his free arm around my waist, holding me up.

"You are soaking, Ellie. Were you thinking about our night during our meeting?" I can hear the amusement in his voice. It sounds like sex and my pending doom.

His finger is moving back and forth in perfect rhythm, torturing me. The entire time, he's nibbling on my ear, and I feel him becoming as desperate as I am. He presses against me, now biting at the nape of my neck.

"I'm so close," I whisper, ashamed of how quickly he got me here.

"So close to what?" he says with a smirk.

My breathing becomes erratic, my uncontrollable moans fill the room, and I've lost all sense of what is happening.

He's in full control and knows it. I know he wants me to beg for it like I had to before. I wish for the willpower to tell him I don't want it, but there is nothing I want more at this moment.

And I'm no liar.

"Please, Chris. Please make me come." The movement of his fingers is pure magic, forcing me to beg.

Like that was a secret password, he places his foot between my legs, kicking my feet apart to spread me wider, exposing my swollen clit. He's hugging me so close his fingers are able to reach all the way past the entrance with his palm resting on my clit, and his movements are pure magic. Pressing his fingers inside me enough to tease my need to be filled, then withdrawing to stroke my center until his fingertips are back on my clit. He does this over and over again, gently pinching my clit before diving his fingers back into me.

I can't take it anymore.

"Chris!" I scream. Loud. So loud my moans echo across the room. His arm releases my waist to cover my mouth, bringing the back of my head to rest on his shoulder as my muffled screams vibrate through his palm.

"Ellie..." His voice in my ear scolds me as my orgasm rips through my body.

"Soon, Ellie. Soon, I am going to take you in every position I've imagined you in, when there are no limitations to the sounds that I will force out of you, and I can't wait to hear you completely unleashed." He releases the pressure of his palm on my mouth as I come back down to earth. I feel like I'm floating down and finally standing back on solid ground. He turns me around slowly to lean back against the wall for the support I so desperately need.

I'm certain at this point in time I look like I've been hit by a train, and here I am, staring at this striking, handsome, well-built Greek god. He's reaching for his belt, unbuckling the front of his pants.

"Tell me, Ellie. Are you ready for me?"

Yes. Yes, I am.

Just as he reaches the top button, a loud bang reverberates through the room and someone yells, "Ow!" behind the door. I jump, wrapping one arm around my breasts and using the other to pull my skirt down. Not like that is going to help the fact that I'm half naked in a conference room with the CEO after he just hired me for a job.

Jesus, what the hell am I doing?

"Chris, Chris! There's a fire in the building. You in there?" A frantic voice yells from the other side of the door. "Why is this locked? Jenny, can you grab the key?"

We both crank our necks toward each other.

"Who the hell is that?" I whisper yell to him.

"Dietrich. He's head of my security." The worry on his face is obvious. Probably for both our situation and the fire he just heard about.

He reaches for my clothes in an attempt to help me get dressed, but I swat his hands away and whisper, "Go."

"I'm not leaving you cornered in a conference room when there is a fire in the building. Get dressed." He adjusts himself as he buckles his belt and pulls his phone out of his pocket. "Seven missed calls," he comments under his breath, shaking his head.

At this point, I've finished buttoning the top of my blouse and I'm fully dressed, but I look far from put together. When I walk out that door, they are probably going to think I just came from the actual fire. He rushes over to the table where he left the controller. The shades start to retract and the lights bloom.

Tossing the controller down, he turns back and grabs my hand to pull me closer to him as he walks. In a gut reaction, I pull my hand away, afraid of what it might look like when we exit the room. He winces like I just branded him in the chest with a scorching trident. His eyes gaze down at the ground, blinking in confusion, but when the sound of keys jangling returns from behind the door, he glances back up and the door swings open.

"Dietrich. What's going on?"

"Someone started a fire on the first floor, sir. Looks like one was started in the main lobby bathroom. They also took toilet paper from the storage space of the bathroom and threw the excess rolls in the elevator, then lit them on fire as well. There is minimal damage, and the fire is all under control, but we're evacuating everyone to be safe until the fire department clears us. I'm guessing it could be those same kids that tried to graffiti the building last week." All of this flows out of Dietrich like he was talking about the latest NCIS show and it's like the most natural thing on earth.

He's taller than Christian, which is a feat in itself, but also broader and more intimidating. He's wearing all black, matching his dark salt and pepper hair, although he has an incredibly young-looking face, so it's impossible to guess his age.

"Good call. Just send everyone home for the day and have Jenny notify everyone to return on Monday. I want the fire department to have ample time to inspect the building before anyone returns," Christian states, like he's done this a million times.

I'm impressed that his first concern is about his employees and not the building or who could have done it.

Dietrich looks at me, confused as to why I'm standing here like a lemur, unable to blink, just bouncing my view between the two of them. Chris misses nothing and introduces me, "Dietrich, this is Elena Jenkins, we've just hired her from Ashford and Stephens for our initiative on XConnect."

"Welcome to the team, Ms. Jenkins. Great to meet you." Somehow my face hides the disgust at being called 'Miss'. Hearing it makes me realize how deceiving I've been, and not correcting them is a blatant lie. Along with not wearing my wedding ring today. I knew Matt wouldn't notice. I could wear a doorstop on my face and he wouldn't notice. Cruz did, though. I told him a diamond was loose and it was at the jewelers. The lie felt like razor blades as it left my lips.

When Jake and I talked about the ring last night, it was a tad awkward, but necessary. I didn't want to wear it and risk Chris seeing it during the presentation, then have him potentially freaking out. I don't think he would do something like that, but after talking out the scenario, we decided against it. And now the guilt is weighing on me.

Most men would be excited and beyond relieved to have no strings attached sexual escapades with a woman who requires no obligations, but not saying anything is literally killing me. It's misleading, and it's not at all who I am. Plus I have no idea where he's at or what he's expecting. It's making me sick to my stomach, and I can't stand how I feel about myself. Especially after my loss of control in the conference room a few minutes ago.

I need to leave.

"Thank you, Dietrich. Good to meet you, too." I give him a polite smile and turn to Chris. "Mr. Ford, you have a lot of things to do here. I'll take the stairs down to the lobby and we can reconnect next week."

"No," he behests. "I'll take you down in the service elevator." Nodding to Dietrich in some silent code before he places his palm at the small of my back. He leads me down a hallway past a few empty offices until we arrive at large metal doors that look like they can hold two sizable vehicles.

The doors open quickly as Chris ushers me in and uses a key card to press the "L" button. His scent is alluring and lingers in the air. It's slightly different from last weekend. Where the whiskey notes of his scent are gone, it's replaced with a woodsy spice and still that hint of spearmint. It invades the small space we are currently in, and I can smell him on every inch of my skin that he just devoured with his fingers.

"I don't trust being behind closed doors with you," I say, with the upmost factuality as I step to the back of the elevator before the doors begin to close. I keep my chin high and study a small smudge on the metal door to avoid all eye contact with him.

"You shouldn't." He steps forward, pressing his hand against my collarbone, guiding me to the back wall.

Slowly, so slowly he leans into me. His lips graze mine feeling softer than cashmere against my skin. "You shouldn't trust me when I don't trust myself." His voice pained with so much pleasure.

Finally pressing our lips together, his tongue parts my lips as he brushes it over mine with delicate precision. I welcome the invasion, it tastes both sweet and sinful. Quickly, so quickly, his movements turn frantic, his hands unable to be in all the places he wants them to. He's desperate and intense. Like he was in shackles until the moment those doors closed and now he's been freed. He reaches underneath my blouse, pinching my pebbled nipple, moaning into my neck and ear.

"Ellie, I need you." He palms my sex, pressing his hips into me, and all I can do is whimper into his mouth as he continues to invade mine.

The elevator doors must open with the grace of a ballerina being that neither one of us heard the gigantic metal doors slide open, exposing us to the expansive lobby.

He pulls away, his dark pupils stretching over his deep amber irises contradicting the smile that begins to tug at his lips. Grabbing my hand, "Come with me."

As he turns around, we're met face to face with a stoic and amused Matt. Slowly, so slowly it feels like watching a slow motion video, a smile forms across his face. His eyes gaze to where our hands are intertwined. "Well, this is interesting. I've never known you to sleep your way to the top but," he shrugs, "maybe this is what you've always done. You've clearly pulled the wool over my eyes. I'm curious though. Does your husband have any idea?"

My neck swivels slowly as I look up to Christian from the corner of my eye. I swallow thick and hard as my cheeks flush with embarrassment and my eyes flood with shame.

He squints at me, confused. I can see all the moments we've shared going through his head as he tries to make sense of what he just heard. Releasing my hand, he steels his spine and places his hands in his pockets.

I don't know exactly how much Matt saw, probably just the hand holding, but clearly there *is* something going on. Matt is playing the card he currently has, which is knowing there is sexual energy between us. Christian is too smart to play into it.

"I was seeing Elena safely to the lobby. You both should exit immediately, as we're unsure of the damage done from the fire." He places his palm out towards the opening of the elevator and I step out.

"Chri..." I shake my head. "Mr. Ford, I..." my words stammering.

"We have meetings starting at eight AM on Wednesday morning. Good day, *Mrs.* Jenkins." His eyes flicker to mine for a moment when he exaggerates the missus.

His tone is unsettling.

He focuses on the panel in the elevator as he presses the button for his floor and holds what I can only assume is the *close this elevator door STAT* button.

"Oh, and Mr. Randall," Christian adds.

"Yes?" Matt peers into the elevator entrance to face him, looking like a needy girl on her first date.

Christian, the alpha that he is, gets the last word.

"Get the fuck out of my building."

The elevator doors close and suck all the air in the room with them.

12

JAKE

"Hey Cruz." I walk up to his desk outside of Elena's office. "Is my blue-eyed bride back from her presentation at Ford yet?"

"Oh, Jake, you are such a romantic." He bats his eyelashes and crosses his hands over his heart as he gushes at the bouquet of flowers I have in my hand. "She's not back yet, but should be any minute. I can totally give those to her for you." He stands up to grab the vase, but not before I shift it away from his grasp.

"You know, I'm not convinced you'll *actually* give them to her." Giving him a knowing smile and a suspicious eyebrow raise.

Cruz is always a handful, but in the best way. He's been the most supportive assistant my wife has ever had and has a great sense of humor. He probably crosses the line more often than not, and I'm sure he is an HR nightmare, but he keeps my girl laughing and happy and that's all I care about.

The elevator dings and there is distinct banter coming from whoever is in there. It causes everyone on the floor, which is only a few people, to stop and look.

I angle my head to get a better line of sight as the elevator doors open, and my pulse starts racing for two reasons. One, Elena is in a fire engine red silk blouse that lays over every inch of her upper body perfectly, tucked into a black knee-length skirt that hugs everything on her bottom half like a glove. Two, Matt is distinctly yelling at *my* wife.

If I didn't know any better, I would think he was trying to sign her to death. Moving his fingers with bizarre flicking motions as he flails his arms back and forth and over his head, clearly irritated and pissed off. Elena has all those same emotions showing but in a silent body language. Even if the grim reaper walked in, she would still be more terrifying.

Stepping out of the elevator, she interrupts Matt during his tangent. "This conversation is over." Her tone sounds as hard as the vase in my hands.

Matt looks at her, astounded. Clearly shocked that she would talk to him that way, but as he opens his mouth to continue to berate my wife, he glances my way, double takes, then cuts himself off. He stumbles over a few words before composing himself, pulling the front of his jacket down and puffing his chest to attempt to establish his self-proclaimed alpha status.

Oh, I don't think so, prick.

I have no desire to pull my dick out and have a cock fight with this guy. But I will knock him the fuck out if he keeps talking to my wife that way.

Curious as to why Matt's behavior changed so suddenly, Elena looks up towards Cruz's desk and her eyes connect with mine. Her eyes flick over to the bouquet, then back again, and the smile that tugs at her lips is intentionally being suppressed. She blinks away, looking down in what looks like shame.

Did they not nail the Ford account?

I would be astonished if she didn't because it was good. Really good. She rehearsed the entire presentation on me and nailed everything from increasing basic account membership sign-ups to implementing integration with other products. It was brilliant.

She waves off Matt, the same way the Queen of England would when dismissing someone, and heads towards me. The curls in her blonde hair match the silk blouse, bouncing with each step she takes. She's like a walking shampoo commercial.

"Hi." The timid curve of her lips conflicting itself with her confident cherry red lips.

"Hey, sweetheart. Everything okay?" I lean in to kiss her cheek as my eyesight moves from her to the relentless man walking up behind her.

"Speak of the devil," Matt's booming voice resonates from behind her. I see the hidden eye roll as I pull back from her.

Not feeding into whatever he's trying to accomplish, I give him a curt nod and a simple, "Matt."

"You know, Jake. You have quite the impressive woman here. Super talented. Smart like a fox, this one. Committed to doing *anything* to get what she wants." The word 'anything' drawn out by a mile.

If the Cheshire Cat had a twin, it would be Matt in his current state.

"Well, I'll leave you guys to it. I'm going to head to Bryan's office to...", a distinct pause and long thought as Matt taps his chin contorting his face, "tell him how everything went." He turns on his heel and stalks off.

I look back at Elena, pure hatred seeping from every pore in her body.

"What in the ever-loving hell was that?" Cruz spits as he sits back down at his desk.

Elena ignores Cruz, which I'm sure is a standard response in most cases when there is drama. She just shakes her head like nothing happened and reaches for the vase.

"These are beautiful. Thank you." She grants me a half smile that doesn't meet her eyes. Something is definitely wrong.

Before she can grab it, I pull the vase closer to me, tucking it into the left side of my body, shifting further away from her reach. "Let me help you put these in your office." I gesture towards her office door and that free hand meets the small of her back to help guide her there quickly.

We walk through the doorway, and I close the door behind us. My soft demeanor morphs into something much more aggressive as I stalk toward her. She is leaning on the back of her desk with her arms crossed over her chest, staring down at absolutely nothing. I place the vase down next to her and cup my hands around her face.

"What happened?" Pulling her face up to look at me. "Did he touch you?"

She once told me that he tried to make a pass at her some time ago and she brushed it off like it was nothing, but I could tell there was more to it that she wasn't telling me. She never reported it, since there was alcohol involved, and according to her, "nothing happened", but I think she downplayed the entire story. I know she can handle herself, but the thought of another man doing anything that makes her uncomfortable throws me into a fit of rage. A stark contrast from the craving I have while watching her with men she desires.

I guess that's the key.

I want her desperate for it. Not despising it.

"No. No, nothing like that." She waves her hand in the air, brushing it off.

"I thought you were heading out with your old college friends tonight?" she asks, ignoring this entire line of questioning.

"I am, but I wanted to see you since I wasn't going to be home when you got home." I release her chin and place my hands over her hips. "Don't ignore the situation. What happened?" I inquire again.

She huffs out a deep breath.

"Christian loved all the ideas. He hated Matt, kicked him out, and hired me. On the spot." Her palms cover her face, spreading them open so her eyes peek through, but her mouth is still covered. She looks up with a smirk in her eyes. "But when I say he kicked Matt out, I mean, he literally kicked Matt out of the building. He said he couldn't stand that Matt kept interrupting me and disrespecting me and since he had nothing good to say, he told him to get out."

Okay, I like this Christian guy already.

"El, you should be so fucking proud of yourself. You're feeling ashamed and guilty that he was kicked out. He caused that, not you. Stop drowning yourself in sorrow for someone else's actions." She always feels bad in situations like these, especially when she is a benefactor of something positive, but she deserves this.

"No, it's not that. Well, not entirely." She looks down at her shoes as she shifts uncomfortably.

I can tell when my wife is timid from being intimidated, compared to her feeling shy and having a hard time finding her words. This was the latter.

My voice deepens. A hum of curiosity leaves my lips as I grip her hips a little tighter. "And what else happened?"

She bites her lip as her ocean eyes stare at me. A tsunami of lust tearing through them.

"He wanted to meet with me privately after the meeting."

Oh, of course he did.

"He told me how disappointed he was in how I left him at the bar and felt the need to remind me again. He... um, fingered me, until I came." Her pebbled nipples are about ready to cut through the fabric of her blouse.

"Was it just as good as last time, baby?" I run a knuckle over the peak of her nipple. She gives me a breathy nod. "And... what else?"

"He started to unbuckle his pants and asked if I was finally ready for his cock."

Oh, Jesus.

I pull her hips into mine so she can feel how hard I am, giving her permission to continue.

"But there was a fire in the building and security was called, and I had to put myself together and run out of the conference room in a freaking total panic."

Well, that was like taking a cold plunge.

"What the hell?" I grab her arms and face and turn to investigate like she's possibly hurt somewhere.

"I'm fine." She half laughs. "Christian saw me out of the building and took us down the service elevator. I think he wanted to try to take me somewhere private to finish what we started, but Matt was standing at the elevator when the doors opened. He saw Christian holding my hand, trying to lead me out through the doors, and pretty much called me a slut for sleeping my way to the top and asked if my husband knew I did that. Now he feels like he has something on me that he can hold over my head. To both you and my CEO." She releases a long huff, defeated of breath. "I just don't know what Matt will try to do."

The raging hard on I just had between my legs is now replaced with an inferno of anger everywhere.

Elena's shoulders slouch forward, and her forehead meets the middle of my chest. What the hell do I say to this? Saying "it's all going to be alright" doesn't feel right because she and I both know that Matt has been dying for a promotion and will probably stab at anything to get it.

"El, you can't overdose yourself on anxiety when you don't know what someone else's actions will be. Matt is unpredictable. I know it's impossible, but try not to focus on what he's going to do, and just keep doing the job you know how to do." I lift her chin to look at me eye to eye. "Maybe he'll do nothing and he's just trying to make you stress." She scoffs at my comment. And she's right. I'd bet my left testicle he'll find a royal flush in the cards he holds. Somehow, someway.

"Regardless, baby, we'll figure it out," I assure her. Which is all I can do.

Then it dawns on me. She didn't mention anything about Christian's reaction.

"Wait." My brows pinch together as I try to recall some of her previous statements. "Did Christian hear what Matt said?"

She pulls away from me, crossing her arms over her torso, and looks away. The same guilt I've seen when she is unsure about someone else's feelings.

"He did..." She shifts her stance and pulls herself upright. "He seemed confused, but just excused himself. Then he reminded me that he is traveling next week, and I'm required to attend his meetings. Then told Matt to fuck off... again."

Okay. I'm not sure what to process first.

"So, you still have the account, and he still hates Matt." I raise my hopeful eyebrows at her trying to point out the positive pieces of that scenario. She bounces her head back and forth like she is kind of agreeing with me but would still rather throw herself behind a truck full of non-strapped porta potties on a pothole covered road.

She has had to travel in the past for some of her accounts, but it doesn't happen often, and when it does, it's usually one night, two max. It sounds like there will be quite a bit of travel with Christian, which actually relieves me more than her traveling with Matt. Although, I can't say a twinge of worry, and dare I say, a pinch of jealousy, hits me.

My wife will be required to stay in multiple different cities for multiple nights with an extremely fit and attractive billionaire.

Awesome.

The flirting and potential sex part, *love* it. The forced proximity of her spending dedicated quality time with said billionaire is a whole other animal.

I reach out and tuck a few wild strands of hair behind her ear. Her eyes are glossed over, staring at a spot on the floor. Her mind is in overdrive. "Why don't I reschedule with the guys, and we can go out tonight? We can do anything except talk about work."

Her face snaps to mine. "Oh, no. No way you are canceling." She pushes herself off her desk and rounds to where her chair is tucked into her desk. Leaning over the top of the backrest, "You've planned this for weeks with your old college buddies, and I've got a ton of work to do. Go have fun." She half smiles at me and I can read her like a book.

She throws herself in solitary whenever she is overwhelmed with emotions or confusion she doesn't know how to navigate through. She pushes everyone away, including me. I run my hands through my hair, knowing this is what she needs, some time alone, but a large part of this is my fault, and I want nothing more than to help fix it. She's already creating distance by standing behind this goddamn desk.

"I didn't say cancel, I said reschedule. They are in town for a few days. I can find another time this weekend to meet up. I'd rather not leave you alone with the internal circus that's running through your head right now."

"I'm fine. I'm just stressed, and I have a lot of things to figure out. I'm really fine. It's fine." She waves her hand dismissively in the air.

It is so not fine.

Abort mission.

"I understand." I walk around the other side of the desk and envelop her hands in mine. I press my lips to her knuckles and take in her scent. Mango and coconut with a surplus of obstinance.

"Then try and come by the bar tonight. You can meet the guys?" Lifting my brows as I plea for her to come with more of my tone and body language.

"Sure, yeah. I'll try." Her four-word response might as well have been the four-letter word with 'off' at the end of it.

"Right, then."

Hello, brick wall.

"I'll plan to be home before eleven, but if the guys get rowdy, I'll shoot you a text," I concede. I plant a kiss on her forehead and turn towards the door to try to hide my disappointment in her wanting to ride solo through this, but she's already created a blockade the size of the Berlin Wall.

I exit through her office door and close it gently behind me. Heading towards the elevator doors, I round my neck to stretch out the tense muscles holding my rather pounding head. The strong, independent woman who I love and adore can madden me faster than Roadrunner on Adderall when she shuts down. I understand why she's spinning, but we're together in this, and I hate that she's isolating herself on an island.

Pressing the elevator button, I glance back towards Elena's office and see Bryan Ashford, her CEO, peering through her window with a two-finger gesture, then turn on his heel back down the hall. The elevator dings and the doors open simultaneously with her office door. As I step into the elevator, her eyes meet mine, keeping her gaze on me only for a moment before stepping out of her office to follow in Bryan's wake and disappear down the hall.

13

ELENA

My heart is thumping out of my chest as I head down the hallway to Bryan's office. When he tapped on my office window and summoned me, he appeared displeased. Although, his facial expressions are never easily decipherable.

Cruz once tried to prank him on April Fool's Day, which happens to be our CEO's birthday. Cruz decided on his own accord, to crumble up hundreds and hundreds of newspapers and old magazine articles and do a complete paper dump all over his office. After all was said and done, Bryan could barely open his office door. It looked like an atomic bomb of paper blew up in his office. It was literally everywhere. Coming out of crevices in his computer, his speakers were wrapped in newspapers like a present. His chair no longer looked like a regular desk chair but a paper mâché figure. Even his scotch bar had strategically placed paper batches coming out of his cups and decanters.

We all thought Cruz was crazy and signed his own resignation letter, but Bryan said nothing the entire day. He acted like nothing happened. He never asked anyone who did it or had anyone clean it up. He might as well have been one of the players sitting at the World Series of Poker table with the look he was giving away on his face.

The next day, Cruz walked into the office with his desk completely missing. Literally gone. Replaced by a ginormous mesh ball pit full of all the crumbled papers. An envelope was attached to the outside of the mesh netting that said:

> Within the pages, hidden from sight.
> Lies a key that brings forth such delight.
> Seek in the pages and you will be told.
> The answer to where your belongings are stored.

NEEDLESS TO SAY, it took Cruz two days to find the key that held the answer to where his desk, chair, computer, and all his personal belongings were placed. We all laughed for days and saw an entirely different side of Bryan for the first time. It was refreshing and a major morale booster. Later, Bryan stated it was the most unproductive thing he'd ever had someone in his company do, but worth every penny.

I know Matt didn't *see* Christian and me doing anything, but Christian's behavior was suspicious in the conference room. Plus, he was holding my hand out of the elevator. I can stand my ground with the entire situation as long as Matt didn't embellish the story or downright lie to Bryan.

As I near his office, the door is open, and I can hear both Matt and Bryan talking about last night's baseball game. Matt sounds overly obnoxious while Bryan spits out player stats and the teams' current standings. I round the doorway and rap my knuckles on the door.

"Hi, you wanted to see me, sir." My voice is kind and

respectful to Bryan, contradicting the snarky look I have aimed at Matt.

"Elena, yes, yes, step in." He waves me into his office.

Matt cocks his head at me and looks entirely way too smug for what went down this afternoon.

I step into his office, leaving the door open in an attempt to avoid getting stuck here too long. He rounds his desk, lifting one leg on the corner to half sit on his desk as he crosses his arms over his chest. I've never paid much attention before, but for an older man, Bryan is quite handsome. He has dark hair with graying at the temples and throughout his short and perfectly trimmed beard. He's tall, with an athletic build, and I bet he was out of this world when he was in his prime. Usually, he is so serious it's hard to even view him as human.

"I'm surprised to have heard this news from Matt prior to hearing it from you." Shit, what *news*? I side-eye Matt, whose arrogant face remains unchanged. He probably told him I'm a two-bit whore spreading my legs for all my accounts and sleeping my way to the top.

"I apologize, sir. I haven't had a moment to come see you since I returned from the meeting." I feel the need to defend myself, but what if Matt didn't say anything at all?

Shit.

Shit.

Shit.

"No need to apologize. I'm certain you're busy working out all the logistics for the account. Matt told me you guys nailed it! We're going to have to shift your other accounts to accommodate the energy and travel required for this one." He pushes himself off the corner of the desk, clapping his hands together as he heads to his scotch bar. "This calls for a celebratory drink!"

I have to prevent my jaw from dropping to the floor. What the actual hell?

Matt told him *we* nailed it?

Stuttering, "Uh, y-yes, Mr. Ford was very pleased with the presentation..."

"Very, *very* pleased, sir," Matt interrupts, raising his eyebrows, bestowing me with a knowing look.

I am dumbfounded.

I thought Matt would throw me under the bus. Instead, he's pretending like he was never kicked off the account. What the hell is he up to?

I glare back at Matt. Oh, fuck this guy. I steel my spine and turn up my nose. "Very pleased indeed. He hired *me* right on the spot." I grant Matt a sarcastic smile.

With Bryan's back to us, Matt creates a circle with his left hand, then pushes his right pointer finger in and out of it.

He is a fucking ten-year-old.

"What a great call Matt made to step aside and have you lead on the presentation. Then, Christian asked for Matt to manage the project while you work closely with his team in the development process. Clearly, he is a great judge of character and knows exactly how to play on the strengths of his team members!"

My face falls. Following my jaw through the floor I'm currently standing on.

You have got to be kidding me.

I'm not going to finish this job because I'm going to go to jail. For murder. Blatant, torturous, first-degree murder.

My pulse is pounding in my ears. The heat radiating from my face is hot enough to fry an egg.

Matt just promoted himself to my directing manager by his own admission and convinced *our* boss of this! How the hell did this just happen after all the work I put in? I have to say something. I have to stand up for myself. He can't do this to me.

Bryan turns back towards us, holding three glasses. The amber liquid sloshes up the sides, matching his exhilarating steps. Holding them in a triangle shape between his hands, he presents them to us, and we reach in at the same time to grab one. He lifts his glass in the air between us. "Cheers to the best damn team I've ever hired."

I sip the scotch while Matt downs it like a shot.

I'm unsure what makes me cringe more. The burn of the bitter liquid or the cheers Bryan just gave us.

"Sir..." I shift uncomfortably in my stance and pause to choose my words.

The pause is short-lived as Matt chimes in.

"I don't know that Elena will have a chance to create a budget for me to approve for the expenses until we have a more definitive travel schedule. However, I'll get that over to you once we do." His smile is menacing. He knows exactly what he wants, and he'll stop at nothing to get it.

Now is not the time to fight on this. I just need to focus on this account and prove what I'm capable of. I have never been so excited to work on a project before, and with the ideas I have for XConnect and the expansion, I can really put it on the map, and myself, too.

"The budget will be higher than other accounts, shoot, probably most of ours combined, but for a project like this, it's completely understandable. Do what you need to do." Bryan waves his hand like it's no big deal.

Matt places his glass at the corner of Bryan's desk. "Oh, she's willing to do *anything*." If Joker had a twin, it would be Matt.

My insides are on fire. If I didn't already have my appendix removed, I swear it would burst again.

"Thank you, Bryan. I'm grateful for this opportunity, and I'm thankful for all your support. I have a lot to work on before next week, so I'll excuse myself." I walk the glass over to his bar and place it next to his.

"Great job, Elena. I knew he would be impressed with you. You'll be inundated with this project, so just give Matt updates. Matt, please report to me every week on the progress."

Hell. No.

"Oh, that's not necessary, sir. I am happy to report to you every Friday on the progress. If I'm traveling, I'll call or we can video conference, it won't be—"

"Nonsense," Bryan interrupts, turning his back towards Matt to talk to me face to face. "I need your full focus to be on Christian and this project." Behind him, Matt places his hand out in front of him, humping the air while pretending to smack an invisible ass. I hide the impending eye roll, but my face is that of a lobster.

I glance back to Bryan. "Absolutely, this is my first priority, and I won't let you down." Staring into his soft gray eyes. His playful energy has faded and the darkness in his eyes replaced with a seriousness that is unmatched in comparison.

"I know you won't, Elena. I have all the confidence in you." He turns around and stalks back towards his desk. Matt stops with the charades just in time. "I don't need to tell you how important this is." His stare burns into me, getting his point across. Then turns towards Matt. "To both of you. Don't fuck it up."

And he's done with this meeting.

"Thank you, sir," I say quietly, walking to exit his office like I've just been scolded by my father. Being that my father passed away when I was teenager, it's been a while since I've been talked to like that. Even in other meetings, when Bryan would need to climb to another level to get his point across, it was never condescending, and he would never swear. Never.

I have an unusual need for acceptance from Bryan. I feel the same as I do when I'm letting Jake down, too. Whenever Bryan gets like that, I fall apart inside, and the few times Jake has expressed disappointment, it's soul crushing for me. Losing my father, the one constant in my life, during the toughest time of my childhood, scarred me. I had to fend for myself and fight for attention from my mother, who loved drinking more than she loved her daughter. It's left me desperate to impress the people around me. Which results in me caring more about their feelings than my own.

Is this why I feel like having sex with other men is somehow acceptable, even though I'm married?

Attention?

Need to impress?

God, I am so fucked.

I have to end things with Christian. Which probably already has happened, considering he now knows I'm married. Thanks to Matt and his big fat mouth.

What have I gotten myself into?

I'm talking about ending my, whatever this is with Christian—my new client, by the way—when I'm happily married and in line for a promotion, while trying to sneak around like an adolescent.

I'll probably end up fired.

And divorced.

Stop going down the rabbit hole, Elena.

Get yourself together.

I'm going to go back to my office. I'll organize the next week and plan everything out. I'll feel better once I have everything out of my head and down on paper. I need to have it perfectly programmed in my calendar and planned out.

I hear Matt whisper yelling at me from down the hall. He's trying to get my attention without Bryan hearing him call for me. I increase my pace to try to avoid turning around, but it's no use when Matt breaks out into full strides to catch up.

"Hey, *Ellie*." His egotistical tone as he uses my not-so incognito nickname makes me wince as he reaches out for me.

"You fucking lied in there, Matt. You lied. I'm not reporting to you." I recoil back to prevent him from grabbing me.

"You had no problem letting Christian's hands grope all over you." He steps in, closing the space between us. "He was pinning you against the wall in that elevator, touching every inch of your body, and you let him." His fingers graze my shoulder and slowly trails his touch down my arm. "I may not be the right person you need to fuck to get what you want, Elena. But you're gonna be begging me for my dick to save your job. You can count on that."

"Fuck you, Matt," I grit out between clenched teeth.

"Oh, you will be, *Ellie*, you will be. You pushed me off this account, I'm going to get something out of it." He snickers as he backward steps towards his office. "I expect you to check in at the end of every day. I need to keep you accountable, my little subordinate." He flicks my nose. The fucker flicked my nose. I attempt to grab his flicker finger, to break it, before he turns around and stalks off towards his office.

Mimicking long strides, I back up and sidestep into my office, closing the door with the weight of my body. Leaning against it, my head naturally tips back and makes a light thud as it meets the thick wooden door. As if my body knew I needed air, my lungs expand, taking in as much as possible before huffing out a long exhale.

Today was...

Today was crazy. Starting next week, I will pretty much have a full-time job with Christian. Bryan was clear that this contract is a priority, as it needs to be. But can I do this?

Physically, yes. Professionally, yes. Emotionally... I don't know. And not because I can't cut off my feelings for Christian, but this overwhelming feeling of expectation from Bryan, desire for these sexual fantasies between my husband and Christian, and then there is Matt.

He's like a rock in my shoe. Such an irritant, and an unpredictable one at that. I always knew he was the type of person to go to great lengths to get what he wanted in any aspect of his life, but if he thinks I'm going to be begging him for *anything* to save my job, he's completely mad.

But what if he continues to dig? The maniacal look in his eyes when he threatened me was beyond just an empty threat. He will do whatever it takes.

There are too many confusing thoughts, too many unknowns. I just need to keep it professional and do my job. *I can do this.*

Finally pushing my weight off the comfort of the door, I walk back towards my desk. Cruz has placed the gorgeous bouquet of flowers on the corner of my desk, and I realize he really missed his calling as a florist. I can tell he's trimmed the stems and perfectly placed each one in a designated spot to bring out the most of this arrangement. It's absolutely gorgeous.

It's inviting and warm. Unlike how I treated my husband earlier.

Jake always gets the brunt of my frustration, even though it has nothing to do with him. I shut down and shut him out but, still, that man loves and adores me, regardless. I've been consumed by work this entire week, creating an unintentional distance between us, yet he still brings me flowers and showers me with love.

Screw this. Work can wait right now.

His college buddies are in town, and I need to make a bit of a grand gesture after my behavior this afternoon.

I grab my spare toiletry bag out of my desk with all my essentials. Makeup, including my siren red lipstick, deodorant, and dry shampoo. I turn to the decorative mirror that hangs on my wall and apply the brilliant color to my lips, bringing some life back into my tired face. Popping the top of the dry shampoo, I spray at the roots and rub my fingertips at my roots, giving me an instant lift.

I don't want to take the time to double back home to

change, so I'm going as is, and hopefully, I don't look too business-y.

I gather up my purse and grab my phone just as a text message lights up the display.

Christian Ford

My heart instantly hammers. How confused he must be after finding out I'm married.

What if he changes his mind about hiring me?

Just open the message, Elena.

> Christian: Is it true?

Christian's maturity is showing. Asking me this instead of just assuming what Matt said was correct.

Even though it was.

I still appreciate him asking. I want to confirm, but it's not a simple answer.

> Me: I can explain

Bubbles pop up and then disappear.

Multiple times.

"Spit it out," I whisper out loud.

He's going to fire me.

Over a text message.

> Christian: My office - 8am on Wednesday. We'll take my jet, so you don't need to book any flights. My assistant will take care of booking the hotel.

The sigh of relief alleviates the elephant that has been resting on my chest.

> Me: See you then

14

ELENA

I'm desperate for a drink after the events of the day. I beeline straight for the first bartender I see as I walk into the bar. It's Happy Hour, and being that this bar is downtown, near most of the financial and tech businesses, it's quite busy with everyone else trying to wash down the day.

I lean over the countertop, looking as desperate as I feel, and try to catch the attention of anyone with access to alcohol.

One of the bartenders slides a delicious-looking martini with cream foam and a mint leaf adorned on top to another patron.

Trying to prevent the drool from my lips, I meet eyes with the bartender, finding my most flirtatious smile. I put up one finger and point to that holy grail of all drinks and mouth, "I'll have one of those." He returns my smile and nods.

"Do you always get what you want that quickly?" a cavernous voice comes from behind me. As I turn to look, he's leaning close to my ear, trying to talk over the loud music and blended voices.

"Not always," I say with a shy smile.

"Doesn't seem that way." He steps to the side of me, placing his elbows on the bar, leaning forward to match my posture. "I'm about a foot taller than everyone here, and that bartender has ignored me for the last ten minutes, but you slide right into home base in less than thirty seconds." He cocks his head at me and smiles.

"My lucky day, I guess." I shrug. The bartender glances back over, and I hold up a peace sign, signaling for two drinks instead of one.

"I hope you like whatever non-masculine foamy topped Happy Hour drink special that is, because that's all the power I've got with this bartender."

"I have no prejudice against alcohol at this point." He chuckles.

This guy is tall, at least six four, very athletic frame, and a smile that could stop a freight train. His brown hair, brown eyes and razor jawline give him a whole Clark Kent picturesque look, save the glasses.

As I scan over his broad chest and arms, I see his head twist enough to catch my attention. He glances down at my ring finger, which still remains bare, since I opted to not wear my ring today. I should have just kept it in my purse, but I was too freaked out I would lose it, so I left it in my jewelry box at home and, again, I'm having massive regrets.

I don't like this feeling. It's so deceiving and I feel dirty. Setting up a proper profile on XConnect for Jake and I is looking more and more appealing.

I cover my right hand over my left, breaking his stare.

"So, are you recently divorced?" He turns to me, leaning on just one forearm on the bar.

My eyes widen at his brazen question. "Why would you ask me that?"

He tilts his head and squints at me, like he's trying to figure me out and decipher what I'm thinking. I shift my weight and then turn to face him, matching his stance. I pull my shoulders back, asserting my confidence.

I'm prepared for any statement you have coming my way, beautiful stranger.

"There's a hint of tan line." He reaches for my left hand, putting his thumb and pointer finger over my ring finger, pressing gently over the skin. "See. Here." He smirks, his eyes deadpan to mine.

His touch is soft, but his hands are rough, and I can tell he works with his hands. I would be surprised if he spent his days working indoors. And if he does, I imagine he spends the other half of his life in a gym. Clearly, never missing chest and shoulder day.

"Oh... yeah. Um, it's complicated. I mean, kind of complicated. But not really. Long story." Annnnd, now, I'm rambling to a total stranger while he holds my hand.

Luckily, the savior of the day–my favorite bartender ever of all time–comes through with two of the drinks I pointed at earlier, but screams over the noise, "We ran out of mint leaves, so I topped with an edible flower."

One brow hitches up as I look over at my new friend and smile.

"Why didn't you just make it pink and throw glitter on the top?" He playfully spats back at the bartender. He hands over his card to the bartender, who swipes it quickly, then hands it back to him. Placing the card back in his wallet, he leans forward, slipping his wallet into his back pocket.

"This round is on me, in hopes that your situation won't be complicated by the end of the night. A preemptive ambition you'll come find me so I can take you home." He leans into me, his lips grazing the shell of my ear. "I'd like to see all your tan lines." He grants me one more gorgeous smile and a wink as he grabs the drink off the bar top and walks away.

Damn.

There is something about a confident, sexy man playing kind-of hard to get. As fun as it sounds, I know I have some making up to do. Actually, Jake would probably love that version of makeup. I raise my eyebrow up and think to myself, he would probably prefer that over getting the real thing himself. The idea of pursuing him in front of my husband sends a few tingles down my spine that erupt in my belly.

I swipe the drink off the counter a bit too aggressively, causing the foam top to pool over the lip of the glass and slowly dribble down the side. I use my tongue to lap up the mess, so it doesn't trickle onto the floor. Perfectly timed to look over and see my new friend holding his drink up in a cheers motion at me, chuckling, as I practically French kiss my glass.

God, how embarrassing.

He shakes his head and quirks up his eyebrow in a *you're such a naughty girl* way, then turns into the crowd and disappears.

Gathering myself back to reality, and the reason why I'm here, I step out from the bar and push the crown of my head towards the ceiling, trying to get a better overall view of the bar. I walk around the outside of the high tables and shimmy my way through a couple large crowds to see my husband sitting down with a group of guys at one of the VIP booths.

Being that this is my first time meeting his college friends, I'm feeling butterflies that I don't normally feel. Jake and I have our separate friends and our group friends that we've developed over the course of our relationship, but I haven't met the guys who knew Jake before I knew Jake. That suddenly makes me very nervous.

Throwing my shoulders back and my chin high with as much fake confidence as I can muster, I head his direction. He glances up and then back to his friends, then does a double take as it takes him a brief second to realize it was actually me.

A slow, sensual smile appears across his face as he stands,

stalking towards me like he's Tarzan and I've just entered his jungle. A few strides and he's front and center, cupping my face with his hands.

"Hello, my wife." A growl leaves his lips as he presses them against mine. He's proud, territorial and dominant.

God, I love it when he's like this.

"Hey, baby," I say, biting my lip as I wipe the lipstick transfer off his.

His smile widens. "Come meet the guys."

He's a giddy schoolboy, grabbing my hand, leading me towards the booth where he and a small group of guys are gathered. They all stand up as we approach, and one of the guys immediately steps forward, grabs my drink and says, "Hold on while I try to get in touch with my feminine side like Hudson." Pulling the glass up to his lips with his pinky pointing outward like a royal would while drinking tea.

The guys laugh and slap the man they called 'Hudson' on the shoulder.

My goddamn beautiful stranger.

I choke on my own spit, but swallow it back.

What. The. Hell.

Why? Why me? I just so happened to unknowingly flirt with one of my husband's college buddies, because why? I like to make things extra awkward and uncomfortable, that's why.

My eyes meet his, and even with the dim lighting in the bar, I can see the color leave his face. Mortified is an understatement. It looks like he wants to crawl under a rock and never return. I don't need a mirror to know that our faces are a reflection of each other.

The guy that took my drink hands it back to me, still chuckling. Knowing I have to push through this weirdness, "Happy Hour special, and it's delicious." I lean in towards Hudson and clink my glass to his, then take a sip. He does the same, hiding his facial expression as his eyes bounce from me to Jake.

He's freaking out inside. I can tell. He might pull a Jerry Maguire and freak out on everyone. I'm half expecting it.

Jake introduces me and then names off all the guys, "Seamus, Dane, Kobi, and Hudson."

"Great to finally meet you guys," I reply with a shy wave and a smile.

"That's all we get?" screams Dane, as he barrels into me, wrapping his arms around my waist, then picks me up and twirls me around. Clearly, this one is the wild, uncensored one.

I'm giggling, trying to save my drink from spilling, grabbing the base of the glass with both hands and he places me back down and gives me a shotgun kiss right on my cheek.

"So, you're the one that tamed this wild stallion?" Seamus push punches Jake with a look only they would know.

I'll have to ask him about that later.

Kobi steps forward. "Oh shut it, Shay." Looking at Seamus, "We all know who the wild stallion of this group really is." He winks at me as he grabs my hand and places a kiss on the knuckles. I melt from not only the touch, but the velvet sound of his European accent.

I blush a bit with the overly flirtatious men surrounding me, which turns into a full-blown shade of fire station red when Kobi pulls my hand away from his lips, squints at my ring finger and says, "Why aren't you wearing a ring? You're going to make me think you're available for some fun."

I glance over to my husband, who is shaking his head as he pinches the bridge of his nose. Clearly, this is normal behavior.

Hudson, who was taking a sip of his Happy Hour special coughs into his drink, misting the foam over the entire group.

Kobi laughs and slaps Hudson on the back. "I'm just playing around, trying to keep Jake on his toes. We've got to make sure he keeps courting his wife, or someone else will." Kobi winks back at me again.

Dane might be wild, but that man screams pure sex.

Jesus. All these men do.

Dane is the shortest of the group at just under six feet tall. All the other guys have to be over six feet. Dane has shaggy, dirty blonde hair and blue eyes. He won the hair color lottery in the genetics department. I would pay a lot of money to dye my hair the same dirty blonde he has.

Physically, Seamus is a complete one-eighty from Dane. Dark, almost black hair that matches his intense eyes. I can barely see his pupils in the dim lighting. He has a distinct scar that runs through his left eyebrow which was probably from him bumping into a door jamb or coffee table as a kid, but I bet if I ask him what it's from, he'll feed me some heroic story of saving a runaway train full of unknowing, helpless citizens.

I'm tempted to ask just to see what story I get.

Kobi is stunning. The most unique, beautiful man I think I've ever laid eyes on. Half Asian of some kind, my guess would be Japanese. Dark hair. Bright, seafoam green eyes. This man is a walking sex billboard.

Standing in this circle of testosterone, the cedar spice whiskey scent engulfs the entire radius I'm standing in. The combination raises my basal body temperature up a degree, or ten. Either that or I'm going through early menopause.

Hudson, still wiping foam froth particles from his face, just smiles at me. It looks like he is still going through the awkward emotions and not sure what to do.

Finally, he speaks up. "Well, I know you guys are all kicking up the charm-o-meter here, but just know that I already called shotgun on this one," pointing my direction, "and told her I was taking her home. So, you guys are about ten minutes too late." He tips his glass up, smirk on display, looking smug as hell with his flower foam martini glass. Like a big, fat, middle finger straight to the group. "If she's going home with anyone, sorry Jake," he winks, "it's me." He clinks my glass one more time, then downs the entire drink in one gulp.

"Jesus, that's actually really bad." Hudson swallows hard through his sour face as he slams the glass down on the table between us.

All the guys crosstalk over each other, hollering at the fact that it's been revealed we met at the bar a few minutes ago, and Hudson not only hit on me and bought my drink, but offered to take me home. So they are all fighting over who should win this competition of taking me home. My husband, not an ounce of jealousy, only pride and genuine enjoyment in the fun, flirtatious banter with his closest friends.

Others might think this is strange, but I think it's adorable.

The night has been so much fun getting to know all of these guys. I've been here for hours, listening to the stories from their *golden* years. Which was referenced along with some crazy story about Dane and an accidental golden shower. Based on his immediate shut down to that conversation, it was not a highlight at all.

As the guys continue to rally back and forth and compete for the craziest stories, both during and after the college years, I catch Jake observing me deeply. I've always felt his unconditional love. The pride that I chose him, that I took his name. He shows it to me in the way he loves me every day, even by the way he looks at me, like he is now.

God, I love this man. He is my better half in all aspects of what that means.

I give him a quick wink and focus back on the conversation. Which has now diverted to the guys giving Jake shit for not inviting them to his wedding, but in all reality, we didn't really have one.

When we got married, we decided to elope. I wasn't into the idea of the whole big wedding thing. Being that I was estranged from my mother and my father passed away when I was fourteen, I didn't feel the need or desire for a big, ridiculously expensive event. We had a small celebration with Jake's family.

Other than that, nothing traditional for the wedding or a bridal party. Now, after meeting these guys, I'm feeling a bit guilty about eloping and taking that experience away from him.

"Okay, okay," I cut in, waving my hands in the middle of the table, because it's so loud in the bar now that if I don't, I would be easily overlooked. "Being that," I air quote with my fingers to repeat one of the comments that Dane mentioned earlier, "I stole your 'Jakey' away for the past couple years, it's only fair that you steal him away for a makeup bachelor party, since he really never got one."

I glance around at the guys as I sip on the sparkling water that has replaced the alcoholic drinks from earlier, and the silence is deafening. The guys glance around at each other like I grew a boob on my forehead.

Hudson finally breaks the white noise. "You'll let us plan a post-wedding bachelor party and take your husband to say, I don't know, Vegas?"

The guys look like they are standing on hot lava for a final confirmation of exactly what I'm saying. I side-eye over to my husband, who is grinning with his head down and arms crossed over his chest, knowing what is about to go down.

"Two conditions." The guy's nod, waiting for said conditions.

"I get treated to the most luxurious spa day Ocean Dune offers..."

"I'll buy you the goddamn spa. What is the other condition?" Kobi, staring at me anxiously.

"No secrets. You guys tell me all, and I mean all, the wild stories from the party, and I get the final vote as to who is truly the wildest one of this bunch." Not only did I give them permission for an unforgettable weekend in Vegas with my very married husband, but I challenged them all to compete for the wet and wild award.

I'm going to hell.

And they are probably going to jail.

The guys literally jump, like they just won a championship football game, and they are grabbing Jake up into a bear hug like he just scored the final touchdown of the game.

Dane is chanting something like, *fling after the ring,* marching around the guys, and Kobi is calling for a round of shots for everyone.

Just based on the short amount of time I've gotten to know these guys, I realize I may have just signed a death warrant for my husband, and by the look on his face, he does, too.

These guys are crazy, but wildly loyal and protective. I felt immediately comfortable with all of them, and my heart feels full knowing Jake has this kind of unwavering friendship with his college friends. That they can come back into his life after years of not hanging out and pick up where they left off.

"Alright, Alright. I'm calling it a night, guys," I announce, trying to rowdy down the group, which did so instantly.

All the guys whine out a long winded, "No", which is oddly adorable. This night out has gotten my mind off everything that happened today, and I was able to make up with my husband after being a complete bitch. Mission accomplished.

Jake stalks around the table, wrapping one hand around my waist and the other at the base of my neck as he pulls me in, slamming my lips into his. He presses his hips into me, making sure I feel his swelling cock against my stomach.

If he tore my clothes off right now, I wouldn't object.

Seconds pass that feels like minutes, and Jake finally releases the tight grip over my body. Hudson clears his throat. "So, does this mean I'm not taking you home tonight, then?" he teases, as he walks around, holding one arm out, offering a chaste hug.

The guy's rally around me, giving me hugs and saying something cute or entirely inappropriate and sensual, but all of them fun-loving and playful.

We all say goodbye, and Jake places his hand on my low back. "I'm walking you out to your car," trailing me as I head towards the door.

I would have fought him on it since I was able to get parking directly in the front of the building, but it's useless, because my husband would never, knowingly, let me walk out of a bar by myself.

Open to watch me fuck another guy? Sure. Possessive as hell when it comes to keeping me safe? Absolutely.

He plants a soft kiss on my forehead and says, "I won't be too far behind you." He pulls back and smiles at me.

"Take your time, love." I creep up on my tippy toes, begging for another desperate kiss like the one in the bar, which he grants me easily.

He growls into my mouth. "Get out of here now before I bend you over the trunk of this car."

"Yes, sir," I whisper, knowing damn well that'll set him off.

He tilts his head to the side, and squints at me, which just makes me giggle. I peck him on the cheek, then finally get in my car and start my drive home.

What an insane day.

I recap the presentation, the elevator, the meeting with Bryan and Matt, which I'm still confused by, and the fabulous end, spending time with Jake and his friends.

It feels like it's been an entire week in one day.

Even with the uncertainty with Christian, the new contract with Ford and whatever scheme Matt is pulling. I feel light and happy.

It's a scientific fact that the eye of the storm is the calmest part of a hurricane. Every time I'm surrounded by it, Jake is my center, keeping me grounded.

As I enter the house, feeling both high on laughter from the banter with the guys and exhausted from the day, I see one of our dining room chairs oddly placed in the middle of the living room. I glance around, checking to see if anything else is out of place, then set my purse and keys down on the entry table.

My heartbeat kicks up a notch as I trudge forward suspiciously. My eyes saucer at the presence of handcuffs and a blindfold strategically placed on top of the base of the chair with a note.

Take off your clothes. Hands behind your back and cuff them to the chair.

Holy shit.

I see another small piece of paper behind the one I just grabbed.

It's a note from my fantasy jar.

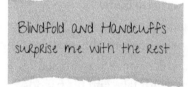

Blindfold and Handcuffs surprise me with the rest

15

JAKE

The guys and I left the bar about an hour after Elena. We had a great time catching up and chatting, but after she left, something felt missing. It's crazy how she just flowed into my old group of college friends like she knew them all along. It was fluid. Easy. Like she's always been there.

The fact that Hudson hit on only one woman in that bar, and it happened to be my wife, is simultaneously unbelievable and so incredibly hot. I noticed the smirk on his face when he returned. I thought it was the ridiculous drink he ordered, but no, it was my wife who gave him that same high that most men feel in her presence.

When I first arrived at the bar, I was stressed and worried about her. What she told me about Chris–Christian–whatever she is calling him these days, I can't imagine how conflicted she is feeling with him finding out she is married. She absorbs others' anxiety, and I know she is feeling guilty and consumed with the "what ifs", and that absolute scum of a human being, Matt. As the thought of him threatening my wife enters my mind, I grip the steering wheel hard enough to snap it in half. I don't even realize how tense my body became until I feel a cramp building in my forearm. I take a deep breath to calm my nerves, which hardly works. I'm sure Elena has to do that meditation stuff she likes to do to get herself in a good mental space when dealing with him.

I would rather just give him a couple of black eyes and a broken nose.

I trot up the walkway, anxious to get home to her, when I see just a dim light through the front window. I see the silhouette of her sitting in the living room, and it fucking hits me that I left out the cuffs and blindfold.

How the fuck could I forget I had left that out for her to come home to?

Luckily, I was only an hour behind her, but fuck, she is going to kill me if she's been waiting too long.

Tread lightly.

I press my key into the keyhole and unlock the deadbolt. Pressing the door open and stepping in, I peek over and see my gorgeous wife sitting in the chair I left out for her. Her arms are pulled behind her, forcing her shoulders back, and her chest is slightly lifted. She's wearing a short silk nightgown with lace hems that lays right at the top of her thighs, teasing me with a close view between her legs.

It's high enough to know it's close to the promised land, but not enough to see if she has panties on, and the anxiety of the unknown is already killing me.

She shifts uncomfortably in the chair as she hears me enter. I place the keys on the entryway table and kick off my shoes. I say nothing and make as much noise as possible. Knowing the unknown is going to arouse her more than anything that would come out of my mouth.

I unbutton the cuffs of my sleeves and roll them up to my elbows as I stalk towards her.

God, she's fucking perfect.

Her hair is down, slightly messy, falling over her shoulders, and resting over the lace trim at the top of her silk lingerie. The glow from the dim lamp behind her bounces off her skin, like the reflection of the moonlight over the ocean. It's radiating, like she's the only thing in this room.

I shift a few things around, making faint noises, before I sit down on the coffee table so I can get a full-frontal view of her gorgeous display.

Her gaze moves in the direction of the sounds, like she's attempting to peek through her blindfold, trying to understand her surroundings, even though she's completely in the dark.

Nothing in my body feels soft right now.

Not my cock nor my mood.

Seeing her like this is turning me into an untrained animal with no desire for restraint.

"Don't move. Don't move a fucking inch. If you peek through that blindfold, I'll see that as an invitation for punishment."

And by punishment, I mean the worst kind of orgasm torture imaginable.

She bites the corner of her mouth, being that's the only thing she can move, and I know she's been ready and waiting and can't wait any longer.

Shifting forward from where I'm sitting, I reach out and cup her breast, rubbing my thumb back and forth over her nipple, already hard from anticipation. She gives me a startling gasp that rolls into an audible moan.

A very desperate one.

Which travels at light speed directly to my strangled cock.

"I distinctly remember instructing you to take your clothes off."

"I thought you would like this," she responds in a whisper.

She's not wrong.

The white silk falls perfectly over her body, except for that damn teasing strap that disobeys her shoulder by falling down over her arm. The only reason that breast is still covered is because the fabric is catching on her taut nipple, preventing it from falling further.

With a weak pull of the silk nightgown, I expose one of her gorgeous tits.

I would pay a shit ton of money for a portrait of her like this.

I stand up and unbuckle my belt, taking it out of the loops and hold the leather in my hand. I circle around her, making my presence known, dragging the buckle on the hardwood floor. Stopping behind her, I test the cuffs, then grab each end of the belt and drape it over her chest. As I pull the belt tighter, closing in on her neck, her body stiffens, her chin lifts and her breath catches. The belt isn't tight, it's just resting snuggly on her neck, giving the appearance of restraint, for now. Leaning down, I nibble on her collarbone and trace my tongue over her jawline to her ears. "Someone was very flirtatious tonight." Shaking her head back and forth, I tug softly on the belt.

"I don't think Hudson would agree with you. He was ready to run off with you by the time he came back to our table." I release the belt, so it lays flat over her chest, and continue to kiss her neckline, then place one hand on her thigh and the other plays with her exposed nipple. Making her feel like she's being fondled completely.

"You were so fucking sexy tonight. I'll never get tired of watching you."

Her head dips back with a groan and a drawn out plea. "Please."

I move my hand up her inner thigh, taking the silk material with me, exposing her bare pussy.

"Please what, baby?" I ask.

Her hips push forward, telling me everything I need to know.

Taking a few steps back, I open the drawer where I placed the new vibrator I purchased for this exact moment. A Hitachi wand massager that I've been dying to use on her since the moment I bought it.

They had a few different versions of this 'massager', I debated between the mini version which was chargeable and mobile but not as powerful, or the standard plug-in version that apparently draws its power from Zeus. I decided on the plug-in version due to the salesgirl using words like, earth shattering and diabolical.

Plugging it in, the cord reaches easily across the few feet to where she sits. I grip the leather straps of my belt, that still dangle over the back of her neck, tugging slightly on the grain.

She sucks in a breath as I lean in closer to her ear, bringing the vibrator around the side of her, gently feathering the crown of it over the thin fabric of her nightgown.

"What I'm about to do to you is going to be intense. Tell me what your safe word is?" My breath is heavy as I nibble at soft flesh under her jawline.

"What are you going to do?" she asks, panic lacing the tone of her question.

"That's not a safe word, Elena. Give me your safe word."

"Pineapple." She whispers.

"That's my girl."

I flip the switch as the base of the wand and it comes to life. Omitting a buzzing sound that takes over the dead space in the room.

Elena startles in her chair, jumping back slightly before relaxing back in the seat. The crown of the vibrator meets the apex of her thighs and she screams, throwing her head back.

"Oh my god, Jake, what is that?" her question is breathy and labored.

I'm only grazing the tip over the fabric of her nightgown,

putting the lightest pressure outside of her lips. She's rolling her hips, moving, moaning, restrained and uncontrolled.

I continue a featherlight touch, moving up and down at the same tempo, teasing her. I hear her heavy breath and pleading whispers over the sound of this magical vibrating wand, that's completely changing her world. Showing me the same desperation she had when Christian made her fall apart in that club.

"I loved watching you with Christian. Seeing him desperate for you. Witness you take his pleasure and receive it. It's the sexiest thing I've ever seen. But wife, tell me, whose fucking pussy is this?"

A moan leaves her lips, then a whimper at the loss of the wand, as I step away and circle to stand in front of her. Seeing her like this turns me into a feral, desperate man. Yanking her gown down, her tits bounce perfectly in front of me. I lean in, grabbing an already pebbled nipple into my teeth and suck in, rolling my tongue in perfect circles, quickly, before pulling back, teasing her again.

"Whose pussy is this?"

"Oh, God. Jake, yours. Yours, always yours." Her head drops back as she arches her back. I place my hand over her sternum, my hand trails down her chest on a runway of soft, gorgeous skin, cupping her breasts along the way. I give each of her nipples shared attention as she continues to moan. "Please, Jake. I need you."

"Finally, she begs," I growl. I grab the underside of her knees, pulling her forward, so her ass is hanging halfway off the chair. Pulling the front of my jeans open so abruptly, the zipper flies open with ease. My dick springs free, and that in itself feels so goddamn good.

I wrap my hand around my cock. It's already so hard the skin is thinned, the crown is shiny and glistening with pre-cum. Dropping to my knees, I bring the tip between her slit, rubbing back and forth over her glistening lips.

"What do you say?" She better say it fast, because I can't hold back any longer.

"Please, please. Fuck, please." The last 'please' trails on as I plunge into her, straight to the hilt.

I'm a man who can usually last longer than most. I can force myself to hold back, but now, I've lost all control. One thrust inside her tight pussy, and I can already feel my orgasm building, and there is nothing I'll be able to do to stop it. It's a bullet train with no breaks.

Pulling out to the tip and driving back in, she lifts her legs and wraps them around my hips. I circle my arm around her waist to give her some support, then replace the tip of the vibrator at the base of where our bodies connect.

She's so goddamn sexy.

The feeling of her walls tightening around me as I thrust into her. The vibration of this device quaking between us. Seconds is all she needs before her pussy is clenching around my cock tighter than I've ever felt. I piston my hips harder and deeper, doing everything in my power to keep her moaning and shaking as my cock releases everything it's been holding back. Still pulsing, I slouch forward over her, growling into her neck, unable to even think straight.

Dizzy. I'm actually dizzy.

"You had me so worked up tonight waiting for you." Releasing her legs from my hips, she melts into the chair.

"I had you worked up?" I chuckle. "Imagine hiding a hard on the whole night, watching every guy at the bar fantasize about fucking his wife and envisioning *that* all night." I pull down the blindfold as she squints, adjusting to the light, then I release the cuffs from her wrists. Slowly moving her arms in between us, as I rub on the area where her wrists were restrained.

"Was this good?" The cuffs hanging off my index finger on one hand and the vibrator in the other.

A shy smile crosses her face. "So good. So, so good." She sits up, pulling the silk gown back over her body, noticing that it's partially torn. "The anticipation of you coming home, and honestly, I didn't think about it until after I was already cuffed to the chair that you might actually bring the guys home. It was terrifying and exhilarating at the same time."

My cock twitches at the thought and it should be dead right now.

"Don't give me any ideas, Elena." I shake my head, knowing that would be my ultimate fantasy. Her, blindfolded, tied up and not knowing who is doing what to her. "I need to go upstairs and take a cold shower already."

"So, you're saying I didn't please you enough?" she says smiling, knowing damn well what she does to me.

"You better get your ass upstairs before I punish it." She grants me one of those classic Elena looks, the playful, bashful one she wears when she thinks she has the upper hand. The one that makes me fall deeper in love with her every time I see it.

"You're in for it now." I stalk towards her as she runs up the stairs. God, I love this woman.

16

ELENA

The Uber driver pulls up to the Ford building just before eight in the morning. I was trying to arrive earlier, but *this guy* drove in circles around my block because he clearly can't read a map. Who am I kidding? It's not a map. GPS literally verbalizes the directions to you.

You have one job. One.

Not hiding my irritation from him, I jump out of the car and go to the trunk to gather my suitcase and tote bag as quickly as I can.

He pops the trunk and stays in the car.

Not that I need someone to cater to me or carry my bags, but at least be a decent human after getting lost, driving like a damn tortoise, and making me late. I barely close the trunk before he peels out like I'm the one who did something wrong.

"UGH." I refrain from stomping my feet like a four-year-old, and thank God for that, because as I swing my colosseum-sized tote bag over my shoulder, it practically clotheslines the Goliath who magically appears behind me.

"Bad day?" The gravelly voice, that feels like cashmere on my eardrums, invades my space. I need zero guesses as to who it is because the emergence of butterflies in my stomach tells me exactly who it is.

"I am completely under control. I have no idea why you would think otherwise." I turn around to face him. Chin high. Spine engaged. An oxymoron, clearly, due to the bangs flying over my face, getting stuck to my lipstick as my luggage case topples over. The handle barrelling into my shin, right before slamming down on my toe that peeks out from my open toe pumps.

I let out a dramatic groan followed by a hiss, then bite down on my bottom lip, hard. I somehow avoid profanities in front of my new *boss* and gift him with what appears to be the laugh of the century.

"Are you laughing at me, Mr. Ford?" I ask, all amusement in my tone completely absent.

"It's good to know that you aren't actually that perfect." My brows pinch together, confused by his statement as he leans down to pick up my abusive bag.

"Every time I've seen you, everything about you is perfect. From your hair to your outfit, your demeanor, from what you say, and how you act. It's good to see you are human, like the rest of us." He smirks, pulling the wild hair back behind my ear. "Really, though, are you okay? Because this suitcase was ruthless. No mercy whatsoever."

I chuckle. "What are you doing out here, anyway? Don't you have some secret bat cave entrance somewhere you should be using?" I joke to keep the mood light.

As much as this is an easygoing conversation, the last time I saw him, he made me come only a few minutes before he found out I was married. Keeping the mood light sounds like a good avoidance tactic at this point. We haven't had any correspondence since the text when I told him I could explain. So, I'm certain he is going to want some answers here pretty quickly.

"The Bat Cave entrance is under construction." His hand waves up in the air like he's trying to shake dirt off of it as he rolls his eyes, then grants me one of those half smiles. "That's cute you think that I'd have some secret entrance."

And just then, in a world where the timing couldn't be any better, a helicopter comes over the top of the building, landing right on top.

I glance back at him, titling my head, eyebrows raised. "Really?"

His half smile turns into a full smile. "Come on. That's our ride to the plane."

If Christian's plan was to impress me, it worked. The helicopter took us to a landing area right at the back of the airport, near a private airstrip. His jet was waiting for us, geared up and ready to go, with Dietrich standing guard outside when we arrived. When I walked into the jet, I thought it would have a few seats and a tv. I was wrong. So, so wrong.

There are white plush leather reclining seats, along with tv screens in every direction you look. The back has a small bar, fully stocked with top-shelf alcohol and a door that leads to a bedroom with its own ensuite bathroom and shower. Everything is pristine. Gorgeous.

I keep my jaw intact, even though it wants to do a Roger Rabbit jaw drop.

After some introductions to his flight staff, the plane taxies for take-off, which is smoother than butter, and we get settled in. Both of us choose seats that face each other as we pull out our laptops and focus on a basic agenda I put together before the trip.

Nothing like avoiding all personal emotion by diving straight into work. A quality that comes natural to me.

The conversation flows easily, like it did the first night we met, but this time about work details and ideas from the marketing campaign that I put together.

"I love your idea about collaborating with NextDoor for local events. It's genius," he admits, as he closes his laptop and moves it off his lap to the side table.

"Thanks!" My excitement shows in my tone at his praise. "I think I'll be able to—"

"Why didn't you tell me?" he interrupts, his tone deep, serious.

I slowly close my laptop, knowing I've exhausted avoiding this conversation. I nibble on the corner of my lip, pulling my hands into each other, and look up to meet his gaze.

"I... my, it's complicated," I stutter.

He crosses one leg over the other and folds his hands together in his lap. "So you said, and I'm listening."

A million ways to try to explain myself come to mind, but none of it makes sense in my own head, so I have no idea what my words will sound like. Will he judge me? Will he feel used? What if he expected more? I can't even fathom a guy like him would be *disappointed* in being used for sex or with a relationship that couldn't go anywhere. I'm jumping to conclusions without even knowing the first thing about him. I just need to tell him and lay my cards out. He's already giving me the opportunity to explain. It's time for honesty, which is going to relieve so much stress that's been weighing on me this week.

Matt was on my ass nonstop this week, too, trying to question everything I was doing and everyone I was talking to. Saying how he owns me. Threatening me. It's exhausting. Honesty sounds like bliss. Even if it's risking the new contract with Ford at this point. This secretive part of myself is not like me and not making me feel good about myself.

"I am married. Happily married." His brows pinch together, and he flinches, shocked that was my first response. "We are... open to explore." Again, he tilts his head, his eyes still focused on mine, trying to decipher what I'm saying. "So, he is aware of this." I gesture, moving my finger between him and I. "Of... you."

His eyebrows raise.

Oh, great. I've managed to shock him twice in one sentence.

Maybe I shared too much. I should have just said, *'I have an open marriage.'* But no, I had to trail on like a bad run-on sentence.

The silence is dreadful.

He leans forward and plants his elbows against the top of his legs as he laces his fingers together and rests his chin on his knuckles. His chest rises and a long exhale comes out, and I'm not sure if that's a pissed off exhale or some sort of relief. He's in deep thought. Clearly trying to process what I just said. Which was minimal in words, but so much in meaning.

Say something.

"When you say he is aware 'of you', does that mean me, specifically, or just of someone?"

Lie, Elena, Lie.

"You... specifically."

Dammit, Elena.

If a jaw could crack by pressure alone, his would. Right now.

"Elena, I can't afford some crazy publicity stunt that comes out of shit like this." His words are abrupt.

He remains seated, eerily calm.

"I understand that, and neither can I. I've worked too hard to prove myself, and I cannot jeopardize my job. What happened between us before–before I knew who you were–will remain completely confidential. Well, and that little thing after... in your conference room." I shift in my seat that feels like a porcupine. "I mean... what I'm saying is I know what we were doing can't happen any longer. I understand that and respect your position as well as my role in the contract we have."

He stops and stares at me. You know that look a shark gets when they smell blood? Their eyes somehow get smaller and the entire iris pools pure black?

That is Christian.

Christian is that shark.

Leaning in closer to me, his voice matching the tenor of his eyes. "I didn't say nothing could happen. I said I can't afford for this to go public."

"Oh." Not the response I expected. "I mean, I'm sure it's wiser for..."

"Do you *stray* often?" he interrupts.

Jesus. I'm certain he didn't mean that the piss poor way it sounded, but after putting myself out there, I'm feeling vulnerable and, frankly, it pisses me off.

Stray? Like a fucking feral cat.

"I know you didn't intend for that to sound presumptuous, like I'm a homeless whore cat in heat, but no. This arrangement between my husband and me is... new." Sitting at my full height to exude the confidence that doesn't actually exist.

He tilts his head, absorbing that piece of information. "How new?"

He is never going to believe me. Like telling a guy they have a big dick when they ask, *"Am I the biggest you've ever had,"* during sex. The reply is always, *"So big, the biggest,"* no matter how far from the truth that is. You know it's what they want to hear.

Who knows whether they believe you or not?

They probably do.

"You were the first experience outside of my marriage since we made that *arrangement*." I pull my lip between my teeth and bounce my head back and forth when saying the last word as I try to describe whatever *it* is.

Looking like someone invisibly slapped him, he sits back, eyes wide, taking in what I just said.

A long pause that feels like a lifetime passes.

"What's his deal?" he asks.

"He has his own company, works from home, and travels sometimes. He's loyal and discreet. We've been married three years." I try to think of some other facts to continue, but if I've gotten to know anything about Christian during the presentations I've done for him, it's the face he makes when he doesn't hear what he wants to hear.

And he's making that face.

Right now.

I bite the corner of my lip, slightly gnawing on the inside.

"He likes to watch," I whisper.

17

CHRISTIAN

The last three days can only be described as a hurricane.

Hurricane Elena to be exact.

We have visited three of my off-site production buildings in three different states. Starting in Arizona on Wednesday, spending the day there, then flying to California on Thursday, and now ending the day in Idaho. The three-day trip has been the most productive trip I've ever made during my office visits. Elena met with the leads of each of the departments, going over the execution of the marketing plans for each of their teams. Explaining exactly how and what to expect from her over the course of the next few months. As well as her expectations of them. How she was able to inspire and motivate them in the short amount of time she spent with them was nothing short of astonishing.

I've never seen anything like it.

She was the lion and the lamb.

I'm both impressed and aroused whenever she's with me, and that's a deadly combo.

The way she works, presents herself, and just... her.

Everything she shared with me on the plane has been sitting in the back of my mind this entire trip. I have so many more questions, but haven't had time to broach them yet.

He likes to watch.

She must love being watched. But does she like being watched in general, or by him specifically? If he likes to watch, does that mean he doesn't explore on his own? Do they explore together with a third? And if so, is it a male or female they prefer?

Too many questions.

I've always been open sexually and probably a little too careless in my younger days. I've had a handful of threesomes in my lifetime, all of them with women, except once with another male. The only downside to that experience was fighting with him for the alpha position; that part was irritating. Although, that little ménage was my favorite threesome experience after he finally gave in and allowed me to take charge, even though I have never tried to go that route again. I've dabbled in pretty much everything. But fucking in public or in front of someone was always something that brought out something deeper in me.

All of my senses are heightened in those moments.

I have always found that strange about myself. I'm comfortable in front of people, and have always taken the lead, especially in business. But I have never relished in the idea of being the center of attention, which is why that's always been confusing.

When I took her in that club, I knew she wasn't afraid of the public display. I figured she probably thrived on the excitement of it all, but I had no idea about her marriage and that she was open *that* way.

Now that I think about it, I wonder if he was there. Watching.

The thought of that rushes blood straight to my cock.

Which is where most of my thoughts go when it comes to Elena.

If she's open sexually, and we've already walked through that door, I have no reason to close it. Other than to torture myself.

Oh, and the little fact that she's a contracted employee.

I deserve a goddamn medal for the restraint I've shown this week, not yanking her into my hotel room to make her beg for my cock.

The same restraint I showed a few minutes ago when we parted ways, as she went to her suite, and I came into mine. My favorite room that overlooks Lake Coeur D'Alene. Still one of my most treasured places in the world. Out of everywhere I've traveled, this place remains to be what feels like home.

Where I spent most of my time. After her. After she ruined me.

This place reminds me of why I need to steer clear of Elena and keep that in the forefront of my mind.

She's married. She's annoyingly perfect. A goddamn wrecking ball.

Elena *is* different. This *is* different.

But it's not.

After this trip, I need to have her report to one of my directors. I can't risk another PR nightmare. Or emotional destruction. I'll never survive.

Who am I kidding? I still haven't gotten over the last.

Walking towards the bedroom suite, I loosen the knot in my tie, pulling it down and over my neck. Unclipping my cufflinks and placing them on top of the flawlessly made plush bed. I free the top buttons of my shirt when I hear what sounds like thumping. I pause, unsure of what I heard, when I hear a couple of light knocks.

I make the short trek to the door and peer through the peephole, and all I see is a blonde ponytail flickering back and forth away from my door. Her feet tip toeing like she is sneaking away from something.

What is she doing?

The click of the door handle makes her stop and turn around as I swing the door open.

"Why are you slinking away from my door like you dropped a burning bag of poop in front of it?" Unable to hold back my smirk.

Her cheeks flush. "I didn't want to bother you after such a long day, and I thought maybe when you didn't answer, you were resting. I didn't want to make any more noise. You know," dropping her hands to her sides and standing up straighter, "it made more sense in my head a minute ago."

Business Elena is fierce, bold, demanding.

Private Elena is cute, adorable, and timid.

I find both completely amusing and totally undeniable.

"It's only six. I haven't even figured out what I'm eating for dinner tonight. Come in." I push the door open wider and step aside.

She walks past me, and the soft tropical hints of coconut and ocean breeze engulf me like a warm blanket I have no desire to remove myself from. Her purse is still over her shoulder, and I question whether she made it back to her room. She either stopped herself because of something work related that's on her mind or it's an excuse.

"Like I said, I didn't want to bother you, but it looks like tomorrow starts really early, and you have calls scheduled during the flight. I was concerned we wouldn't have time to connect to summarize our visits. I was hoping to get some goal setting done, so that when we part ways tomorrow, there were no unanswered questions or missing expectations." She sits down on the sofa, pulling her notebook out of her purse, primed and ready.

So, it was work related.

She's so fucking good at what she does it blows my mind that she hasn't advanced further at her company. I think her being at a company with old mindsets and substandard precepts is holding her back, and she needs a place that will give her the wings she deserves.

But that's for another day.

All I can think about is how it's taken all my willpower not to find a reason to knock on her door every night. Now that she's here in my room, it will take me cutting off my own arms to not touch her.

"We will have time tomorrow to discuss the logistics for the next steps." I cross my arms over my chest.

Fuck it.

"Is that really why you came by?" I shouldn't be asking her that. I should give her a reason to leave. I know her situation. I know the proper thing to do. I shouldn't risk an inevitably bad outcome.

But I can't stop.

"What else did you need, Ellie?" I call her by her nickname, knowing exactly what it means. Her eyes look up at me from her seated position, the same look in her eye when she was on her knees in front of me. Her tongue darts out to lick her bottom lip, pulling before it in between her teeth. Tearing my gaze away from that tempting mouth, her eyes burrow deep into mine, and we both know what's about to happen.

Obnoxiously, an awful ringing from her phone pulls us out of our hypnosis. She fumbles with the notebook, losing her pen to the floor in an attempt to silence her phone.

Glancing at the screen, then back at me, "I'm sorry. We've been playing phone tag all day. I'll just be a second." She stands and walks towards the corner of the room where the desk and a large standing bookshelf sit. It's about six steps away, providing less privacy than a Japanese rice paper barrier would, so I have no idea why she even tried.

"Hey, honey." Pause. "Good. Great, actually." She blushes and sneaks a glance my way. She is proud of how she did these past few days. She fucking should be. "How was yours?" Pause. "We finished the day at the office. We were just going over notes in Christian's room before calling it a day."

She's fidgeting with her hair. The phone is against her ear, and her eyes side-eye my way, probably to see my reaction since I know she's speaking to her husband.

I've fortified my defenses against her these past few days. Remaining completely professional. But my determination is vanishing and all the reasons to stop disappear along with it.

I have no idea what comes over me. The smell of her wafting around my room. The seductive look in her eye. The possessiveness I feel wanting to take her in front of her husband. My feet have a mind of their own as they tread towards her.

Her brows arch up in a knowing curiosity.

"Put him on speaker." A demand, not a question.

Her breath hitches as she stares at me. A tsunami of confusion in her ocean blue eyes.

"Do it," I say with even more clamor.

"Hey, uh... love. Christian has a question. I'm going to put you on speaker." Pulling the phone from her ear, she presses the speaker button, and I hear the end of his statement. "...strange, but okay," he finishes.

There's a pause. A long fucking pause. My eyes plow into Elena. I'm silently praying she's fully honest with him about *everything*. Even though I don't think I need it, there isn't a proper way to get *approval*. I still need it for myself.

"We good?"

Two words. So much meaning.

Elena knows it. I know it.

The air is dense and heavy. The silence is thundering.

A short moment later. "We're good." The confidence behind his smirk I hear comes through the speaker like a foghorn.

"Good." I walk back towards the couch, unbuttoning the rest of my shirt, shrugging it off with one swift move, then turn back to face her.

"Turn the camera on."

18

JAKE

Did he just tell her to turn the camera on?

"What?" Elena questions, echoing my thoughts.

"You heard me." His voice is distant, but deep and commanding.

A bit of rustling and white noise comes through the phone. I urgently pull the phone down to look at my screen.

I can hear moving around like maybe she, or he, is setting things down in the distance. There is some shifting of objects on what sounds like a glass table. A sound of a click like a lamp switch.

God, this is killing me.

I'm alternating between pulling the phone down to see anything on screen and pressing the phone to my ear hard, while plugging the other ear with my finger, leaning as far into the phone as I can so I don't miss a thing.

This is what it must have been like for Elena when I blindfolded her the other night.

It's excruciating.

Keeping my eye on the screen, it flickers, and asks me if I would like to accept and switch to a video call.

Yes. Yes, I do.

The video appears through my screen, pixelated at first, but then as the clarity gets better, I see Elena is still holding the phone. It's at an upward angle, and I have a clear shot of her gorgeous face. She's biting her lip, her eyes larger than normal from this point of view as she looks forward. Curiosity is written all over her face.

"Set it down here, facing towards the couch," he instructs as her eyes peer down to me. I turned my camera on so she can see me now as well. Pressing her lips into a thin line, the corners of her mouth lift with a hidden smile, and I return it with a look that tells her I'm all in, if she is.

The background starts to move behind her as she walks to wherever he told her to place down the phone.

After a few gradient changes and auto-focusing occurs, she perfects the degree of where the phone is pointed, then takes a few cautious steps back to make sure the phone doesn't move from where she planted it.

As she distances herself from the camera, the rest of the room comes into view, along with a very tall and very shirtless Chris.

He looks like a giant in the room next to her. His chest and shoulders are as wide as the Grand fucking Canyon, tapering into chiseled-to-perfection abs.

What the hell.

I'm a confident man, but this man is a descendent straight from the Greek gods. Minus the beard and armor.

Elena is fully dressed. A white button up top with long sleeves is tucked into a snug, high-waisted pencil skirt that hugs her hips and legs flawlessly. Her heels give her another three inches, and he still towers over her. The iron straight strands of her honeycomb hair are pulled back into a tight low ponytail that drapes down her back.

She is absolutely flawless.

"Take off your skirt." Somehow, his voice is a few decibels deeper than earlier.

The sound of her zipper sends tingles straight to my cock as the skirt pools at her ankles and she steps out of it. The bottom of her blouse spreads out, splaying over the top of her thighs.

Chris steps towards her, and their profiles adorn my screen as he carefully unbuttons her blouse, one by one. She looks up at him, unblinking, biting her lip. Her fingers toying with the hem of her shirt. I want to say something encouraging, but I don't want to ruin the mood. The chemistry is palpable. I can feel it even as a spectator behind a camera.

What feels like a year goes by when he finishes unclasping the last button. Their eyes focused on nothing but each other. He spreads the shirt wide open, then takes the top and gently pushes it back over her collarbone, so it hangs just past her shoulders.

God, she's beautiful.

She shimmies her shoulders and performs a light shake with her hands, allowing for the shirt to meet the same demise as the skirt on the floor behind her. Her bra and panties are a matching light pink color, and she looks like a goddess.

My entire body is on fire and my cock is aching. I open the zipper of my pants, tooth by tooth, to avoid making any noise that can take them away from that room.

When he said, '*We good*', I knew two things immediately. I would have absolutely no control over my cock and even less control over what happened in that room. His '*we good*' meant this is his show, not mine.

I am simultaneously apprehensive and exhilarated at the loss of control.

Chris hooks his fingers under her bra straps, pulling both of the thin straps down her arms, then trails his fingers over the cups. Pulling down the fabric, her gorgeous full breasts are now exposed, nipples pebbled and hard.

She releases an audible gasp when he cups his hands around her tits. His thumb moves back and forth slowly over the peaks. Her eyes close and her head tips back with another groan. He is slow and calculating and driving her absolutely wild.

Trailing his hands down to her hips, he turns her whole body to face the camera, then steps behind her. The change creates a blur in the screen as it attempts to refocus, making my heart skip a few beats in panic. Worried I'll miss a moment or our connection will fail.

I would die. Literal death.

She's on display for me now, and she looks universally sublime. Nervous yet confident. Flushed and ready. From behind, he unclasps her bra, and it tumbles to the floor.

I'd like to think his purposeful change in that angle was specifically for me. I'm certain it wasn't *just* for me, but he is acutely aware of their location and where the camera is, so I know he is being mindful of my presence.

I have an unusual amount of respect for him, considering he is fondling my wife at the moment.

Pinching her hardened nipple, her head rolls back onto his shoulder as he dips his other hand into the front of her lace panties. His fingers reach the apex of her thighs. I can see his knuckles move through the mesh of the fabric, bending, rubbing back and forth. She's looking down, watching his fingers move, her lips forming a perfect "o" shape as he massages her. I know the moment he rubs over her clit when she gasps out a long moan, grabbing onto the back of his neck, like she needs it to keep standing.

"Jesus... Fuck," I whisper out loud, unable to stop the thought from turning into words.

Pulling his hand out of her panties, he hooks his fingers on the sides and pulls them down her legs, dropping them at her ankles. Stepping out of them, not taking her eyes off of me, she's now standing in front of us, completely naked. A gorgeous display of tan skin and perfect curves, obstructed by absolutely nothing.

Bending at the knee, she reaches down, gripping the stem of her heel before Christian interrupts her.

"Leave your heels on and turn to me," sounding tortured but loving it.

I grab the shaft of my dick, needing something, anything. Pre-cum is already leaking from the tip, and I have no idea how I'll get through this without pre-ejaculating.

He takes one step towards her, placing his finger over her bottom lip, pressing it into her mouth and rubbing it over her tongue. "See how wet you are, Ellie? Tell me, is that for me or for your husband?

It's a rhetorical question, really.

She answers, anyway, in a muffled and breathy moan, "Both."

My eyes squeeze shut as I take in a deep breath, trying to calm myself. It feels like lava is moving through my veins and everything is flowing to my cock. He's barely touching her and I'm hardly able to maintain control.

When I reopen my eyes, he's looking at the screen, and he knows the loose thread I'm currently hanging from. He cups Elena's jaw and shifts her gaze at me.

"I'm going to make you come. You're going to tell me how, but he has to give you permission first."

How I hold back, I have no idea.

Taking his lead, knowing Elena is terrible about asking for what she wants sexually, I ask, "Do you want to come, baby?"

"God, yes." Her voice, raspy and desperate. I open my mouth to respond, but the words she speaks next send lightning strikes in both our directions. "I need him to fuck me."

Holy shit. She's never been forthcoming in the bedroom, so

I have no idea what's come over her right now, but I'm all fucking for it.

Chris tilts his head back and huffs out a long breath, peering up to the invisible sky of their ceiling with what appears to be a silent prayer.

Welcome to the club, man.

She turns towards him, both of her hands gripping his hair as she pulls his mouth closer to hers.

"Please fuck me, Chris."

Watching him fall apart is almost as exciting as watching her. Spying on them in the club, hidden in a corner, was a turn on, and something I never thought we could top. But this. Him knowing. All of us together. My entire body is burning with a desire I never knew it had. It's an out-of-body experience, and I'm barely hanging on.

He grabs her waist and picks her up; her legs wrap around his torso as his mouth meets hers in a feral kiss. He takes a few steps forward towards the couch that runs vertical to the one that faces me. Leaning down he gently places her on the top of it, where I have a full view of both of their profiles. As he leans back up, she reaches for his belt, unbuckling the leather strap and letting it fall to the sides, then unbuttons the top and pulls both his pants and boxers down in one swoop.

His goliath-sized cock springs loose from the cloth cage it's been locked in and, Christ, it's big. A low "hmmm" escapes his mouth as she stares up at him from the couch, biting her lip.

"Put your mouth on my cock, Ellie." She reaches forward, grabbing his hips so the tip of his cock meets her lips. She circles her tongue around the crown before opening her mouth, pulling his hips closer as it slides deep down her throat.

"Fuuuck." His voice is deep and desperate. He leans forward, catching himself on the armrest of the couch. She bobs her head back and forth, taking him all the way down her throat to the tip, repeating it over and over.

"Jesus... Dammit. Fuck." His words roll into one long description of how wrecked he is.

My cock is the size of the goddamn Titanic. Harder than the iceberg that fucking hit it. I can't stop stroking myself, feeling an overwhelming sensation pool at the base of my spine. I want to beg him to fuck her myself so I can come, but I never want this to end.

"Oh God, Ellie, you have to stop." He hisses as he cups her chin and pushes her back, gripping onto his cock tightly to hold back.

I've been there before and damn, that was close.

The smirk on her face is both adorable and the spawn of the Devil.

"Are you ready to fuck me yet?" Yup. Devil incarnate.

He kneels down, pulling out a foil wrapper from his pants pocket, quickly teething it, ripping it open and sheathing himself in latex. Still on his knees, he grips the back of her calves, pulling her towards him.

"Say it again," he demands.

"Fuck me." He tilts his head at her, giving her a knowing look. "*Please*, fuck me," she begs.

He presses his cock against her slick entrance, inching the tip in. She moans at the initial invasion then he pushes into her, all the way to the hilt. Both of their moans vibrate through my speaker, a mix of husky and desperate whines. He continues to piston his hips, switching between a teasing pace and steady tempo. The sounds coming from Elena are anguished and desperate. She's in need of a release, and I can see in his face he knows it.

He circles his hand around the base of her ponytail, taking her hair in his palm, pulling her closer with his other hand, then yanking her pony down so her neck is completely exposed to him.

She looks like a goddess.

"I've been waiting a long time to feel this pussy wrapped around my cock. It feels so fucking good." A breathy moan escapes her lips in response.

"You're clenching around me so tight, Ellie. Are you going to come on my cock?"

I can see where they connect as he pistons into her, stretching her open. He's so hard and she's so wet. The sight of them together is almost too much. His pleasure is completely at her mercy and the sounds of their bodies slapping together, mixed with moans of pleasure, has me at theirs. I feel my orgasm begin to pool at the base of my spine. My hand is desperate as I stroke myself, gripping tight around the base all the way to the tip.

He's got an anaconda grip on her ponytail that allows her only the ability to shift her line of sight to mine. Her once Caribbean blue eyes are now the darkest of sapphires. Our eyes connect, and the exigency in my face must blare through the screen like a silent foghorn as she moans, begging for release.

Knowing she'll never ask and my need to have some control over this uncontrollable situation, I say, "She's too shy to ask you to rub her clit, Chris."

His lip turns up into a smirk as he moves his thumb over her glistening bud, and she whimpers, causing him to moan, forcing groans from me. It's a mix of feral, anguished sound effects, and we're all desperate for more.

"Come for him, baby. Come for us." Giving her the permission I think she needs.

She squeezes her eyes shut, relinquishing the power she was holding onto.

"Oh, God. You're going to make me come." Her voice trembling.

"Fuck," is what I think I hear from him as he releases her hair and drags his hand down to her nipple, rolling it between his fingers as his finger drums on her clit with more pressure.

"Chris! Oh, God. Fuck, Jake, I'm coming." She's calling for him, calling for me.

I've lost all control. I grip my cock harder, swiping my thumb over the top to use the excessive amount of pre-cum leaking from the tip. In two weak pumps, I explode all over myself, ropes of white liquid spilling over my hand and fingers. Groaning and mumbling words all the way through, I leave my eyes pinned on Elena and Chris as he chases his own release. He is seconds behind me. Throwing his head back, groaning into the air, mumbling inaudible words as he grips her hips, driving into her like he can't get deep enough. Falling forward, he visibly relaxes on top of her, panting.

I had no idea when I called Elena tonight that *this* was going to happen. I look at myself and can't help but huff out a short chuckle. Half my buttons are undone, my pants splayed open by the zipper, a mess all over myself, but I couldn't feel more relaxed with the intensity of the orgasm that I just had.

I stand up and grab a towel to wipe off my hands then peer back through the phone. Chris is still resting on top of Elena. His hand bearing some of his weight on the couch with his forehead resting on her shoulder.

My gorgeous wife and her sexy as hell lover laying there spent in each other's arms. I should feel jealous, but I don't. I feel fulfilled. Conflicting feelings battle each other in my head. This isn't normal. I shouldn't enjoy this. I have no idea what we just started. I just know I never want it to stop.

19

ELENA

The flight home is quiet and a tad awkward. Not as awkward as departing from his hotel room last night, though.

What do you do after your new *sort of* boss fucks you until you see stars while your husband watches while getting himself off on FaceTime? Yeah, I'll let you know when I know. Because whatever it was that I did was not graceful, nor was I playing it cool and collected.

I think Christian may have actually laughed at my awkward body movements as I tiptoed around the hotel, picking up my clothes scattered over the floor. Grabbing my belongings and saying bye to my husband while not trying to be too distant but not trying to be lovey. Instead of doing either of those, I mumbled something that I still can't figure out, then just hung up on him.

I actually attempted to reach out for a handshake during our goodbye process. A freaking handshake. Like a, *thanks for the great dick, nice doing business with you,* handshake. Luckily, I realized that I was crossing into the realm of total weirdo and slyly wrapped my hand around his waist, giving him a shy chest hug instead.

God, I was a complete lunatic.

I started to leave his room before he stopped me to remind me that I didn't have my purse and I was still pretty much naked. With the exception of my underwear and blouse, that was still unbuttoned and barely covered the tops of my legs. I stopped to calm myself, sucked in as much air as possible to regroup my thoughts, before finally gathering my things like a halfway normal human being, and left his room with some poise.

He shot me a knowing smile, which eased some of the guilt I had blanketed over me. But not enough to get any kind of decent sleep last night. I couldn't stop the rampant thoughts of shame.

I slept with a man, who wasn't my husband.

Yes, my husband was present. *Sort of.* Everything was consensual. Still, it all felt surreal.

Plus, this man–technically–he's my boss. A man that I work for and have to talk to daily *and* see multiple times a week. How has my willpower failed me so badly?

The other overbearing stress was Matt. He had pestered me the entire trip, asking for check-ins multiple times a day. I even questioned if he was having me followed because he demanded to know where we were going and what time everything was scheduled. If we changed up that schedule in any way or went somewhere else, I would get another text from Matt asking for an update. Like he knew I wasn't on track. Mind you, I felt like he just asked for updates all the time regardless, but it felt off. He even asked for pictures of my chosen outfits "*for approval*". He's been so inappropriate and over the top. A part of me wanted to report him to HR, but then I went and fucked my client during a business trip, so my own guilt is blanketing my decision making process. Plus, I have a feeling Matt would just turn it around on me and find something he could use against me. The man is a total idiot, but annoyingly resourceful when he wants to be.

I know I can't risk anything further, at least during the time I'm working on Christian's project. I need to cut this off now. It shouldn't have even started in the first place. Okay, the first time, I had no idea. But the second... and third. Jesus. Yeah, my willpower definitely sucks.

The plane taxis and we are waiting for the green light to exit. Like the procrastinator I am, when it comes to emotional communication, I wait until the last minute to share my thoughts. I begin packing my bag without looking at him so that I can look as busy as possible.

"Christian, I'd like to thank you for the opportunity to represent your company on this project. This trip has been wonderful in getting to know your team and expectations. I won't let you down." I peek a glance his way and he's sitting forward in his chair, staring at me. I'm unsure if laser beams will come out of his eyeballs or if he's going to stalk over to me and rip off my clothes. It's like a fifty-fifty chance, either way.

I continue, "I know the circumstances of how we met are... unique. And then there was last night." I bite my lip at the memory as heat floods my cheeks. "However, I think it'll be best for us to remain completely professional throughout the remainder of this project."

A lopsided smirk appears with a slight shake of his head, so small I almost miss it, then he pushes his hands off the tops of his thighs and stands abruptly. Walking over towards me, he holds out his hand to help me stand, which is weird because I don't need help standing, then leans down and grabs the handle of my laptop bag.

Holding it out to me, he says, "I understand, Mrs. Jenkins."

No Ellie or Elena. *Mrs. Jenkins.* So, this is what professional feels like.

I hate it already.

He turns away from me, heading towards the door of the plane. I follow behind him, crouching through the opening even though I don't need to, but the door feels tight and restricted.

Maybe that's just the energy in the room after what just happened.

The airstairs of the plane are expanded open, and he's exiting down swiftly. My steps are slow and calculated, being that I'm in three-inch heels, and all I need is to misstep and crash land at the bottom. I hold the railing and keep my eyes glued to each step I'm coming down on. As I reach the bottom, I peer up to see his entire body blocking the final step of the staircase.

Keeping my gaze locked on his arms that have caged me, he closes in on me. His spicy woodsy scent invades my space, the same scent that lingered on my tongue all night. With his lips on my earlobe, I can feel his breath on my neck, and it sends tingles down my spine.

"If you think I'm not going to want more of you after feeling your tight cunt around my cock, you are out of your fucking mind. Depriving us of something so good is a terrible mistake, Ellie. But if you want to remain professional, I will respect your decision. Just know that every time you are in a room with me, all I'll be thinking about is how desperate you sounded screaming my name while your husband came all over himself."

Holy shit.

Everything in me malfunctions completely.

His hand cups my jaw while he kisses my cheek. As he steps back, for good measure, his hand trails down the front of my silk blouse, palming over my breast, brushing over my tight nipple, before giving me a sexy smirk and turning away.

What. The. Hell.

Within an hour, I'm home and walking through my front door. I place my keys and purse on the entry table. "Honey, I'm home." Jesus, that sounds so domestic.

Unexpectedly, hands wrap around my hips and spin me around. Jake's mouth crashes into mine as he yanks up my skirt and pulls my legs around his waist. Carrying me up the stairs to our room, it feels like he has eight hands roaming feverishly all over my body. In my hair, my neck, hips, wrapping his arms around my back, pulling me flush with his body. His fingers pinch my nipples, and he's grabbing anything he can, as his lips and tongue wander all over my face and neck.

Placing me on our bed, he strips off his pants, then pulls his shirt over his head, and in two rapid movements, he's on top of me. Placing his forehead to mine, his eyes shut tight, and he inhales deeply. The weight of his body is nothing like the emotions I feel coming from his actions. He's excited, uncertain, worried, and absolutely wild.

Cupping both of my hands around his face, I pull his lips to mine, running my fingers through the stubble on his jawline and my tongue parts the seam of his lips.

"I need you."

And that's all he needs to say. Emotionally and physically, he takes me. Spending the rest of the morning in bed together, reminding each other that no matter what our relationship status is–open, closed, shared, or complicated–our love and respect for each other goes beyond anything else. And knowing that no matter what happens, we're in this together.

20

ELENA

"You've been way too busy. It's Friday, we need to go out. And you need to buy me drinks for all the shit I do for you all day," Cruz whines, placing my cinnamon latte on my desk.

My attitude at work this week has been nothing short of nasty. I've been ridiculously short tempered, and since Cruz is who I work closest with, he's felt the wrath more than most.

Matt has been nonstop on my ass, daily. Multiple times a day, actually. The project itself is amazing. That's where I thrive. It's the underlying pressure from Matt and his snide sexual comments that have me on edge. Instead of taking it out on Matt, I've been taking it out on Cruz, with my horrible attitude at work and pretty much giving Jake an undeserved silent treatment at home.

"You get a paycheck for that, Cruz." I stare at him so I can see his jaw drop to the floor, which it does.

"Girl, I don't make cinnamon lattes, perfect temperature, with a dash of love, for just anyone. Do you think everybody gets the love you get?" I shake my head, unable to hide my smile because he's so goddamn adorable, and I actually don't know what I would do without him in my life.

It's been a week since I came back from the business trip with Christian. I should really call it a pleasure trip since it did involve a mind-blowing orgasm, but I've still kept that little secret to myself.

"You're even in your hot maxi dress today, and those wedges." He brings the tips of his fingers to his mouth with a chef's kiss to the ceiling. "You don't even need to go home to change."

"Okay, okay fine. I'll let Jake know we're going out for drinks tonight. But I'm not helping you hit on that bartender again. So don't even think about it." Cruz raises his hands in the air in celebration.

"Hallelujah!" he praises. He's going to be wild tonight. I can feel it already.

"Don't forget you have your Friday follow up meeting with Christian at his office at one o'clock, then an accountability call with Matt. He called me earlier and asked if you were in the office, and I stupidly said, 'yes'. Sooo... he told me the meeting would be in person." I throw my head back in frustration that Matt has had such a tight rope on me since the start of this project. I am literally drowning under his micromanagement, and I think I might projectile vomit on him if I have to see his face.

When I bring my head forward, I glance at Cruz, and if looks could kill, Cruz would drop dead. And probably in the most dramatic fashion because he knows no other way.

"I know, I know. But if I told him you weren't in the office, he would have just started stalking you on your phone, so, really, I did a good thing." I roll my eyes. Not at Cruz, but at the thought of Matt and his recent tactics.

Remembering that Cruz doesn't know anything about

what's happening, I have to pretend like none of this bothers me as much as it does.

"It's fine. I've been avoiding him all week with how busy it's been, so I'm sure he just wants a face-to-face update. I'm going to head over to the Ford building, then when I come back, I'll slam out the meeting with Matt, and then we'll head for Happy Hour as early as possible." I smile at Cruz, who is currently doing some kind of mamba with himself in the corner.

"Hallelujah squared!" He places the updated Ford portfolio on my desk and waltzes out of the room while blowing me a kiss.

He deserves a medal for putting up with me this week.

When I arrive at the Ford building, Christian's assistant, Jenny, sees me to his office. It's a large corner office, floor to ceiling windows, with a separate sitting area beautifully decorated with a plush leather loveseat and couch. A coffee table adorned with tea, coffee, and small French pastries. She leads me to the sitting area and tells me to have a seat, gesturing me over to the couch like Vanna White.

"He's just finishing up a call. He'll be right over," she whispers to me. I smile and nod back.

I watch Christian as he paces back and forth on his call. His week looks like it's been as rough as mine. His sleeves are rolled up to his elbows, tie is absent from his collar with the top buttons of his shirt splayed open, exposing the hard line of his chest. His dark hair is unusually untidy, and he's got more than his standard five o'clock shadow decorating his jawline.

He looks as edible as these miniature pastries.

He glances towards me. My heart rate kicks up a few notches before I give myself whiplash, trying to turn away. Embarrassed by my blatant staring, I fiddle with an empty coffee cup and start to make myself a coffee I don't need. Cruz probably brought me three lattes today, which is pretty much all the calories I've consumed. Any more caffeine and I might as well Tasmanian Devil myself through the middle of Christian's office.

So, instead of pouring myself the standard liquid lead, I opt for some organic tea made with a bunch of herbs I can't pronounce and let it steep on the table.

Christian holds up a finger, indicating he'll be just another minute, and I grant him a close-lipped smile and a small wave of my hand indicating, it's no big deal.

I can't help but appraise him and wonder what his story is. He's a great guy, amazing in bed, and beyond sexy. His aura is so well balanced, I find it hard to believe that he doesn't have women throwing themselves at him. There is hardly ever anything in the media with him and other women. He seems to keep a low profile and prefers it that way, but I can't imagine him not having a plethora of girls to choose from whenever he desires.

He finishes on the call and starts to walk towards me. I stand to greet him, pushing into tippy toes to press a kiss on his cheek.

Although it wasn't sensual and just a friendly hello, it probably crosses over the line of professionalism, but doing nothing would have been totally awkward.

"How's your week going? Or ending, I guess I should say," I ask as I sit back down and remove the tea bag from my cup.

"Busy, but good. My teams have never been so productive since meeting you. I think I need to bring you to all my off-site meetings." Smirking, he winks at me and pours a cup of coffee for himself.

I can't help but blush and cross my ankles together at the reminder of how our off-site meeting field trip ended, and what he felt like.

Oh yes, Elena, crossing your ankles is really going to prevent you from spreading your legs.

I press my thighs together in an attempt to reduce the arousal that begins to stir.

He's more than aware of my internal thoughts as his smirk turns into a full-blown smile as he shakes his head.

Jesus, this whole keeping professional thing is going to be so much more difficult than I expected.

"I connected with each of the team leads on Monday to confirm the weekly plan and then again this morning to confirm all those deadlines were met. All the teams completed everything I had laid out for them and a few of the team members even came up with some additional ideas I think we can incorporate into the overall project. You truly have great people working for you." I smile and hand him the portfolio. "Here are the updates and the plans for next week, so you can go over them at your convenience and let me know of any modifications you think are needed."

He grabs the portfolio and places it down on the table without a glance.

And because my brain doesn't keep up with my mouth whenever I'm nervous, I blurt out, "Why are you single?"

There's a pregnant pause and a curious look on his face. It's times like this I wish my superpower was mind reading.

"I don't have time for a relationship," he says simply and abruptly.

I may not be a mind reader, but that's a basic bullshit answer.

My brows pinch together as a reflex and my lip turns up at him. My facial expression is calling him out on said bullshit.

"For someone as professionally passionate as you, I can see work takes up a lot of your time. But sexually, you are just as passionate, and I know that's not reserved for just random women." There goes my mouth again, detaching from my brain.

What has gotten into me?

He stalls, stirring the cream in his coffee for a brief moment, looks at me, blinks away, then continues to stir his coffee. He taps the spoon, creating a sharp ping that echoes through the deafened room, and places it on the saucer.

"Sexually passionate, huh?" He smirks, raising the cup to his lips.

And cue more blushing.

"I just mean, you're a great guy, Christian. Your life is very public, but there's nothing known publicly in regards to partners in your life. What's stopped you from relationships in the past?" I ask honestly.

"At first, it was just time. I was so busy building this company I didn't have time for much else. That is still the case, but it's a little more challenging than that now." He pops a tiny French cookie in his mouth.

"Why is that?" I ask, finishing the rest of my tea.

"If I go out, it's most often to events where everyone knows who I am. Women are... easily accessible," he pauses, "but they're interested in the money or lifestyle, and after a while, they all look the same. Boring and untrustworthy."

That is an odd word to describe these women. "Untrustworthy?" I repeat.

He shrugs. Just shrugs. Like that is the answer to my question.

I watch him chew and lick his lips after eating some of the table snacks and, Jesus, how is everything this man does sexy? That familiar sensation in my core starts to tingle, and the temperature in the room has increased 100 degrees since he sat down.

"Feeling okay there, Mrs. Jenkins?" His eyes bore into me, playful yet seductive.

"I think you pump pheromones into the air to kick me off kilter, Mr. Ford," I reply back as professional and playful as he did.

"No, you did that all by yourself by drinking tea." And the sexy smirk returns.

"What?" I squeal.

"The tea, you must have known. It's an aphrodisiac. Makes you horny as shit." If you look up smug in the dictionary, it would say Christian Ford.

I huff out a breath as my jaw slacks, and I urgently grab the empty ripped tea bag. Some of the ingredients listed are Ginseng, Maca Root, and some other herbal names longer than my arm.

"How the hell was I supposed to know that?" I hold up the tea bag like it's the bane of my existence. "And why the hell do you have this in your office tea selection, you lunatic?"

His laugh is infuriating but contagious.

He finishes his coffee and wipes his lips with the petite napkin that was placed on the table.

"You're making it difficult for me to honor your *let's remain professional* request." He air quotes with his fingers.

Uncrossing and crossing my legs, I shift in my seat, trying to find a comfortable position, but who am I kidding? Nothing is going to calm the burning desire flowing through my veins.

Instead, I sit to my full height and tilt up my chin.

"I know you want me, and you can't blame the tea. I sensed it the minute you walked through my door." He leans forward, crowding my space, and whispers, "Just say yes."

Fuck me.

No.

But words escape me, so I just shake my head.

He grins. Fucking grins. Smug bastard.

This is the point in time when the human psyche is completely questionable. You start thinking things like, *I've already done it once before* and *one more time won't matter*. When you start making excuses for the things you know you want, but shouldn't have. It's already too late.

Fuck it.

"Yes," I pant.

In one swift movement, he's kneeling in front of me. One hand on each of my legs slowly spreading me open. He lifts the flowing fabric at the bottom of my dress and folds it over my knees, inching himself between my legs as he pulls my hips forward and flush with his. Crashing his lips to mine, my uncontrollable moans are swallowed by his mouth as our tongues explore each other frantically.

His hands trail up my thighs under my dress until he reaches the apex of my legs. "You're wearing panties," he states factually. "You're going to regret that," he states with even more factuality.

Hooking his finger into the side of the lace, he yanks them forward, ripping the delicate material, then ducks his head under the curtain draping my legs. His flattened tongue meets the hardened peak of my clit and I gasp out, covering my mouth to stifle my whimper.

"Ah, fuck," escapes through my lips.

My head falls back over the back of the couch, one hand gripping the soft grainy leather while the other tries to grip his hair through the fabric of my dress.

"Oh my God, that feels so good." My moans louder than I intend. "Don't stop."

Why is everything in this room glass or tile? My sounds are just bouncing off the walls like ping pong balls trapped in a trampoline box.

His tongue works in me and through me over and over again in perfect rhythm. Everything is building quickly, pooling in my center, and I've lost any control I had over my body, my mind, my mouth. Quickly, oh so quickly, everything explodes. A loud groan echoes through the room. Christian moans into my pussy with approval as my orgasm peaks and my body trembles under him.

Removing himself from under the tent of my dress, he comes up with a look that tells me he's even more pleased with himself than before. Releasing the death grip he has on my hips, he cups my face and pulls my lips to his. I taste myself on him, sweet mixed with his spice.

Jesus, this man is insatiable.

I press my hands into his chest, making space between us so I can reach for his pants. He stands so I can quickly unzip him, pulling out his cock and wrapping my fingers around the base. My fingertips barely meet as I pump my hand from base to tip, spitting on the crown to add to the pre-cum lubrication pooling at his tip. He's so sexy with his jaw slacked and eyes desperate, as lick my lips, preparing myself to take all of him. Sitting on the edge of the couch, I gaze up at him with his cock so close to my mouth he tries to angle himself so it's easier for me to devour, but I just smile. Teasing him. Knowing exactly what he wants, but instead, I stroke him up and down, in a slow, languid rhythm.

Keeping my hand at the base, I open my mouth and stick out my tongue, beating the pre-cum laced tip on my mouth, teasing him further. He hisses in approval, then grabs my hair, forcing my mouth at the perfect angle so he can fuck my mouth. It's only moments and a few thrusts before he is cursing under his breath.

"Fuck, Ellie. I am always in full control until your mouth is on my cock."

I can feel his cock harden in my mouth. The tip is fuller

than it was just moments ago. Challenging my gag reflex, I grab his hips and push him further down my throat, convulsing slightly at the size, but that little heave provides enough pressure to make him lose all his restraint.

He pulls out of my mouth and falls forward, breathing heavily as he steadies his forehead to mine. "I need to be inside you." He grabs a handful of my hair, yanking my head back and crashing his lips to mine, completely ungoverned by anything but his sexual hunger. He quickly sheathes himself with a condom. Then, in a move so swift my brain can hardly keep up, he wraps his arms around my hips, turns me around and pulls the weight of my body up so my knees are resting on the edge of the cushions. I'm facing the back of the couch when I feel the distinct texture of latex trail over my wet slit as he urgently pushes inside me. I didn't think there was any way I would come again before he did, but as he pushes in and out of me with such a perfect tempo, I realize what an amateur thought that was.

My hands are gripping the back of the couch with white knuckle force, and as my orgasm crests, the sounds escaping me are tamed only by Christian's hand covering my mouth.

He simultaneously pulls me up as he leans down so we are flush, back to chest.

"I've been craving this since the moment you left my room. The feeling of you tightening around my cock. Making you unravel all over again." Leaning closer, his lips graze my ear. "It's fucking addicting, Ellie."

I don't know if it's his words, the way he's fucking me, the desire, or the fear of getting caught, but everything builds into an all-encompassing explosion which has me moaning uncontrollably into his palm. His thrusts are punishing as he shoves his face into the crook of my neck, muffling his own sounds as he shatters behind me.

After an atomic bomb of orgasms, we both relent, and our

bodies fail us as we slump in defeat. I melt deeper into the sofa since he apparently took all my bones with that last orgasm.

"You are... wow. Just wow." His body slides beside me, as boneless as mine.

I huff out a laugh at him, which quickly fades when the desire fades, and I realize I never considered asking Jake about what would happen if Christian and I were alone. He keeps saying the ball is in my court, but this feels... adulterous. I lost control, and I shouldn't lose control.

Sure, we've messed around. But this sex is different. This feels different. It feels... emotional.

Jake already watched us during the video call. I don't know that he would want us to continue pursuing this with Christian.

And Matt. Ugh, fucking Matt.

Knowing Matt is beyond suspicious of whatever is happening between Christian and me, this could just give him more ammunition. Even though he doesn't know the details of what is happening, the fact that I do makes me feel even worse than I already did. And if he ever finds out, he'll completely ruin me.

Pulling my, now ripped to shreds, panties off and placing them in the pocket of my purse, I continue to silently scold myself while I make myself presentable.

I glance up to see Christian looking my way, studying me in the same way someone with basic math skills would study a calculus problem.

"What happened in the last minute?" Christian asks, pulling me out of my head.

"What do you mean?" I ask the annoyingly handsome billionaire, who's already put back together other than the wildness of his unkempt, just-fucked hair.

"It looks like someone just told you your dog died." His eyes squint, assessing me, then widen suddenly.

"Shit, does he know you are here?" he asks.

My face flinches with his tone.

"Don't say it like that. All accusatory," I snap back.

Pure shock blankets his face. He wasn't expecting that reply.

Placing his hands out in front of him like a surrender. "It was a simple question. I'm just not sure of the boundaries here."

I huff out a breath. "Neither am I," I say, with more defeat than I intend. "This is all new to us. He says everything is flexible, but I don't know if I should be telling him beforehand or if he always wants to... witness." I run my hands through my hair nervously.

"Maybe we should all meet, talk about this." His tone is even and irritatingly reasonable.

I must look at him like he grew a turnip out of his head because he puts his hands up again in surrender again and says, "Just so there is no confusion or guilt."

Guilt. I'm not guilty.

Okay, I feel guilty. Because he's right. Jake and I talked about being open and the ball being in my court, but my loyalty to my husband is being questioned by my own actions, and I'm drowning in the shame of all of this.

I can talk about anything, unless it's sex or emotions. God, what is wrong with me?

So instead of being a rational human and agreeing to his complete and utter logical stupid nonsense, I lash out.

"It doesn't matter because this isn't happening anymore. It can't happen."

"Elena..." He takes a step towards me.

"Don't." That halts his movement. His pleading look is devastating, blanketing me further with remorse.

"I can't do this anymore, Christian. Please assign me someone else to report to." I grab my purse, and, before walking out the door, I turn to him. One hand is on his hip, the other at the nape of his neck. Those desperate pleading eyes full of lust just moments ago, now desperate with something else. Pity, maybe? Sorrow? I don't know, but I can't care.

"You can't tempt me anymore. Just please... stop," I beg as I hang my head. It's pathetic that I need to ask him and can't control my actions myself.

"I don't want to," he whispers.

"You have to."

21

ELENA

I still feel at odds with myself as I punch the elevator button in my office building. Normally I would have just gone home, but I still have that meeting with Matt, which I'm dreading more than I would be if I were skydiving naked.

I would like to blame Christian for how I'm feeling, but I know I can't. My own actions are to blame completely. The push and pull of emotions is confusing, and I can't navigate how I'm feeling. I enjoy myself with Christian. I shouldn't. Right? How can something wrong feel so right? I'm sure Jake would condone my actions, but my emotions are something different. Maybe that's why it felt wrong doing something with him alone.

So what does a respectable, conflicted woman do when she is baffled by her emotions?

Start a fight and cut that shit off at the knees.

But now, I have the guilt of my childish behavior to add to the rest of my current emotional status.

Happy Hour with Cruz is looking better and better.

I exit the elevator and head towards my office. Cruz is inside it joined by none other than the egomaniac himself, Matt.

Normally, I wouldn't be concerned about Cruz's flailing hands and dramatic demeanor but their banter is hostile.

Channeling my clashing emotions into anger, I enter my office with purpose. "What are you doing in my office?" The depth of my voice matches my mood, slamming my purse down on my desk for extra effect.

Cruz's eyes widen and he looks over at Matt, unsure.

I'm always kind, well put together, and level-headed. Sometimes a little moody, but I never raise my voice. It shocks Cruz, but just fuels Matt.

"Get out." Cruz exits immediately. Matt just stands in the middle of my office, assessing me.

"You smell like sex." He smiles.

"Get the fuck out of my office. Now."

He takes a few steps back, and I'm relieved in his retreat, until he turns around and shuts my office door. Locking it. "We have a meeting."

What the hell.

When he turns back around, his entire demeanor has changed. I've never met anyone with a split personality, but I imagine it feels something like this.

I stand to my full height and cross my arms over my chest. "Our meeting doesn't start for another thirty minutes."

"It starts when I say it starts." He strides back towards me.

As he nears closer to me, his scent wafts through the air. That of cheap cologne, musk and... whiskey. Someone could perhaps miss that grainy fragrance if it didn't smell so sour, like it's coming from his pores and radiating off his breath. As he steps closer, I see his bloodshot eyes and flushed cheeks.

The flashback of his behavior at the Christmas party hits me immediately. I drop my hands to my sides and fist my fingers into my palms. My defiance transforms into worry. I find myself scanning the room in a fight or flight response.

I stand behind the protection of my desk as he nears. He

motions to the top of my desk. "Come here." His tone is understated, but insistent.

"I'd rather we reschedule this meeting," I return.

"I said fucking sit!"

My neck bounces back like his words physically hit me in the face. I sneak a glance around the room again, ignoring my flight response in order to just get through this conversation. I walk around to the front of my desk and give in to his demand, but I stand to retain some sort of power in this moment. Of course, he's having none of that and places his palm against my breastbone, pushing me back until my ass plops down on top of my desk.

The disgust and confusion are written all over my face, but he either doesn't notice or doesn't give a shit. He keeps his gaze down at his palm, still placed between my breasts, and starts tracing the lines of my top. Silence engulfs us for what feels like minutes as he crooks his finger under the fabric and pulls, exposing the lacy rim of my bra.

"What the fuck are you doing?" I yell, smacking his hand away.

That does nothing to deter him. His hand simply boomerangs back around and lands firmly against my throat. He steps forward, trapping me between his body and my desk, as his fingertips tighten against the sensitive flesh under my jawbone.

What the fuck is happening? My heart is beating out of my chest, and I'm completely immobilized by shock. I grip the arm that's choking me, but it's as if it's cemented in place.

"Matt..." I whisper, trying to plea with him.

"He's good enough for this pussy, is he? Willing to cheat on your husband with him, but not with me? I'll fucking give you a cock you'll never forget." He takes his free hand and places it between my legs, trying to pry them open and pull my dress up at the same time.

Using all my strength, I pull away, crossing my arm under his, then pressing my shoulder and elbow towards him to loosen his chokehold. In an effort to protect myself, I pull my knees up and kick my feet forward, landing a blow between his legs. It wasn't hard, but enough to get him to step back and crouch.

I place my palms at the base of my neck, trying to catch my breath, trying to inch away from him. "Why are you doing this?" I'm able to ask between breaths.

His eyes are still dark; his entire demeanor is like nothing I've seen from him before. I'm even more terrified by the look on his face now than when he was choking me. I need to scream for Cruz, but I'm worried what Matt would do to him if he came in here. At least Cruz and I could take him on together, then run out of here. Jesus. How is this happening?

As I open my mouth to scream for Cruz, he lifts up his phone with the screen facing me. My heart drops as I see the picture come into full view.

Me and Christian, on his couch a mere hour ago. Christian's hand haphazardly sheathed over my mouth as he pulls my hair and fucks me from behind.

"Oh my God..." I breathe out. "How..."

"You're a fucking slut," he interrupts.

"A FUCKING SLUUTT!" His voice bellows through my office. Spit and saliva mist over my face and I flinch.

I'm paralyzed.

How did he get that picture?

Does he have more?

I don't understand all the thoughts that are rapidly flashing through my mind.

My breathing is labored, not because of his recent grip on my throat, but because the walls of the room are closing in. The air in the room feels thick and heavy, and I can hardly catch my breath.

Matt stands to his full height, regaining his composure as he pulls his phone back towards him, swiping right dramatically over the screen.

"Wow, you must *really* like his dick or you've just got a great porn face and fake that shit really well. Either way, these speak for themselves."

"Don't..." I lunge forward, trying to stop him from continuing to browse through pictures of me.

Pulling the phone back out of my reach, he reaches his other hand out, locking it around my arm tightly, holding me back.

"You get to go home and give your dirty cunt to your husband. I'll get to go home and jerk myself off to pictures of you getting railed by Christian fucking Ford." His tone is conniving and condescending. The same way a parent would scold their child in a, *I told you so* way, but the crooked smile on his face is dark and twisted, saying more than his words do.

Giving my arm another hard squeeze, before he releases it, he pushes me back to the front of my desk. "Sit the fuck down."

I obey because I'm lost. Devastated. Ashamed. And I'm so goddamn confused.

How did this happen? How could this happen?

Rubbing my hand over the arm that he definitely bruised, I lean back on my desk with my head down and shoulder slouching forward. It's the total opposite of Matt's composure. Standing tall like a king in the middle of *my* office.

I know this wasn't Christian. He wouldn't risk the exposure. Christian is a single man, but the last thing he would want is pictures of him floating around fucking a married woman. Fuck! What the hell was I thinking doing that in his office? We were so exposed. Except it was in his office–his private fucking office.

"How did you get those, Matt? How?" I grit through my teeth.

I once heard that if you ever feel threatened and you know the name of your attacker, you should use their name and look them in the eye. It makes them question their motive when you remind them you know who they are.

"Do you really think that's the most important question, Elena?" He exaggerates my name like a joke.

He steps forward again, this time slowly, placing the tip of his finger at my temple. He traces an invisible line down the side of my face as his eyes bounce over me. Tears begin to pool at the bottom of my eyelids. Tears of worry, the unknown, and flat-out fear.

I turn my head away from his touch, but he follows, leaning closer into me as his lips graze my ear.

"The question is, sweet Elena, what am I going to do with these pictures? There are so many options I have, you know. Show them to our boss, show them to your husband, release them to the media. All have... repercussions." He takes a hold of my chin, gripping my cheeks as he pulls my face back to his. "I'll get my promotion with or without these, so holding on to them is just a nice little perk for me. You'll be my little puppet. And after I get what I want, maybe you can have these back."

He leans deeper into me, and I feel his erection pressing against my hip.

I squeeze my eyes shut as a tear escapes, falling down my cheek. I feel sick to my stomach.

"You are blackmailing me," I manage to mutter as he releases his hold on my face.

"Call it whatever you want. I'd like to say I'm just using my resources." He moves his hand down the front of my dress, popping the top two buttons, exposing the trim of my bra line, then grazes his fingertip over the peak of my breast.

A mix of a huff and grunt fall from my lips out of disgust, which only eggs him on more. He swiftly moves his hand to the back of my neck, taking a handful of my hair, pulling it back as a show of power.

"Touch yourself," he whispers in my ear.

What the hell.

"Fuck you," I spit back.

"I said fucking touch yourself!" whisper yelling into my ear. He yanks his grip on my hair down my spine so my face is parallel with the ceiling, placing the other hand back on my throat.

I've never felt so powerless.

So exposed. So vulnerable.

I want to cry and scream and thrash around like a fish out of water, which is exactly how I feel. Completely absolved of any oxygen.

I reach down the front of my thigh, pulling the fabric of my dress up with my fingers. As I reach the hem, I place my hand underneath and trail up towards the apex of my thighs, allowing the material to fall over my forearm. I circle my wrist, but I don't touch myself, knowing he can't see what I'm doing underneath the cloth that hides my body.

He crooks his neck back to get a better view of my lower half. "That's it, you fucking whore. How does that feel?"

He's pulling harder on my hair and grips my neck viciously.

"You're hurting me." The hold on my hair is so tight I'm barely able to move my mouth enough to mutter the words clearly.

He releases the hold on my throat, sweeping his hand down my sternum and pulls one side of my dress down, taking the cup of my bra with it, baring my breast. He slaps the exposed flesh, and the sting makes me whimper in pain. I squeeze my eyes tighter, shedding another tear.

If I don't open my eyes or see anything, it won't be real. I keep my eyes glued shut. I have to.

"Keep going, slut." As he steps back, I feel the distance

between us. The relief is overwhelming, freeing. He releases my hair, but my neck stays crooked back. I can't seem to gather the courage to do anything but just keep my eyes closed and shut everything off.

I pretend to roll my wrist and touch myself while cursing myself for getting into this position. I hate myself. I hate myself so much.

"Open your eyes, Elena." I can't. I fucking can't.

"Fucking look at me!" he clamors.

Using some invisible force within myself, I crane my neck forward, pulling my chin all the way down to the front of my neck. I flicker my lashes, letting in a little light, then open my eyes fully to see him standing a couple feet away, one hand rubbing himself over his pants and the other holding his phone, aimed straight at me.

"What the fuck!" Pulling my hand out from my dress and covering my arms over my chest.

A smile turns up that covers his entire face. The Joker of all smiles.

"Oh, puppet. A little too late for shy. Don't you think?"

22

JAKE

The week was absolute mayhem, and my development team has been working nonstop to find the bug that's currently making my life a living hell. In the past, it's taken a few hours to locate a bug and fix it, or at least find a workaround for it. It's been two days, and there are thousands of active users that are completely blocked from logging in. If we don't get this fixed today before we go into the weekend, the risk of losing these people as users permanently, triples.

People are fickle and easily replace conveniences at the first sign of turbulence.

Loyalties extend as far as their annoyance will allow. Which is typically in short supply.

Not that I truly don't have faith in the site that I've built or the application's value. There is really nothing else out there that offers what we offer all in one place. But the whole "grass is greener" thing occurs in every aspect of life. Phones, computers, products, jobs, life, love. Especially where emotions are involved.

My phone pings, interrupting my thoughts with a text message from Seamus. Reminding me of that night with the guys and how Elena showed up for me. Even though it was probably the last thing she wanted to do after that shit day at work. It felt like a declaration of love, and I felt so proud that she is mine.

> Seamus: We're planning your very belated bachelor party with blessings from your wife. You free the second weekend of next month?

> Me: This is a very bad idea.

> Seamus: I'm telling your wife you said that.

As I start my reply, my phone rings, and Cruz's name appears. I flinch back, shocked because he never calls me for anything, which has my concern instantly skyrocketing.

"Cruz?" I answer.

"Hey Jake, sorry to bug you but um, Elena... she's... being weird."

"What do you mean, weird? Is she okay?" I ask, with obvious worry in my tone.

"Yes, I think so, but we were supposed to go out for a drink after work today. She had a meeting with Matt, and right after he left her office, she stormed out and left and looked... frazzled. Her hair was a mess, and her makeup was, well, I think she was crying, and Elena doesn't cry." He does a little hmm thing, and I can picture him looking at his nails with his eyebrows raised in such factuality. Because, no, she doesn't cry.

"What was the meeting about, do you know?" I inquire, standing up to get my shoes on.

"It was just an accountability meeting regarding the Ford account, which he seems to have seized the whole boss role in like the arrogant prick that he is." I squint, confused by his statement.

Matt is not her boss. So, I'm not sure why she's having an

accountability meeting with him and not her CEO, that she reports to. She mentioned he was the one that got the meeting, so maybe he's still involved. Clearly, she's not telling me something.

"Thanks for calling me, Cruz. I'll let you know when she's home and that she's okay," I tell him, genuinely happy that he called me.

I hang up the phone and walk through the house to grab a few of my things. Slipping on my shoes in a rush and grabbing my jacket along with my keys and wallet.

She's been a little distant this week, but nothing that I've noticed out of the ordinary. Although an alien could have landed on our roof, and I probably wouldn't have noticed in the last two days.

Shit.

For someone who likes to watch, I definitely haven't been paying attention to the details that matter.

I pull my phone out of my pocket to locate her phone. We use this app to find our phones when they are lost, but this is the second time I've used it to locate her, and I hate that I feel like I have to.

When the map comes up, I see her phone symbol, which is hovering mine, like a duplicate reflection. I use two fingers to zoom in and see that she's home.

Confused, I look around the house, in case I was that inundated with work and completely missed her coming home, then peer out the window and see her car is in the driveway. She's fixing her hair and running her fingers below her eyes, wiping evidence of any tear-stained cheeks and smudged makeup.

I already know she's in the process of her typical retraction. Hiding everything she is feeling and withholding anything that happened today.

Goddammit, Elena.

Storming out there demanding answers isn't going to help anyone in this case. Fighting every single cell in my body to avoid going out there, I place my keys and wallet back on the side table and kick off my shoes.

It takes another couple of minutes for her to walk through the door. By this time, I'm in the kitchen, pouring a glass of wine for each of us.

Our home is completely open when you walk in, so there is a full view of the living, dining, and kitchen areas. It's a blessing when we have people over, but does nothing for trying to privately walk in the front door.

"Hi, my queen. I just opened a bottle. I hope you feel like red tonight," I say, as I finish pouring the second glass. I push her glass towards the front of the island as she walks towards me.

"Sounds great," she replies with the emotion of a sea urchin.

"Bad day?" I look at her over the top of the wine glass as I lift it to my lips.

"A long week. I'm glad it's Friday," the tight-lipped smile doesn't reach her eyes.

Well, that is the most bullshit generic response I've ever heard. The one you feed strangers when they ask you how you are doing. She's infuriating when she is closed off, and sometimes, I wish I was a man who lost my temper so she could see how much it pisses me off.

"Cruz called." She snaps a look up in my direction, her eyes wide like saucers. "He said you guys had plans tonight, but you left... suddenly."

"He was confused," she replies quickly.

"He seemed concerned," I bite back just as fast.

"It's next week. We're going to Happy Hour sometime next week." Whatever happened is locked in a vault and she has thrown the key into a black hole in another fucking universe.

"Okay." I blow out a long breath of defeat.

I round the island to stand behind her, moving her hair behind her neckline and wrap my arms around her shoulders. As I lean in, I physically feel her shudder.

She fucking shudders.

It has me pause long enough for her to step out of my embrace.

"I just need to shower, wash off the day." She sets down her wine glass and walks towards the stairs without a backward glance in my direction.

I know this is how she processes things, but something feels off. Really off.

As she ascends the stairs, I grab my wine glass and instinctually down it like it's a shot. Which goes down as easily as water at this point.

Pulling out my phone, I text Cruz to let her know she is home, and he replies with a thumbs-up emoji.

I decide to jump back on my computer and get some more work done while she's cleaning up to give her the privacy I know she needs. Although, my thoughts keep drifting back to her. Her red-rimmed eyes and blotching cheeks and that goddamn shudder.

I Google Ford Enterprises and Christian Ford's name, digging to find something–anything. I have no idea what I'm even looking for or why I'm looking into the guy who was in my wife last week. I should have no business doing this, and wouldn't have to, if she would just open up and communicate.

I find myself getting more and more flustered by the fact that the guy is literally squeaky clean–at least on paper–according to the whole trusty internet. He's 38, never married, no kids, went to Yale, graduated top of his class, *of course he did*, and started Ford Enterprises, building it from the bottom up. He's pictured at a few events with a couple of different women, but no over-the-top scandals that I can find, and I'm not getting any weird psycho vibes from him. Only, I'm now annoyed at the perfection that is Christian Ford.

I close down my computer and realize it's been over an hour since Elena went upstairs. I refill my wine glass and grab hers that's been sitting on the island since she left to take a shower. When I walk into the room, she's in bed, rolled over on her side in a fetal position, sleeping. Or at least it appears she is.

What the fuck.

Placing the wine glasses down, I crawl onto my side of the bed. My weight shifts her body slightly towards mine, and I wrap my arm around her stomach.

"Baby, what's going on?" I nuzzle into her neck, pressing my nose to the back of her earlobe.

"Just hold me," she whispers.

So that's what I do. I hold her all night, for as long as she needs.

23

ELENA

This week, and by that, I mean the first two days of the week, has gone by painfully slow. Not as slow as last weekend, but it's still a torturous feeling. The weekend was entailed of Jake's probing questions, about how I was feeling, and a couple of questions hinting around Christian, but nothing regarding the Friday afternoon meeting with Matt. I was unsure if he knew anything about that when he mentioned Cruz called him, so I kept to myself and remained as vague as possible.

I also haven't mentioned anything to Cruz, and probably won't because his concern was valid, but I'm still a little peeved that he called my husband.

Cruz and I had our weekly roundup meeting on Monday, where I completely ignored any question of Friday afternoon and bailing on him that night. I've had a few texts with Christian, which have remained awkwardly professional. Only speaking about the project and jumping on calls with his offsite teams.

Then our company's Monday morning meeting, which was me sitting in a room with that disgusting, self-important, walking dick stick. I tried to avoid sitting next to him, but he made Cruz move by making some stupid excuse about sitting with his *teammate*. Then as he sat down, I got that familiar whiff of musk and cheap cologne when he leaned in and whispered, 'Good Morning, Puppet'.

The use of the nickname makes me cringe.

The thought of the evidence he has, and our encounter, pushes bile further up my throat, which feels like it has made a home there since Friday.

Fortunately, I wore pants on Monday, but it didn't stop him from groping my leg and caressing my thigh under the table during the entire meeting. I've worn nothing but pants and long-sleeve sweaters every day since. I still feel exposed. And so dirty.

Never have I felt like a weak woman. I have weak moments, like everyone. But this... nothing has ever made me feel so powerless.

I almost went to Bryan on Monday after the meeting. Career be damned. But the shame of everything stopped me at his office door.

Jake doesn't care who knows about our extracurricular sex activities, and I wish I could feel that same way. I wish I didn't care so much or have so much riding on the fact that everyone would judge my personal life.

When Jake and I first tried this out, I don't think either one of us thought it would be more than once with any specific person. It might be fun adding a regular partner to our sex life, which I never thought of until after meeting Christian. That is something that I would consider now. And Jake... I don't think Jake cares about whether it's a regular or just something we explore from time to time, as long as I'm happy and comfortable.

But that makes no fucking difference at this point.

Everything feels soiled.

Matt could completely ruin everything I've built in an instant, and I hate him for that. It doesn't matter if everything with Christian was condoned by my husband, people are going to think I'm a cheating slut who sleeps with her clients. Besides, what's my defense? *'No, no, it's totally okay; my husband likes when I fuck other men.'*

Everything is absolutely fucked. The heaviness in my chest is feeling more and more debilitating every day.

And the more I go down this rabbit hole, the more trapped I feel. I don't know what drowning in quicksand is like, but I imagine it feels something like this.

A knock on the door rips me away from my thoughts as my heart jumps in my chest and my pulse quickens.

I hear the creak of the door handle before I see it turn. I hold my breath until Cruz steps through the door, easing the tension twisted on my face. The air stuck in my lungs releases, and I slouch back in my chair, realizing how exhausted my body is from running so tight and rigid all week. Even my fingers feel tight. I open my palm to a full stretch and close it shut, repeating that over and over again as I grab my forearm, squeezing the stiff muscle.

"Holy shit, are you having a heart attack?" I shoot a look his way as he stops dead in his tracks.

"What? No. God, Cruz, you are so dramatic. I'm just..." I stand up, shaking out my hands and rolling my neck around in a circle, "tense," I say simply.

"Well, no shit, you've been tighter than a nun on a Tuesday, girl."

Pinching my brows together. "Why, Tuesday?" I ask, confused.

"Oh, I don't know. It sounded good," he says, waving his hand in the air, swatting away my question like a gnat.

I huff out a laugh, shaking my head. No matter what is

going on in my world, he always makes me smile. I truly love that about him.

"So, here is all the work I do for you to make your life easier." I flash him a look as he places a binder and a couple of manila envelopes on my desk. "I know, I know. I get a salary for that. Also, Christian's assistant called to confirm your meeting on Friday, and Matt wants to have the accountability meeting in person again."

My stomach drops to my feet and my breath catches in my throat.

"You know, I knew that would be your response when I told you that." Pointing at me as he draws an invisible circle at me in the air.

"What's going on? What am I missing?" he asks, his voice soft and serious.

"Nothing, I'm just stressed. That's all," I blurt back defensively.

"You can talk to me, you know." He leans into my desk, closer to me, like he knows if I did say anything, it would be a whisper.

I could tell him. I know he won't judge me. It might actually make me feel better, but all of my words get stuck in my voice box.

"Hm, okay, then," he mutters, pushing himself upright. "I told him you weren't going to be in that afternoon and scheduled time before the Monday morning meeting, so you should probably make yourself an appointment or something on Friday afternoon."

One side of my lip lifts in a half smile as I peer up at him in admiration.

"I don't deserve you." It's honest and true.

"Yeah. Yeah." He waves me off again, unable to take a meaningful compliment. Turning on his heel to leave my office, "I don't care what you do on Friday afternoon, but we *are* going out for a drink Friday evening. You're buying. Oh, and the top shelf stuff, not the well shit that they mix with rubbing alcohol. I'm going to lunch." He leaves and shuts the door behind him.

Oh, the confidence he has. The bear trap that my heart has been in this week feels looser now, and I realize how much he's always been there for me. I make a note to buy him something to thank him. He's more of a friend than an assistant, and I truly can't imagine working without him.

I reach for the stack he left on my desk and pull out the reports, taking a quick glance through them. I scribble a few notes on the face page and scoot my chair back, turning to the credenza behind me to file it away. As I finger through the file folders, I hear the familiar creak of the door handle turning.

"Are you back to ask me for lunch money?" I giggle, waiting for no doubt a witty comeback that Cruz always seems to have loaded in his verbal arsenal.

But it doesn't come.

"Silence is unbecoming on you... " I turn in my chair and freeze, as Matt stands front and center in the middle of my office.

We stare at each other for a minute. Maybe an hour.

Every cell in my body is hitting the panic button, but the anger and resentment I feel towards this man is taking over that fear. I stand, straightening my baby blue blazer as I lift my chin, refusing to back down to this sorry excuse of a man.

"Get. Out." Crossing my arms over my chest to close myself off.

His lips quirk up briefly, like I'm a toddler having a tantrum and he finds me amusing.

"So, you're not ready to beg for it yet?" I flinch in disgust, taken aback by his question.

"You have lost your fucking mind if you think I'll be begging you for anything," I quip.

Finding his way to the side of my desk, he walks over slowly, creating more tension with each step.

"Matt, stay the fuck away from me. I will report you. I don't care about the repercussions to myself." I step back, my strong stature failing me, and he sees it.

"You won't, because you can't. And you know it." He draws nearer, rounding over to my side of the desk. I take another step back, but my heel slips on the wheel of my office chair, and I fall back into my seat.

"Right where you should be. Below me. Looking up at me. Except you should be on your knees." Unbuttoning the jacket of his shit-colored suit, he pushes it open to expose the cheap starchy white shirt beneath it, contrasting the black tie laying uneven in the center.

"No." Sitting to my full height.

"No?" He cocks his head. "You'll get on your knees to get a contract, but not to save your reputation? Your morals are quite confusing."

He hooks his finger behind the lapel of my blazer and trails down the border of the hem until he reaches the peak of my breast. My heart is pounding out of my chest, and I want nothing more than to kick my shin in between his legs.

I tilt my head away, my chin nearly on my shoulder, and squeeze my eyes shut. Taking myself anywhere but here, but then I quickly remember how he was able to turn the tables on me last time. I shoot my eyes open and turn to face him.

"You don't know the first thing about morals." The sour taste from the bile rising in my throat helps the excess saliva build, so... I spit in his face.

He barely flinches. Like it's just another day with spit in his face. Frozen with a smirk, he uses his fingertips to clean the dribble off his cheek and flicks it away.

"I will expose you with everything I have. I will fucking ruin you. Your husband will leave you and no one will hire you.

You'll be too ashamed to do anything in this business because everyone will look at you like a fucking sex toy." Bringing both his hands around to the base of my neck, he caresses the top of my blouse as if he's drawing invisible lines over my collarbone. "And if you think I've shown you all my cards, you aren't nearly as smart as I thought you were."

My eyes flicker, thinking back on anything and everything decently inappropriate that I could have done in public since meeting Christian. He's trying to scare me. Trying to make me think he has more than what he already showed me, but it doesn't matter. What he has is enough to destroy everything I've worked for.

Fuck.

An overwhelming feeling of sadness hits me. Already grieving the loss of my privacy and sense of security. Tears form at the corners of my eyes, as they have threatened all week long, but I'm unable to continue to push them away.

He sees the defeat in my face. And like the devil he is, he continues to push, regardless of seeing the light in my eyes fade.

"That's it, puppet." He smirks.

His brawny body is like a tree, blocking me in the small confines of my chair. I have never considered myself to be a claustrophobic person, but the dense air and throbbing in my ears provides me with a panic I've never experienced before. I move my hands to the edge of the armrests, gripping the ends with such force, the skin over my knuckles becomes thinned and white.

I realize instantly that it was a mistake when he presses both his hands over my wrists, leaning the full weight of his body into the chair, trapping me.

"You're hurting me," I wince out, attempting to move my hands from his powerful grip.

"The physical pain I can induce will be nothing compared

to the emotional destruction I will cause you if you don't give me what I want." He leans his face into my neck, pressing more weight into my petite wrists. The weight he is bearing on the delicate joints feels like they are completely dislodged at this point.

He sniffs deeply. Like a fucking dog. Breathing heavily into my ear. The full body shiver that runs through me is tangible, seeping with pure disgust.

"What is it that you want, Matt?" I grit through clenched teeth.

"You'll see soon enough. Just two more days, to be exact." He leans up and releases my wrists.

The relief is painful, and although he's no longer pinning me down, I still feel stuck.

"Friday?" My brows pinch. "What's on Friday?"

His lip lifts up in a crooked smile and he takes a few steps back before turning to head out of my office. With his back turned at me, he reaches his arms out, wiggling his fingers like he's controlling puppets.

"You'll see, little puppet. *You'll see,*" he singsongs as he walks through the doorway, leaving it wide open.

Just like all my secrets.

24

CHRISTIAN

It's been a week since I've seen Elena. I shouldn't be so concerned about how she's doing or what she is up to, but I can't help my thoughts wandering that way. Fortunately, work has taken up most of my brain power this week, and in my downtime, I've been doing nothing but working out or running. Which is when most of my thinking happens.

The thoughts of the situation that have become us. And by *us*, I mean Elena and her husband. Everything feels honest and open. Even though I've yet to meet Jake in person, there's a distinct connection. A silent understanding between all of us. But then, Elena breaking down after what we did in my office confused me. She's all over the place, and I want nothing more than to try to figure things out.

The feeling of her in that hotel room was so heightened by him. Every inch of my body was burning for her, to take her and make her scream for both of us. Usually I wouldn't care about him or the fact that he was watching. It should have just been about me and Elena and what we wanted out of each other. But with her–with them–it felt... different. I needed to please him like I was pleasing her. Not physically, but in a way that I knew he would appreciate.

I kept my eyes on her but stole glances at him watching. The overwhelming desire of his fixed eyes on us pushed me to the edge so quickly that I had to slow my thrusts to avoid embarrassing myself. The desperation in his face as I pleased her, his need for her, it was otherworldly.

I've had threesomes before, but this one was far beyond anything sexual. It was sensual, and intimate, and by far the best sex I've ever had.

I have no desire for a relationship, and I've never been a relationship guy. But what they have to offer is, strangely, ideal for me. I've pushed that thought away more than I'd care to admit. Especially considering my past history with so-called relationships.

I can't go back there again.

Was it my fault?

No.

It has taken years of therapy to be able to answer that with confidence.

Did my actions cause one of the biggest catastrophes of my life?

Yes. God, yes.

It has to be one in a million, the irony of the first woman that I've been remotely interested in pursuing since then, is married.

Regardless, I push those thoughts away yet again. It doesn't make sense for her, for me, for her husband, and certainly not for her career.

I don't know which of those caused her to completely freak out last Friday, but either way, the outcome is inevitable.

Someone gets hurt. Someone always does.

She's been checking in this week only by text messages and emails. Her work is impeccable, which only makes my desire burn even deeper, and I keep going back to the possibility of some kind of relationship with her... with them.

I shake my head yet again, shoving those thoughts into a black hole where they belong, as I finish up my run, rounding the corner to my penthouse. Slowing to a walk, I interlace my fingers behind my head, taking in a few deep breaths of the crisp morning air. The sun is just making its appearance over the mountains that surround this gorgeous city, allowing a few rays of light to beam through the clouds.

Is that a foreshadowing of what could come? Light in the darkness.

Dare I say it. Hope?

I've been in a state of despondency for... well, since Madeline.

Elena has brought out hope in me, and the irony of that is not lost on me.

It's Friday, the day I've been looking forward to all week. For most because it falls before no work and all play days. I'd like to use that as an excuse, but I can't when it's the blue-eyed bombshell that has plagued all my thoughts this week. The look on her face last week is a look I'll never forget. She was disgusted with herself. I could see the distaste of our actions emanating from her like a beacon from a lighthouse.

She asked me to have her report to someone else. I'm not doing that. Not until I can talk with her more clearly about our... situation.

I need to make a decision on how to handle this because I can't keep drowning these thoughts for them just to float back up to the surface. I need to lay my cards out to her, to both of them, so they know. It could be more. If we wanted it to be and it could work.

"Elena Jenkins is on her way up, sir."

"Thanks, Jenny. Bring her in when she arrives and no interruptions, please," I reply back to Jenny over the speaker before disconnecting.

She is going to be all business today and try to cut this as short as possible, but I'm going to need her to listen and hear me out. If she cuts herself off like she did last week, I definitely have my work cut out for me. I've never seen someone's walls fly up so goddamn fast. Every time hers appear, they are fortified with steel and regret.

I run my fingers through my hair, realizing how shaggy it's getting, and along with my twenty-four-hour stubble that I failed to shave this morning, I look like I've roughed it a bit too hard this week.

The moment Jenny opens the door and Elena walks through, my face drops.

She looks conquered. Like she's flown from halfway across the country to be here and the jet-leg is still draining her. Her makeup is perfect, like usual, but not enough to hide the dark shadows and hollowing under her eyes. It's the first time I've seen her wear something other than a skirt or dress. The powerful yet feminine woman I've gotten to know over the past few weeks is not the same woman who just walked into my office.

"Elena?" It sounds like a question. I ask, almost unsure if it's really her even though I know it is, but there is also a *how are you* and *what's wrong* in that question mark, too.

Her brows pinch in confusion. Then she glances down at

her watch and back up into the room, but not in my direction. "We have a meeting today, right, Mr. Ford?"

Fortified fucking titanium steel.

I don't want to push her, but if I don't, I'll get nothing out of her.

I round my desk to walk directly in front of her so she cannot avoid my presence. Her eyes peer up for a brief moment as she pulls her shoulders back and straightens her stance, ready to fight.

There she is.

She holds out a black binder to me, similar to the portfolio she gave me last week, with, I assume, the weekly updated reports that I don't need. I know she's done a phenomenal job managing every single unit and keeping the teams motivated.

But something is killing her spirit.

"Everything is on track for the product release and I'm—" I snatch the binder from her hands and toss it on the leather couch closest to us. The same one I fucked her on just last week.

"What's going on?" I ask sternly.

She looks at the binder resting halfway off the couch, where it landed haphazardly, then back at me before taking her gaze to the floor. She shakes her head, like I'm actually going to believe that nothing is wrong.

"Nothing, I just wanted to keep this short. I have some other obligations to get to this afternoon." She checks her watch again, which pisses me off.

I pinch the bridge of my nose and find myself huffing before trailing my hand down my face.

"Look, there is a history here. Albeit a short one, but one, nonetheless." I pause, tilting my head to the side, trying to get her to look at me. "I know it's new to you... and your husband. This is new to me, too, but..."

Distantly from the hallway, Jenny's frantic voice interrupts me before I can finish.

A muffled, "Stop. Don't go in there," before a figure appears behind the frosted glass door. It opens, and Matt Randall walks through it, uninvited and clearly hostile.

Elena looks over her shoulder at the door and turns to the side, now facing him, and steps back to stand next to me. Everything in her demeanor deflates. Her shoulders slouch and her body stiffens. I don't think she's even breathing.

I'm confused as fuck. And beyond furious. My eyes bounce between Matt, Elena, then over to Jenny standing in the doorway, who is mouthing an apology to me.

"Didn't I fire you?" Looking at Matt, with a rage in my eyes I'm unable to hide. "Jenny, call Dietrich and the police."

"You don't want to do that." A sinister smile grows on his face. His chin is tilted down as he stares up at Elena, looking nowhere else but at her. His laser focus could burn a hole the size of Texas through her.

I look back and forth between them again. Elena is... scared. Terrified, actually.

"You think you're special?" He looks at me to tell me that's a question for me and not Elena. He reaches into the inside pocket of his jacket and I airplane my right arm out to move Elena back behind me.

I breathe a sigh of relief when it's his phone and not a weapon.

Facing the screen towards me, he shows me a picture of Elena in the same dress she wore last week. She's on a desk, the strap of her dress draping down her arm, her breast exposed as she's touching herself underneath her dress.

"You're not fucking special." He looks from me to her. "She's just a whore," he spits, glaring at her with such hatred.

The shock pummels through me like a bullet tearing through flesh. Is she involved with him, too? Is he pissed she's here because he found out there was something going on between us? Where is her husband in all this? Does he know? Is this history repeating itself? The questions coming faster than I can register them.

He pushes the phone closer, trying to taunt me further. At a quick glance, she is touching herself for him, for someone. But digging deeper, her face is contorted and eyes are squeezed shut. Nothing like the pleasure I've pulled from her. She appears to be... suffering.

I force myself to pause and glance over my shoulder at her.

Feeling a pull on my arm, Elena grips the fabric of my shirt. Turning my head to face her, the answer is written all over her gorgeous, terrified face. She shakes her head. "It's not true; it's not what it looks like." Her breathing is labored, there's a desperate solicitation in her face as she begs me with her eyes. It's the first time I've seen them today, her once bright piercing baby blues, now faint and feeble.

I have no idea what's going on or who to trust. Fuck, I don't trust either one of them at this point, but I do know I trust her more than him. He's the chauvinistic ass who tried to have the upper hand in everything she said during our first meeting. And got off on running into us in the elevator, finding her in my arms, and tried to make her look bad even then.

Everything I've done in business has been about hard work, knowledge, leading the right people, and most importantly, following my gut.

Looking back towards the loose fuse in front of me. "Get the fuck out, now!"

His smile drops, then retracts itself into a lopsided grin as he shakes his head.

"Man, I was really hoping you would have my side here. I didn't want to have to do this." His tone is less menacing and more like he thinks we're forgotten friends who I just betrayed.

He swipes the photo of Elena away, and in slides a different one. One of Elena and me on *my* couch. The one just a few feet away from us.

What. The. Fuck.

How did he get that? There are only a handful of people who could have taken that picture. My mind is racing, my blood is boiling, and I'm ready to grab him by his fucking throat and choke the life out of him with my bare hands.

I feel Elena's hands grab my forearm, sensing my anger, trying to pull my attention away from the impending dead man in front of me.

She succeeds as I turn to look at her again.

And I see it. The defeat. The fear. The plea in her irises that I hear what she is trying to tell me through the silence.

"You're blackmailing her." It's almost a whisper, but I know he hears it, even though I'm still looking into her troubled eyes.

Her relief is unmistakable. She releases a long breath, like she's been unable to breathe for days. She squeezes my arm as she closes her eyes, comforted by the knowledge of that.

I turn to look at him, and his center of attention is now completely on me.

"Not her. You."

25

ELENA

"Well, both of you, really. Originally, it was just you," Matt says as he flicks his pointer finger at Christian, "but then when you didn't hire me, and I found you two fondling each other in the elevator, well, you both made it way too easy for me." He shrugs, like none of this is a big deal and he hasn't been tearing my entire world apart.

At some point, Christian must have waved off Jenny, and she left. The door is now closed, and Christian and I are parked up against the back of the couch as Matt circles the room like a vulture.

I can feel the heat radiating from Christian, and I swear if it were possible to see steam from his ears and flames from his eyes, I would.

"I was never going to hire you. I only agreed to the meeting as a favor for..." Christian fades off as his shoulders drop. I've seen that look once before. The look of shock and disappointment. It's the same look he gave me on the plane when I told him I was married. But this, this one is laced with sadness.

"You have nothing but a few scandalous sex pictures. If you

think you're extorting anything out of me with that, you are out of your fucking mind," Christian snaps back.

In the last few weeks, I've realized something about Christian. His passion drives him. Not just a base level passion for work or a hobby, but it's embedded deeply in his personality. This passion is what drives him to be the successful leader that he is, but also not back down to someone or something when he feels threatened.

It's always about the principle.

And he won't go down without a fight.

The guilt I'm feeling over him being dragged into this has weighed on me like a brick blanket, but the relief of no longer being alone in this feels like drinking ice cold water after walking through the Sahara.

"You think I'm that stupid?" Matt asks.

An oxymoron if I've ever heard one.

He paces the room. Back and forth. Back and forth.

"I've been waiting a long time for this. Way too long." He mutters the last part under his breath.

"Waiting for what?" Christian questions. Placing his hands on his hips as he glances back at me. We're both prepared for... well, we aren't prepared for anything. We have no idea what the hell he is thinking or what he's talking about.

Matt reaches behind himself, into the waistband of his pants, and Christian instantly jumps in front of me. The spicy woodsy scent engulfs me as he wraps his arms behind himself, attempting to cover me fully. I know in my heart that Matt isn't a kind man, but I never took him to do what he has done to me these past couple weeks. Abusing me mentally and sexually.

I definitely never anticipated violence.

I wonder what the headlines will read on this one. What kind of interpretation the media will put out there on this. I think of Jake and wonder if he'll forgive me. For this, whatever *this* is, whatever it might look like. I think of Christian and his gallant behavior at this moment. He owes me nothing, yet he protects me.

I flinch at the sound of fluttering and a light thud as something hits the floor at Christian's feet.

I open my eyes, that I didn't realize I was squeezing shut, as Christian bends down to pick up a pile of papers, which I see now is simply a stupid newspaper.

He flips open the front, and displayed there in black and white.

HUSBAND SHOOTS WIFE BEFORE SHOOTING HIMSELF IN MURDER SUICIDE

I squint to read the title and my brows pinch together in confusion. There is a picture of a beautiful woman on the front, smiling and happy. The paper is clearly weathered and old. When I glance at the date underneath the headline, it's dated almost two years ago.

What does that have to do with anything?

Christian's entire body tenses, and he fists the sides of the paper he is holding, then tosses it back at Matt, directly in front of his feet, mirroring how Matt had presented it.

It's something.

"How did you find that?" Christian whispers.

"Go ahead and tell her." Matt tilts his chin at me. "Tell her what you did."

I back away as Christian turns to face me.

"It's not what it seems." He reaches for my hand as he whispers in a defeat-laced undertone.

"What's not what it seems? That you fucked my married sister and her jackass fucking husband killed her for it?!" Matt's voice booms through the room as Christian's eyes widen in realization.

"Madeline was your sister?" he says in painful shock.

"Oh, God." I cover my mouth. "You... she...?" The words are stuck in my throat, unable to come out.

"I didn't know," he whispers.

"Didn't know what?" I question.

"She never told me she was married." He drops his head.

"My sister was not a liar!" Matt belts out, the depth of his tone echoing off the walls.

The following silence is deafening. Each of us pondering our respective thoughts.

When I look up to Christian, his tormented eyes reach mine, and I see nothing but regret, sadness, and sorrow. A haunting in his eyes that was buried so deep it's struggling in the daylight.

Matt, on the other hand, is reveling in the suffering that fills the air. His eyes are red-rimmed and alcohol-glazed, overflowing with revenge.

"You killed her. Not with your hands, but with your actions. You never had to pay for that, but you will."

Christian's posture changes instantly with that threat. The torment that caused his temporary moment of weakness is now overshadowed with power and anger.

"She lied to me. She was sleeping with multiple men, taking advantage of all of them. Seducing every single one of us for her own financial benefit. You two are cut from the same cloth. The same disease runs through your veins that ran through hers. That's what fucking killed her." I can see the exhaustion of the last couple years pour out from his words. He sits down and relents.

Matt doesn't.

"I won't back down. I've worked too hard to find a way here. To shatter you. *The* Christian Ford. The almighty Christian Ford and all his fucking perfection. I know everything about you and everything about the people who work for you. Don't underestimate me.

"Oh, and hey, whore. I left my," his head bounces back and forth, finding his words, "ransom note in your office. If you ignore my request, your secrets will get blasted in a company-wide memo, with visuals. I'll share these pictures on every social media platform I can find and make sure no one questions who and what they are seeing. I'll fucking ruin you."

He leans down to pick up the newspaper, throwing it over to Christian's desk. Tattered pieces fly away from the bulk and fall to the floor before landing at the corner of his desk.

"I was dumbfounded when your name never came up in the papers after he killed her, since you know it was your fault. But, of course, I know you had to have paid them off. So, in true form, you will be sending me money, *a lot* of money, if you want to keep your past... in the past." He advances towards the door. "I'll be in touch after *Mrs*. Jenkins here complies with my first request. Then I'll let you know how much you'll be sending me. You wanted to be *partners*, after all."

He opens the office door and stalls before looking back at us.

"I hope *Ellie* is as generous with me as she was with you. She will be if you both don't want your world completely destroyed. I will not hesitate. I will not hold back." Bile rises to my throat, thinking of the things I would need to do for him, to him. And even then, there is no guarantee he won't always hold this over our head. Tears rim my eyes, blurring him into a haze for a moment until I blink them away, just as he steps through the door, and it closes behind him.

The moment I hear the click of the door, the air thins and my bones evaporate. I no longer have the ability to stand. Placing my hand on the side of the armrest, I use it as a clutch, trailing my hand over the side to find a seat on the other side of the couch. I melt into the leather and my hands start to tremble before my entire body follows suit.

Christian rounds the couch, sitting next to me. He leans forward with his forearms planted on the tops of his thighs and intertwines his hands in mine, attempting to calm the tremors.

He pulls my hands to his lips, the heat of his breath floats over my fingertips.

"Does your husband know what Matt has been doing?"

Does my husband know? I repeat his words in my head.

Does he know what Matt has been doing to me? Does he have any idea of the suffering, degrading, and harassment I've endured the past couple weeks, day in and day out? The stolen, unwelcome touches and groping. The threats. God, all of it.

No.

Does he suspect something is going on and has been worried every single day when I get home what condition I'll be in? Wondering if it's something he's done or if I'm having an affair with another man. Has he asked time and time again what is going on?

Yes.

And I've treated him like a distant stranger. Trying to keep him away from all of this when I've needed him more than ever. I was so scared of what he might do or what it would do to him, and I thought I could bear through it myself.

I've pushed him away like I do every time I struggle beyond my control.

Still unable to formulate any words, I shake my head softly.

He lets out a frustrated huff. And believe me, I feel the same. But I'm more disgusted with myself.

"Why didn't you say something?" His forehead wrinkles as his eyebrows knit together, as if that was painful to ask.

I'm at a loss for words. My thoughts are still catching up with themselves, and I'm unable to keep one at the forefront to focus on anything that's actually happened.

The fact that Christian was involved with a married woman who was killed by her husband due to her infidelity. How did he even muster the courage to continue things with me, considering his past?

Am I really going to be forced to give myself to Matt to avoid public humiliation? Do I physically give myself to him to prevent him from slandering my reputation? Could I live with myself if I did? He said it's not one without the other, holding both of us accountable to each other. It's not just myself I have to worry about protecting anymore.

He's demanding a ransom. A fucking ransom.

How did we even get here?

I shake my head at Christian., "I... I didn't know how."

Out of everything that just happened, he's worried about me. He's so much like Jake, and I am slowly realizing why I was so drawn to him. He's a selfless protector. Jake provides me with that same safety net, and it's something I've always needed, but fail to admit because I'm too stubborn to accept it.

Glimpsing back at Christian, he's angry, but his eyes are laced with sadness. I didn't need to know the details about the article or the people in it. I could see the torment in his eyes the moment he saw it. It was more than regret. It is so much deeper for him.

"You loved her?" I whisper.

He unwinds his fingers from mine and presses into the tops of his knees, pushing away from me. He's sitting at his full height for a moment until he blows out a long audible breath. His shoulders slouch and his head follows suit.

"I thought I did, but how can you love someone when everything you knew about them was a lie?" he concedes.

I'm at a loss for words. I want him to be able to speak freely and openly with me, but I don't want to push him. This is the first time since everything happened that my mind isn't racing through the what ifs and wondering what is going to happen. Instead, worrying about Christian's headspace and recognizing the emotional challenge he had to put himself through by getting involved with me and Jake.

Before I can ask a question, he continues, "We dated for almost a year; it was easy and fun. I've never been able to dedicate much time to a relationship, but I also don't like just hooking up with random women. What we had was casual, but consistent. It was perfect." He stands up and runs both his hands through his already disheveled hair.

"I left for a business trip and had planned to see her when I got back. I thought at one point during that trip it was strange that I hadn't heard from her, but figured she was busy. I was busy. I just pushed the thought aside." Sorrow covers his face like a blanket.

"When I returned, I rummaged through the newspapers I missed and saw her face. That," pointing to the paper on his desk, "same article."

"Oh my God," I mutter, my lips barely able to move to pronounce the words.

There's a pregnant pause between us, registering what happened and how he could have felt. Being with someone for a year to find out in the newspaper that her husband killed her. The husband you knew nothing about. The regret, the shame, the denial, the deceit. All the unknowns, wrapped up in one twisted reality. I don't know that I could have emotionally survived such a thing.

"I went to the funeral, knowing no one knew who I was to her. Just to find out I was one of many men in that same situation." He shakes his head, still in disbelief.

"She used men to get what she wanted. Whether it be for sex to spite her husband or the financial benefit she reaped out of the relationship. I always thought we shared a strong connection. We had... chemistry. To find out I was just an unrequited prey for her was a realization I was not prepared for. It ruined me.

"I'm good at reading people, judging people's character. She completely deceived me and it destroyed me. It has made me question... everything." His confession is heartbreaking. I'm sure he's already used to being used for his money and his status, but he can probably see that from a mile away when he meets someone. To be in a year-long relationship to find out all of this after the fact with so many unanswered questions. That is unthinkable.

"How could you even consider getting involved with me after what happened to you?" I have to ask. I can't not ask.

Huffing out a chuckle. "Oh, the irony is not lost on me, Elena. I've been asking myself that same question every day since the moment you told me."

My face falls and a cold shameful shiver sweeps over my skin. What must he think about my marriage–about me? I don't want him to regret the moments we've had, but how could he not? He must literally be a glutton for punishment, putting himself through a similar situation, but this time knowing it could end not just badly, but in the worst way, if someone is mentally unstable like Madeline's husband was.

If this gets out, his unbeknownst affair with Madeline years ago and our relationship, it'll ruin his reputation and his image. I don't think he cares all that much, but the corporate world is mercurial. If you aren't on the straight and narrow, you are judged, possibly looked down upon, and in some cases, outcasted. Then people start digging for all your skeletons, and everything is over-interpreted and embellished.

I pick at my fingernails nervously and bite the corner of my lip. I've always had such a nasty habit of that and consciously try to stop myself when I realize what I'm doing, but right now, I can't.

Reading me like a book, Christian's long legs close the space between us in a matter of seconds.

"Your honesty is what made me feel comfortable, Elena." He grabs and holds my hands to stop my nervous tick. "I felt so much regret after what happened to Madeline, but I also felt ashamed of how happy I was with the type of relationship we had. The only reason we had that kind of relationship was because she was married. We spent time together, but we had our own lives. It was selfish in its own way, but it really worked for me. When you told me about you and Jake, I felt that same shame, thinking I could have something similar."

My brows pinch together involuntarily. That is a whole lot to register. He looks at me with both sadness and relief. Like he's wanted to say that for a while but couldn't or didn't know how. A frown-laced smile graces his handsome face, and like a contagious yawn, I mirror his smile.

It's the first time since I walked into his office together that either one of us has attempted such a feat.

"Now, we need to get to your office to find out what *ransom note* Matt left for you. I can drive you." He helps pull me up and keeps his hand on mine as he guides me through his office. Business Christian is back, and I can already see the wheels turning. Whatever it is we've gotten ourselves into, we've got to stick together to get through it.

"I'm disgusted to even think about what he wants me to do." A ripple of nausea rolls through me as those words leave my mouth. The thought of willingly doing anything with Matt actually makes my insides want to implode.

"You're not going to do anything with him. He wants to play games with our lives. We're going to play back."

26

ELENA

It's late in the afternoon when we pull up to my office. Cruz nicknames Fridays at our company Forty Percent Friday, because typically only that percentage of the staff is working, if at all. Those who are working are dressed down, and if they are present, they are socializing more than they are working.

The parking lot is almost empty, with just a few cars spread out, and Christian finds a spot near the front entrance. I scan the parking lot for Matt's car and don't see it, which brings me immense relief. I'm confident he's not here because he typically parks near the front, and if he can't find an open spot, he's one of those jackasses that makes a spot clearly not intended for parking.

"I'll just run up and come back down," I tell Christian as he puts the car in park. This *car*–a ridiculously nice Bentley–that makes me feel like I can't touch anything in it. The interior is all beige and black leather. What isn't leather is some kind of high end shiny lacquered wooden accent, and all I can envision is the finger smudges I'll leave on it if I even look at it.

"I should come up with you. What if he is up there?" he

questions, as he is looking around and ducking his head lower to look up through the windshield to the windows of my building.

"He never works this late on a Friday, and he wouldn't come back after everything that happened. Plus, his car is nowhere to be seen." I place my hand on his forearm, providing a little comfort.

"Ehhh, I don't like it." He pushes back with me in his protective way, still glancing around.

"I know, but for those who are here, I don't want it to look suspicious that you are with me. Christian Ford doesn't make office calls." I wave my hand like a prince to a peasant and he rolls his eyes in return.

"Really, an eye roll?" I give him shit. "Channeling your inner rebellious teenager?"

He tips his head with a shrug. "You make me feel like that in more ways than one."

I laugh, shaking my head. At least we're able to joke now. There was so much tension earlier, but since we left his office, he's done nothing but try to make me feel comfortable.

I know I have to talk to Jake and share with him everything that is happening when I get home, but I'm not even sure where to start. I'm embarrassed that I let everything go as far as it did and didn't open up to him earlier. He's going to be... God, so upset. He doesn't get *mad*. But he'll be massively disappointed, and that might be worse.

One thing at a time, Elena.

"I'll wait here. If you're not back in ten minutes, I'm coming up," Christian stipulates.

His tone is that as if he were talking in a board meeting with a bunch of his colleagues.

"Yes, sir," I reply, like a sexy subordinate.

I was searching for another eye roll, but this time he closes his eyes tightly and inhales.

When he finally opens them, he leans forward over the center console. "You shouldn't say things like that. It's been a long week, and I can't trust myself with such powerful words in such a small, confined space."

Biting the corner of my lip with a smile, I reach for the door handle, because if I don't leave this car, I don't trust myself either. Plus, I can't breathe. The woodsy leather new car smell, along with the sexual tension, fogging the air. I'm suffocating in the best way possible.

Before the door closes, I hear Christian shout, "Ten minutes!"

I hustle as quickly as my three-inch heels will let me, shuffling my legs towards the entrance of the building. The elevator is already open and ready, so I pop in and quickly press my floor. I feel nervous, like I shouldn't be here. Which is totally ridiculous.

I swing my purse from one shoulder to the other and hold my hands in front of me, thinking about not picking at my nail beds, but failing at that whole mind-body connection thing.

Whatever note Matt left, I'll just pick up and go. I'll read it with Christian, and we can just figure this out and move on. God, if only it could be that simple.

As the elevator door opens, the ding echoes through the open floor. It sounds louder than usual, being that the floor is completely deserted.

I beeline straight to my office, passing Cruz's desk, which is spotless as usual. He's one of those people who always has a clean desk, no matter how busy he is. You'd never be able to tell if he's here or not based on his desk.

I step up to my office door with my key in hand and slide the metal through the knob. The metal on metal sound zips through the office, and again I feel like I shouldn't be here. Like I'm sneaking into an office that isn't mine. Matt has me so on edge I think I'd be more comfortable walking through the mall naked on Black Friday.

As I open my door, I see in my periphery streamers and decorations hanging around and over my desk. I relapse for a moment and have to think of what day it is. It's not my birthday, which would be the only reason Cruz would decorate my office. He would maybe if I got a promotion or something, but that hasn't happened.

As I step through, flashes of the papers hanging from the streamers come into full view. They are hanging from the ceiling of my office, taped to the streamers, and some are strewn across the floor. Panicking, I shut my door and see the back of my office door plastered in printed papers with pictures of me. Different stills of the video that Matt took of me touching myself on my desk. And more of me on my knees in front of Christian. Another one with him behind me, both of our pleasured faces in full view.

"Jesus," I mutter. "No, no, no. Oh, God." I panic, tearing the pictures that are taped to the back of the door. They rip in pieces, some of the tape and corners of the picture stubbornly clinging onto the door.

I crumble what I have in my hands and pick at the stray pieces, scooping them up in my arms. Frantically picking up the loose pictures on the floor and snatching the ones hanging from above.

Oh, God.

I. Am. Everywhere.

These pictures. They are horrible. Some are zoomed in closer to show just my face or Christian's. Another few photos zoomed in are showing just my breast hanging out of my dress. Others have the word 'Whore' written in a red sharpie.

An invisible band tightens around my chest, and everything feels heavy. The room is dense and too goddamn small, but impossibly vast, full of nothing but flashbacks of my indiscretions.

I collapse to the floor, weak and dizzy. Still trying to pick up as many flyaways as I can, but losing the ability to move my arms or any other body part for that matter.

How could I have let this happen? I never should have continued things with Christian. It was supposed to be a onetime thing, but serendipity really has a sardonic sense of humor.

That bitch.

There was no way I could turn away from the opportunity to work with him, but I should have stopped everything.

How is my willpower so weak?

I'm fucking married. The enraged part of my brain is running rampant inside, feeling like there is no reason for us to be doing what we are doing. Why couldn't we just conform to the normal marriage rules and a standard sex life? There are too many risks involved. Too many emotions. And for a brief moment, I feel angry with Jake for this quandary, but this is Matt's creation, not Jake's. I know this.

The other side of my so-called intelligent organ, the side that believes in autonomy and free will, wants to tell everyone to fuck off. I should be able to do whatever the hell I want in my own marriage without rebuke or judgment.

But now all of this. Blackmail from someone I considered to be a teammate. Humiliation from someone I should have been able to trust. It's truly unfathomable that *that* one decision brought us here.

Choice and Consequence.

The familiar sound of an elevator ping tears me from my thoughts as I turn my head to stare at the back of my door. I tilt my head so my ear is in direct line with the door, like that is going to help me hear anything any better. Like turning down the music in your car when you're trying to see where you're going.

All I can make out are muffled voices, and as the sound grows louder, I panic. I scoop up the crumbled papers in front of me, gathering them haphazardly. As I look around the room, I know this is going to take so much more time than I have.

I glance back at the door to listen for the voices and realize it's unlocked.

Dropping the pictures I have scooped in my arms, I press my hands into the floor to attempt to push myself up at the same time the handle clicks and the door sways open as Cruz peeks in, stopping mid-step through the partially opened door. Shock cloaks his face as his eyes bounce from me, to the ceiling, to the floor, and back to me. I am somehow relieved and horrified at the same time. I stare at Cruz, the emotional pain showing physically on my face.

His eyes widen as he pulls himself back through the doorway. "It's actually not a good time right now," he states, certain with uncertainty.

Oh, God, who's with him?

Suddenly, the door swings open a full 180 degrees, banging against the back wall as it opens. Cruz and Christian stand in the doorway. Cruz's normally tight jaw is on the floor. Either from Christian's behavior or the sight of my office, I'm not actually sure.

And Christian. Christian looks like the goddamn Terminator. Save the sunglasses and leather jacket, the death stare full force. His legs are hip-width apart, aligning with his broad shoulders, fists clenched at his sides, and his jaw bones might actually explode from pressure.

He stalks through the door and squats down in front of me, grabbing a few of the wrinkled papers, inspecting them.

He lets out a long exhale and holds out his hand.

"Come on, we'll get this cleaned up." His tone is so even, it's frightening.

A gentle tug and he has me back on my feet, cupping my jaw and looking at me with concern. "You okay?"

"Yeah, I-I was just overwhelmed." And freaking the hell out. I should probably be doing more of that right now with these two in the room, but it doesn't feel constricting and immense anymore. It feels like solace.

"Umm, I'm sorry. What the fuck is going on?" Cruz waves his hand between us and the room, popping his hip for extra effect.

Christian and I turn to face him, then side-eye each other, trying to find the words to even begin to explain.

"We can explain that later. Help us pick this up." I have to give it to him, Christian knows how to boss people even if he's not their boss.

"You can't dismiss me that easily. Explain *while* we pick this up," Cruz banters back, in his true fashion.

Standing up, I straighten my blazer and brush off the front of my outfit, even though I don't see any particles. I just feel dirty. Literally from being on the ground and figuratively from my surroundings.

Cruz somehow locates a large waste basket bag that he is shoving all the pictures into with whispers of, *oh my,* as he obviously looks at them without trying to be too obvious. He crumbles the pictures inwardly so you can't see anything even when they are bunched up, then throws them into the open garbage bag.

"I thought this guy," pointing his finger at Christian, "was in the parking lot to come by and see you for your meeting, but clearly there is something else going on. That's been going on," Cruz spits out.

Both Christian and I still for a moment. He only met Cruz a few minutes ago, so I know he questions whether or not he can trust him. He looks to me for an answer to his silent question, and I meet his gaze. There is a battle in his eyes. Lust from being surrounded by pictures of us and anger for our circumstance.

Cruz continues to pick up and clean, then throws the open bag on the floor, some of the contents falling out onto the ground.

"I'm not helping you fix your problem unless you explain yourselves. I've been way too loyal to you for too long for you to give me the silent treatment on this, Elena." He turns around and stomps his foot like a four-year-old. "What the fuck is going on?"

He's not wrong. I mean, his temper tantrum is funny and adorable. But his feelings are justified, and he's right. He's shown me nothing but loyalty and allegiance since he started here. I know if I ever left this company, he would want to come with me wherever I landed.

"Jake and I opened our marriage up, sexually. Christian and I fucked. Matt found out and is blackmailing us both." Not sure how I summarized everything in twenty words, but I do hate communicating about emotions, so there's that.

He's frozen. Staring at us.

"That's a hard core cliff's notes version, El." He waves his hand at himself to fan himself off. "I need to sit down."

He crosses the room to the chaise lounge chair he loves and sits down. "Explain."

I take a few minutes to explain everything in detail, as I walk around the room grabbing and cleaning. I stand near the desk, craning my neck up to Christian, who is standing on my desk pulling the streamers from ceiling tiles and handing them to me to place in the garbage bag.

I finish telling Cruz the story of how we got here right as we are finished picking everything up.

Cruz takes in everything I say, with his eyes rounded and brows plastered to the top of his forehead.

"No wonder why he *gifted* me his spa treatment," Cruz says to himself.

Christian turns to him. "What?"

"He told me that a client scheduled him for a free spa treatment. Full body massage and facial–the works–but he couldn't make it and couldn't reschedule. He told me he cleared me to have an extended lunch and gifted me the appointment. That's where I was this afternoon."

Sneaky little bastard. Making sure Cruz was out of the office so he could desecrate mine.

"Where do you think he would have left the ransom note?" Christian asks, looking around my desk.

"I have no idea." I walk around and nothing seems out of place. I glance behind my desk, where there are a few trinkets and pictures of my friends and family. There is one of Jake and me that is not only in an unusual spot, but the actual picture itself is upside down in the frame.

I pick up the frame and open the back pegs to retrieve the photo. At the same time, Christian picks up one of the photos of Jake and me when we went to Italy, standing in front of the Colosseum.

"This is Jake?" I just nod my head, biting my lip, to both concentrate on the picture frame I'm opening and out of nerves when he sees Jake and I smiling together, happy and in love. He stares at the picture, stoic and unreadable. I'm not sure what feelings are normal in this situation.

Awkwardness sure is.

"I didn't get a good look at him the night we FaceTimed," he states factually.

"Oh, okay. That's hot," Cruz says, then realizes his mouth spoke without the approval of his brain, which is not unusual.

"I mean, if you didn't see his face, then what were you looking at?"

"Cruz!" I scold.

He just puts his hands up in surrender.

The glass portion of the frame finally pops out, but I wasn't expecting it to since I was too busy yelling at Cruz. The glass falls to the floor, shattering into pieces.

I glare over at Cruz, blaming him for distracting me.

"I'll get the broom," he relents, his tone annoyed.

I expect to find a note or something behind the photo, but when I remove it, there is nothing there. Upon turning the photo over, his serial killer chicken scratch is graffitied all over the back. My eyes bounce to Christian, who straightens to his full height in response. Like he's getting ready to fight.

"All it says is *'Call Me'*," I say aloud.

"This whole dog and pony show for theatrics. What a fucking joke," Christian grits through his teeth.

I pull out my phone and select him from my contacts list. Calling him, then pressing the speaker button. A half a ring echos through the room before he picks up, clearly expecting my call.

"Did you like my gift?" He avoids even saying hello, getting right to the point. "I have taken up scrapbooking and thought you'd appreciate the new way of expressing myself."

"Fuck you, Matt. Where is this note you talked about? What do you want?" I hate him. I wonder if there is a way to kill a man through a phone call. I wish I had some Jason Bourne style skills. I'm sure he could do it.

"You think I would put that shit in writing? You're out of your fucking mind." He laughs, and the sound vibrates my eardrums in the most painful way.

Cruz walks back into my office and freezes, looking around for Matt, not realizing he is on speaker. He glances up at me, and I press my pointer finger to my pursed lips, shushing him.

"Tomorrow night, you are going to let me fuck you raw in your matrimonial bed. I want to come in you and all over you in his bed, while you beg me for it. Oh, and I'll be recording this consensual event, so I always have something to look back on and..." he singsongs, "use it against you in case you get any ideas."

"You are out of your goddamn mind, Matt. My husband is home tomorrow, and I'm not letting you fuck me anywhere, especially in our fucking bed," I snap back, my blood boiling, the rage burning like an inferno.

"If you don't want the entire company and everyone in this industry knowing what a slut you are, your husband *won't* be home. Christian's relying on you, too. He'll pay me to keep his name out of the press; he'll just pay me a shit ton more if you don't do what I ask. I'll blast not only his love affair with his married employee, but his contribution to the death of my sister. I will bankrupt him and break him. It's what he fucking deserves."

My eyes don't need to see the visible change in Christian's demeanor; I can feel the tightness in his body that mirrors my own. Still, he just listens to Matt unknowingly threatening him, but remains quiet.

I open my mouth to reply, but nothing comes out.

"I will accept your silence as compliance. See you tomorrow night."

My phone disconnects, and I stare at the screen of my phone, the light fading before going to a black screen. I pick up my slacked jaw and look over at Christian, who is leaning against my desk with his arms crossed, staring at nothing on my floor.

Cruz raises his hand, like he's still following my shushing request. "I have a fabulous idea." The smile he couldn't hide while he said that tells me otherwise.

"I doubt that," I reply too quickly to not be offensive.

"Heyyy," he whines. "I might not be the one being threatened here, but I've had my fair share of revenge fantasies when it comes to bullies, especially when it comes to men like Matt, who are homophobic."

My brows pinch together as I look at Cruz. "This isn't some high school game, trying to devise a plan to get back at a bully."

"You're naïve to think I haven't gotten *bullied* after high school," he replies with a sad tone, a few notches more serious than usual.

I am a prick.

"I didn't mean that, Cruz. I'm sorry," I reply, my voice light and honest.

He waves his hand off, but doesn't reply.

I think about all the things Cruz has done for me out of love and respect. His daily help to make my life easier. Having my back when Matt would try to call unnecessary meetings. Glancing in here and seeing me broken on the floor, then trying to push Christian out to protect me. Picking up the dirty photos scattered across the room, without judgment or question. He never brought Jake up to withhold the fact that I was married in case Christian didn't know, protecting me again.

I walk over to him and wrap my arms around his neck and pull him in for a hug.

"Thank you," I whisper in his ear. "I don't deserve you."

He returns my hug and stays still for a minute, then replies, "I know," in true Cruz fashion, making me giggle.

"Seriously, though, you need to give him a taste of his own medicine. There's no going to the authorities or our boss, unless you want him to blow both of your reputations to oblivion. The only way to fix this is to play his game. Just turn the table."

"I like the way you think," Christian replies, using the weight of his own body to push himself off my desk.

"You hear that?!" Cruz bumps my hip, gloating. "The billionaire likes the way I think."

I roll my eyes with a smile and look back at Christian, who is back to his power stance. He's all business, with a side note of sex, as I stare straight into his darkened irises.

"We need to call your husband."

27

JAKE

When Elena called to have me meet her out tonight, I was taken aback. I knew she was planning to meet with Cruz tonight, so I wasn't expecting to see her, at least not until late. That surprise was nothing compared to the shock of seeing her walk in Cruz-less, with Christian Ford at her side.

The roller coaster of emotions I felt in a matter of seconds could have set a Guinness World Record. My thought process was some type of organized chaos.

There she is. *Happiness.*
God, she is beautiful. *Enamored.*
Who's with her? *Confusion.*
That's Christian Ford. *Shock.*
Jesus, is he really that tall? *Envy.*
He's even better looking in person. *More Envy.*
I bet his calves are puny. *Jealousy.*
Why is he here? *Uncertainty.*
Where is Cruz? *Skepticism.*
Does she want a threesome? *Rapture.*
She has been so weird and distant this week. *Doubt.*

Is she... leaving me? *Distress.*

No, she loves me and our life. *Confidence.*

What is she going to tell me? *Curiosity.*

What the fuck is going on? *Frustration.*

By the time she reaches the table I had snagged for us, which was far too small for three, my knee is bouncing vigorously underneath my high top chair. I stand to stop the uncontrollable knee bobbing, and she walks straight into me, her face burying itself into my chest. I wrap my arms around her, engulfing her in my hold and involuntarily kissing the top of her head.

I can feel her steady breath and racing heartbeat. My lungs feel like concrete. It's hard to take a full breath, confused with the events that have unfolded in the past minute.

Christian walks up behind her with his hands in his pockets, non-intimidating and casual, but his gaze doesn't leave the two of us.

His eyes boring into us so deeply, I wonder if a part of him is a voyeur as well.

I need answers now.

I trail my hands down the sides of her arms and gently pull her away from my hold. It feels like a magnetic pull, not wanting to separate. Cupping her cheeks, I lift her face to mine.

I study her for a brief moment, the shade of her sapphire eyes a few shades lighter, even in the dark space, looking drained and tired.

Elena is not one to cry. But when she does, I always know because the telltale signs stay with her even hours after. Her red-rimmed eyes are as stubborn as she is, and an unavoidable pink tone touches her skin and borders around her eyebrows and the tip of her nose.

I know instantly something is wrong. My entire body tenses and my face snaps back up to Christian, anger piercing my eyes and laser focused on him.

"Christian is helping me," she replies to ease my tension.

Sharing my wife. Sure. Love it. So goddamn sexy.

Having another man *help* my wife with a problem that I'm completely in the dark about.

Do not love it.

Forcing my cement lungs to take in some air, I let out a heavy breath and pull her back into me, holding her because I need the comfort just as much as she does.

I open my arm up to pull out a chair for her while Christian grabs an empty one from the table next to us. Elena scoots slightly closer to me at the already small table, and we're ironically sitting in some twisted triangle, representing us in more ways than one.

I suddenly realize why Elena moved closer to me when Cruz walks up with beers in his hand and a huge smile plastered on his face.

"That bartender, ten outta ten, you guys. I bet money he'll be calling me Maverick by the end of the night." Elena has told me in the past that's his version of *'Daddy'* in bed. Cruz never fails to make an entrance.

But now, I'm really confused. I force a smile at Cruz, but my eyebrows furrow in contradiction, not understanding why he is here.

Elena palms my forearm while Cruz replies, seeing my confusion.

"Don't worry, we'll explain everything. Well, they will. I'm only here for moral support and a really fabulous idea to help the cause." He sips his beer with a smug look on his face, his eyes bouncing over the rim of his cup between the three of us.

"Okay. Explain." The mystery of all of this has hit its peak.

Elena reminds me of the run-in she had with Matt at Christian's office after the first presentation and how strange he was acting in the beginning when she first got the account. How he manipulated the meeting with Bryan to spearhead overseeing the account. She goes into clear detail, speed-talking me through all the events, until she pauses for a brief moment and looks up, her beautiful blues flowing with a bit more color and life again, but then she squints as if she is in pain.

"I met Christian at his office last Friday for an accountability meeting." She looks away and back down at her fidgeting hands on the table. "We had sex, and someone in his office got pictures of it." She glances over at Christian and back to me.

The reasons I should be pissed battle each other silently in my head.

She had sex with him and didn't tell me. To me, that feels a lot more unfaithful than the act itself. I know I gave her the freedom to run with this and make decisions that she was comfortable with, but that feels like a secret, a lie, a shameful indiscretion that she didn't want to share with me. That feels... hurtful.

But someone apparently has pictures of this encounter? Of course they have to tell me. It's probably gone public or will.

"Is that why you brought us here together?" I look between the two of them. "To tell me something you should have told me last week when it happened? Now you're caught, and I realize it's hard to be caught doing something I condoned in the first place, but keeping it a secret is what pisses me off." I inhale sharply. "Who is going to see these pictures?"

"No one," Christian speaks for the first time. His voice is deep and raspy from remaining quiet this entire time.

"I don't understand," I question his response.

Elena places her hand on mine and cups my jaw, turning my face to hers. Her palm is soft against the longer than usual stubble gracing my cheek.

"I had every intention of telling you, Jake. He..." She removes her hand and folds it into her own fidgeting with her nails. "Matt came to my office after my meeting with Christian and had the pictures. He showed them to me and threatened to share them if I didn't... If I didn't... cooperate."

What the fuck.

"Did... did he..." Every cell in my body is exploding. My skin is on fire, like there isn't enough oxygen getting to the outer reaches of my body, and my heart is thumping hard against my veins.

"No, Jake. No," she assures me, shaking her head profusely. "But he did make me do things to myself and has evidence of that. He's using all of this against us." She and Christian continue to share the details of what he made her do. Including the last couple weeks of harassment she has endured, through today when Matt showed up at Christian's office and he got the bomb dropped on him about his ex-girlfriend slash mistress. Then finding the photos strung up in her office like explosions of confetti before locating the ransom note he left for her.

"It's really only been a week." She shrugs, throwing her hands up like it's no big fucking deal or it doesn't matter because it was *only* a week.

I think back on the entire week's events and how distant Elena has been. She came home last Friday and pretty much went straight to bed. How she must have been feeling after what Matt made her do and threatened her with. The constant moments in her days that he has consumed her by physically doing something to her and leaving her with the dreadful memory of it.

'It's only been a week,' is a bullshit statement. A week or years, abuse is abuse. The memory of it lasts a lifetime.

My heart is breaking a little for her, but my mind is reeling. Battling between empathy and anger. How could she not open up to me? I get that she has a hard time sharing her feelings and doesn't communicate well or tell me when there is a problem. But she has been getting bullied by a sexual predator and walked around like a zombie all week, not saying a fucking thing.

She reads my expression instantly, seeing *that* look on my face. The look of disappointment. She knows her biggest flaw has always been lack of communication. "I felt ashamed of myself that day when I left his office." She looks over at Christian. "Not that I regretted what happened. Everything was just unknown, and I didn't know how to handle it. Then with Matt afterward. I was lost."

I pull her hand to my lips, silently telling her I get it and whisper, "We're going to talk about it later," because I'm fucking pissed.

I release her hand and down the rest of my beer more aggressively than I should, just as Cruz is bringing another round. I grab the next and drink it halfway down. The dull carbonated liquid feels like a boulder going down my throat, but that's nothing compared to the discomfort that has settled in my stomach.

"What is it that he wants?" I ask.

Cruz speaks for them, clearly loving the drama. "Something about fucking El raw in your bed and wanting all of Christian's billions." He says it with a nonchalance I'm quite jealous of.

"Matt has lost his fucking marbles if he thinks he's fucking my wife in my goddamn bed. And raw, for that matter."

I'll cut his fucking dick off.

Elena tries to hide her smile behind her glass. I know how much she loves it when I get protective over her, but this is more than that. Thoughts of his untimely brutal death run through my mind, but I also wonder if this is all really about revenge and money for Matt. I don't know him well, but what I do know of him is that it goes deeper than just greed. There is a drive to be on top. To be superior to others. He'll do anything to get there, and I know, in my heart, even if he gets what he wants out of Elena and the money he wants from Christian, he wouldn't stop.

The kink to watch my wife is something I'll probably never fully understand. The push and pull of desire and guilt. I love it, but is it normal? I've never been one to care what others think, but the guilt that I shouldn't enjoy something like that has weighed on me more than a time or two.

I truly love seeing her pleased and seeing other men pleased by her. But the thought of someone taking advantage of her in any way, forcing her to do something she doesn't want to do, has me seeing red. I round my head in a circle, stretching the tight muscles in my neck, feeling a few low cracks as I toss it side to side like a boxer getting ready for a fight.

"I'm disappointed that it's come to this. We have minimal options, and the options we do have are mediocre, at best. Everything we could do would just ruin your reputation," I tip my chin at Elena, then turn to look at Christian, "and put you in a public nightmare. It's like we're starting a game of strip poker, already naked."

"We might be naked, but I think we can even the playing field," Cruz says. Oddly, there's a bit of seduction to his tone, which is weird and worrisome. Christian and Elena are smiling at each other as they sip their beers, and I realize they have already talked through, at least some, if not all, of this plan. Cruz continues, "Maverick wants to play."

28

ELENA

We stayed at the bar much longer than we originally planned. I actually don't think we had a plan for how long we would stay, but Cruz decided to leave first. Well, let me rephrase, he decided to go hit on someone he referred to as a cub. I just love his confidence, both inside of the office and out. We all need a little wild Cruz in us. Figuratively speaking, of course, not literally.

He sauntered off in his signature walk and left me, Christian, and Jake at the table that Jake had originally grabbed for us. I swear it was the tiniest table I had ever seen in a bar. Oddly enough, it worked out well, being that we had to talk about our plan loud enough to scream over the music and other voices, but low enough so no one else could hear what we were scheming. It would have been instinct to move when Cruz left and give the three of us a little more space between each other. But the guys remained stationed in their chairs, inches from either side of me.

We fell into a natural conversation, talking about anything and everything, likes and dislikes, favorite bands and sports. Turns out Jake and Christian like all the same sports teams except hockey. Which drew up a fun banter, being their favorite teams were massive rivals.

It was easy. Really easy.

Jake and Christian acted like old high school friends, similar to the way I saw him interact with his college buddies. I watched them, feeling light and happy, a stark contrast to the feelings I possessed this past week.

After my father died, I taught myself to shield my feelings. I was only a teenager and everyone felt so sorry for me. I could feel their sorrow and pity, and I hated it. I learned to brush off their condolences and ignore any feelings, so I wouldn't be asked the dreaded *how are you* questions.

You know there are a lot of those.

"How are you doing?"

"How are you feeling?"

"How are you holding up?"

When those questions are paired with a whiny tone, and you're asked multiple times a day, you learn to mask yourself and the response becomes uniform. I hid them so the world didn't see an emotional weakness and closed myself off completely.

I have never truly learned to open up again, and I've realized in the last few months how important that is to Jake. So, that is something I really need to work on.

At some point, Christian received a phone call and excused himself. He returned a few minutes later, saying he had something come up and had to leave.

A small wave of jealousy weaved through me, being that it was close to midnight on a Friday night, so I could only assume that meant one thing. It wasn't an emotional type of jealousy, more of a physical one. I had some straying thoughts of Christian coming home with us, and I would bet that Jake had the same passing thought throughout the night.

We decided to Uber home and leave Jake's car at the bar,

since both of us had far too much to drink, which worked out in our favor. Well, at least favorable to the Uber driver, who I hope is a secret voyeur, since we couldn't keep our hands off each other, and I wouldn't have been able to go down on Jake if he were driving. Okay, I probably could have, but let's be real, giving your guy head while he's driving is just as bad as drunk driving. Plus, nothing is more terrifying than a death by impalement of a penis to the back of your head.

Once we made it home, Jake fucked me eighteen different ways and gave me more orgasms than I could count. It was deep, intimate, sexy, and raw. We fell asleep naked, dirty, and hungover, since most of the alcohol had worn off by the time we were finished with each other.

After a week of tense meetings, brutal encounters with Matt, and so much unknown, it had felt like the zip tie that had been cinching tighter around my chest each day was finally cut loose, and my body expanded like a Pillsbury biscuit can. The relief was palpable and so desperately needed.

Until I woke up this morning realizing it's *tomorrow*–Saturday. The day Matt demanded that he is coming over.

Even with our plan in place, it's not foolproof. And we have no idea what other sneaky shit Matt will pull. He might not be the brightest crayon in the box, but I won't underestimate him. Not when there is so much on the line.

I rub my salted eyes open, squinting from the light shining through the blinds. It's minimal, but enough for my brain to hate it mixed with the hangover from last night's alcohol.

Rolling over, the bed is empty and cold, so Jake must have gotten up quite a while ago. It's not unusual for him to wake up early, but on a Saturday and a post drinking night, he must have woken up with a lot on his mind.

I don't blame him.

Just then, the door creaks open and I push myself up on my elbows to peek at the door.

Jake walks in with the most beautiful thing I've ever seen. A tray donned with a bottle of ibuprofen, a glass of water, a piece of toast, and a steaming cup of coffee. The aroma of the roasted beans arrives before he does, and I close my eyes, inhaling the scent filling my lungs to its full capacity.

This smart man grabbed the largest coffee mug we own, so there must be at least thirty ounces of rich, warm liquid gold just waiting to be ravaged.

He remains quiet, his eyes on mine, as I take the first sip and moan in so much pleasure his eyebrows rise to his hairline.

"That's my second favorite type of moan that comes out of your mouth." Leaning in to press a kiss to my forehead. "How are you feeling?"

"Good," I reply too quietly and too quickly.

His eyebrows raise up again, but this time with a condemning look.

"I'm nervous about tonight." Which sums up everything I'm thinking about.

"Don't be. It's going to work." He places the tray in front of me, opening the bottle of drugs I need more than I need my second kidney. He replaces my trough of coffee with a glass of water in one hand, then places two pills in my other.

I drop the pills on the top of my tongue. "And how are you feeling?" I muffle before I gulp down some water.

"Good," he replies with a smirk, damn well knowing he's just mocking my bland response.

I tilt my head to the side with a playful yet disapproving look.

And that apparently allows him to unleash everything he was feeling.

"I'm pissed I was the last to know what happened to you. I'm mad at you for not telling me what was going on and what Matt was doing. And I'm pissed that it had to come to this for you to share your feelings and be open about everything."

I hate when he reprimands me. He rarely does it, but when he does, he's beyond a reasonable doubt, correct. So it's annoyingly deserved.

My shoulders slouch on their own as my chin tips down. Looking back, I know it was hard to share what Matt was doing, but to tell him about Matt means I would need to admit to having sex with Christian without him knowing beforehand. That was shameful to me at the time.

"It all started because I couldn't stop myself in Christian's office. It felt wrong, like I was cheating. I didn't know how to tell you." I keep my gaze down at the pool of dark liquid in the mug that I'm cupping, following the small streams of vapor until they fade. My thoughts mirror the steam, coming in waves and fading into other thoughts.

I feel the mattress dip as he sits beside me, and I shift my gaze up to look at him. I need him to see how sorry I am.

He cups my face and brushes his lips to mine, comforting me. Always comforting me.

"I knew that was a possibility. When we opened up our sex life, I had to mentally prepare myself for a lot of things, but the most important thing was that you were honest with yourself, and honest with me. You need to, and should always, have control over whatever circumstances happen. I shared with you what I wanted, and I trusted you to decide what you were comfortable doing. I don't ever want you to feel ashamed of those choices.

"Would I rather watch? Yes. Absolutely. But just hearing you tell me about it..." he squeezes his eyes and inhales deeply, "does more to me than you'll ever know. So, if that happens again, you're going to tell me, and I'm going to fuck every single dirty detail out of you."

Wow.

Well, that does things to me.

I think back to when he snatched me out of the bar the first night I met Christian. He was starving and insatiable. He was grabbing everything, everywhere, yet couldn't get enough of me, and he needed to hear me tell him everything. How I felt, how he felt, what he did. All of it.

I hum at the memory.

"That sounds like a really good deal," I reply with a shy smile.

"Good. Now get your sexy ass up. We've got a lot to do today." He pats the top of my thigh and heads out of the room. He should have just thrown me into an ice bath with that transition.

The day went by fast, too fast. Jake and I spent most of the time cleaning and getting ready for tonight. Matt is still coming over to our house, which was part of his original plan. We want him to feel like he's in control and I'm being fully compliant, so it only makes sense to keep that as it is.

It's actually quite a silly plan on his part. Going into enemy territory. If he wasn't being such an alpha male about fucking me in my husband's bed, he would have an upper hand at his house. But greed is getting the better of him.

I don't know how I feel about parts of our plan, but like Cruz said, we have to even the playing field, and that means playing dirty.

I walk around to the kitchen island, grabbing a bottle of wine. I cork it and begin to pour myself a glass so I can get some kind of alcohol in my system to ease the tension.

Glancing around the empty house, it's quiet and oddly

serene considering the circumstances. I'm rarely here alone, since Jake works from home, and it feels peaceful.

I hate that it's going to be tainted with the presence of a man I despise.

Just as I bring the dainty glass to my lips, the doorbell rings, and my heart lurches to my throat. My body involuntarily tenses everywhere. I take a deep breath, then release a long exhale, which ripples some of the wine in my glass. Closing my eyes, I tip the rim onto my lips, taking a sizable sip and downing the glass in one mouthful.

Apparently, I'm just taking wine glass size shots now.

Another impatient ring from the doorbell, too quickly after the first, and I wonder if Matt is impatient or nervous.

I'm going with nervous.

I trudge to the front door. My steps are heavy and attempting to rebel against my decision. I manage to unbolt the deadlock and grip the door handle, taking another deep breath before opening the door.

Matt is glancing around to the street like he was going to rob the place, checking to make sure no one was around. He leans to the side, looking past me, then to my driveway, only seeing my car. Oh, and his car. That is parked right next to me. In my husband's spot.

The nerve of this fucking guy.

"You're alone." Satan smiles.

"Not by choice," I reply.

"Oh, you had a choice, and I think you made the right one." He steps through the doorway, forcing me to step back. I spin on my heel and walk away from him to be as far away as possible.

I round the kitchen counter to pour some more wine for myself. When I look up, he's locking the door–every lock on the door–and closing the blinds even tighter than they already are.

Slithering towards me, "You're drinking?"

I side-eye him with a sarcastic chuckle. "Oh, yes, I need to be very intoxicated for this." I round my finger in the air, loosely throwing my hand up, referring to him and this room in a *what the fuck* sort of manner.

The first shot of wine is clearly already hitting my system when I start talking. It's probably closer to a yell than a talk, but who cares?

"What the fuck is wrong with you, Matt? You need to blackmail women for sex." Pouring the wine a bit too aggressively, it sloshes out of the top and splashes on the countertop.

"You're sick and disgusting," I say, ripping a paper towel out of the holder, wiping up the mess.

"Some would say the same about a woman who sleeps her way to the top." He shrugs. "Can't say I wouldn't do the same if I had a pussy and a set of tits, especially tits like yours." His eyes stare directly at my chest, that is fully covered.

"And now I'll know what all the rave is about that pussy." He licks his lips, and it makes me want to stab myself in the eye with the corkscrew.

I roll my eyes as I sip down the bile creeping up my throat with more alcohol.

"Aren't you going to ask me if I want something to drink? You aren't being a very good host, Elena."

I smile, a fake yet pleased smile, because that's exactly what I wanted.

Pulling out the glass, I strategically placed behind the island, I pour a few ounces, then push it towards the front of the counter. The glass scraping against the smooth granite countertop.

He manhandles the stem and tips the glass up in the air. "Cheers." He takes a long, slow sip as his eyes burrow into mine, angry and eager.

Bringing the wine glass down from his lips, he wastes no time. "Take off your clothes."

Even though I knew this was coming, I am still stunned by his demand.

I either need to say no and push back with him, or comply, but very slowly. If he gets mad, he won't drink, and I need him to drink. So, I comply.

I decided to wear something that covered pretty much every inch of skin on my body, and the farthest thing from sexy as possible. An oversized button-up blouse tied in the front, with a pair of leggings and comfortable ballet flats.

He continues to sip on his wine, since he has nothing else to do with his hands, which I'm thankful for.

I circle around the kitchen island and stand across from him. We're about six feet apart, but his overpowered musky scent, that matches his personality, is swarming around me like he's holding me hostage.

"I don't want to do this, Matt," I whisper. A final plea for him to stop. I don't care if it sounds like begging at this point.

"See, that pisses me off," he belts out. "You don't want to fuck me, but you'll fuck everyone else. Take your fucking clothes off," he says impatiently as he throws his head back, drinking what's left of his wine.

Thank God.

I close my eyes and force myself to breathe. I untie the front of my shirt and let it fall over to the tops of my thighs. I tuck my thumbs into the waistband of the leggings and bend down, peeling the leggings off to my ankles. I pull one over my ballet shoe then release everything to the floor as I lean back up and step on them to pull the other side off.

In my head, that was the least sexy way I could remove them, but as I look at Matt, I realize it didn't matter if I undressed with the grace of a walrus; he would still enjoy this. It's about the compliance for him, not the action.

I begin to unbutton my top, going slowly as I fight through

the slight tremble in my hands. He sees it and smirks. "Nervous, Ellie?"

"Don't fucking call me that," I spit back at him.

"I'll call you whatever the fuck I want, slut." Losing his patience, he takes three large strides over to me, gripping the collar of my shirt and ripping the buttons wide open.

I gasp at both the action and the abrupt cold air that grazes over my newly exposed skin. The sound of tearing fades and the silence is donned with the echoes of the plastic pieces bouncing on the hardwood floor. I move to pull the shirt closed, but he pats my hands away, gripping the middle of the hem, then pushing it over my shoulders and down my back so my arms are pinned at my side with my own fucking shirt. He's dangerously close to me, but somehow pulls me closer, so his body is flush with mine.

"I've waited long enough. You've teased me for far too long, and now it's time to give me what's mine." He leans down, tearing the shirt from behind my arms and throws it on the ground so I'm standing in nothing but my bra and underwear. My ballet shoes feel like an extra layer of protection, which is pathetic, since they are equivalent to a tiny ankle sock.

"Take me to your room." I squeeze my eyes shut. My heart is racing and I'm questioning this whole plan. I take a small step back from him, keeping my gaze to the floor, afraid to look at him, to look at the monster he's become.

I turn on my heel, walking quickly towards the stairs, and I realize he's keeping up with me, anxious and ready.

There have been a lot of uncomfortable moments tonight. Walking up the stairs in a thong, with his face right at my ass, as I stride up each step, is probably up there at the top.

I reach the last stair as he smacks my ass, my fists clench on their own, and I want to turn around and punch him in the face, so he flies down my stairs and breaks his goddamn neck.

A girl can dream.

I turn through the doorway into the solace of my room. The scent of my husband lingers in the room, giving me an overwhelming amount of comfort. I need that as I turn to see Matt coming through my doorway, glancing around the room, taking in the surroundings of our sanctuary that he intends to defile.

"Put on a pair of your heels." He walks in the room like he owns it, heading towards the bench at the end of my bed. He sits down and has a direct line of sight into my walk-in closet.

I slowly walk in there, grabbing the first pair I see, placing one hand on the wooden panel of the closet, as I start to slip one on.

"Not that one. Those." He points over at my black and gold, four-inch strappy heels.

So, Matt has a shoe fetish or a foot fetish. A feetish I like to call it.

Maybe he'd like a kick in the face with these.

Slipping them on, I walk through the closet, and I notice him squeezing his eyes tightly as he opens his eyes, blinking hard repeatedly.

I smile internally.

He palms his eyes and continues to blink, looking around at the floor, then around the room. He zones in on me, or what he can see of my silhouette, squinting and blinking.

He shakes his head and presses the backs of his fingers into his eyes again.

He brings his hands down in front of him, flipping them back and forth, then looks back at me.

"You fucking bitch! What did you do to me?" He lunges forward at me, then falls chest first into the floor. He presses one arm into the floor, shaking his head once more, and I'm frozen, watching him work through the confusion.

Not realizing how close he is, he reaches his long, Gumby-like arm out and grabs my ankle, pulling my body towards his. I lose my balance and fall to the floor in front of him, and I flail, trying to push him back, but he has more strength than I realized.

He yanks me closer, then wraps his hands around my neck, pushing me onto the ground.

Shit.

He drops his weight on top of me, using all his remaining energy to press into the soft, sensitive flesh of my throat. Even with the drugs I gave him, he's still ridiculously strong.

My vision starts to fade as I gasp for breath. The tightness surrounding my eyes is painful, and the pressure feels like nothing I've ever experienced.

I close my eyes, fading into a dark space. My eyes see nothing but pricks of light that match the tingling sensation on my skin.

Suddenly, the pressure is gone, and my body jerks to take in air and cough simultaneously. I hold my head up for a brief moment to see Matt on his back next to me, blood dripping from his nose and mouth as he looks up at Jake standing over him with a look a murderer would be proud of. Matt manages to mutter, "W—what the fuck," before his head drops to the floor and he passes out.

I'm no longer able to hold my head up, and although I can't say the same, I feel that, as I my head drops back and I fade out alongside Matt.

29

ELENA

I hear distant noises and some indistinguishable clattering. My brain is stuck somewhere between waking up and dreaming, and I'm not sure what side the noise is coming from. Hearing the faint ripple of duct tape toggles me over to the reality side of things when I remember where I am and what happened.

Matt attacked me. He fucking attacked me. Which is clear now that I'm blinking my eyes open, but my immobilized muscles are unable to lift my neck.

I groan in pain, moving slowly, attempting to push myself up to a seated position on the chaise lounge I somehow ended up on.

"Woah, Woah. Slow down." Christian comes to my side, placing his hand on my thigh.

Jake follows right after him, crouching down in front of me.

I'm looking between both of them, their faces full of concern.

God, they are handsome.

My lips inch into a smile over my face, seeing both of them like this.

Adorable. Worried. Sexy as hell.

The relief is palpable when they somehow synchronize their smiles back at me, telling me our plan is working. I glance over at Matt, who is currently tied to my bed, which makes me pleased and repulsed at the same time.

"Are you okay, baby?" Jake asks, cupping my cheek and lifting my jaw, examining my neckline.

"I'm good." He instantly leans his head to the side and rolls his eyes, hearing my default response.

"I mean, it's a little tender, but I'll be okay." I smile.

Cruz comes to Jake's side as he hands me some horse pills, that look like prescription ibuprofen, and a glass of water, which I take and chug down immediately. The first sips that go down feel like spiked boulders, but after that clears, it surprisingly feels, well, good. But I won't dare use that word again.

I look at the three most important men in my life and feel an overwhelming amount of love and support. I've always gotten that from Jake, but to feel admired by these three, all in totally different ways, is a comfort I can't explain.

"You guys are amazing," I say the exact thing I'm feeling.

Jake and Christian glance at each other, then back at me.

"Jake got here first, thankfully, otherwise you'd probably be dead," Christian says as he gives a murderous stare over at Matt, who is still passed out.

"Christian was seconds behind me and saved my ass from going to jail," Jake replies, standing to his full height, but not before stopping to kiss the crown of my head.

My eyebrows pinch together, a little confused because the last thing I remember is Jake standing over Matt, who passed out right before I did. *I think.*

"Oh yeah, that man..." Cruz points at Christian, "for sure saved your ass. In literal terms, because you would for sure become a meat rock in prison."

I giggle, because in true Cruz fashion, he makes me laugh in any situation.

"I walked in to you two half dead on the floor." Cruz points back and forth between Matt and me. "And Christian bear hugging Jake, pulling him to the corner with a goddamn kitchen knife in his hand. You almost needed a full remodel in this place, El."

Christian is only a couple of inches taller than Jake and relatively the same size. I imagine that was not the easiest task, pulling back a large and very angry Jake. Cruz grabs the water glass from me and retreats from the room.

I look over at Christian, who's still staring at me, worry hidden behind those golden irises, tinged with a hint of pride as well.

I rub the stubble that's taken purchase over his entire jawline, and in the lightest of whispers, "Thank you."

He leans up to me, pressing his lips to my cheek, before going to check on Matt.

An hour goes by as we all wait for Matt to wake up. He's tied to the bed, his shirt unbuttoned and his pants unzipped. His arms are tied above his head to a rope that descends behind the headboard, tied to a hook we installed behind it.

Which I'm sure will come in handy at some point.

His legs are also roped together and tied to the edge of the bedpost to prevent him from kicking and flailing around too much.

There's duct tape across his mouth, which is probably going to rip off half his top lip and wax that area of his chin, but I shrug to myself. He deserves it.

A groan comes from low in Matt's belly, and we all spark to life. I swear we suck in all the air in the room, and none of us breathe, so we can hear every movement.

His head sways forward, heavy and weighted, then bounces up, and he tries to hold his neck upright. He looks like a decapitated bobblehead for a few seconds before finally opening his eyes.

Squinting tightly and blinking a few times, he finally starts to look curiously at his surroundings. First at his legs, then up at his arms, pulling aggressively at the restraints. Realizing that is pointless, he looks around at the room, finding me, Jake, and Christian. His eyes widen in confusion as he passes over each one of us, muttering something inaudible behind the thick barrier of the tape. His eyes bounce back and forth between Jake and Christian, and when I glance at them, they are grinning. Close-mouthed smiles, but ear to ear.

Smug bastards.

Matt screams in frustration. Then looks down at his exposed belly. Matt's not a big guy, but he doesn't have the washboard abs my guys do.

My guys.

I shake that thought away for a moment. Well, technically, Matt rips that thought out of my head when he starts bucking and screaming, noticing the translucent milky streaks painted over his stomach. Paired with the painfully hard-looking erection, courtesy of the Viagra-laced Rohypnol I snuck in his drink, he's having an absolute breakdown.

The homemade spunk mix, made of an egg white, some water, and cornstarch, was a last-minute idea Cruz had and is working like a charm. I'm not sure I want to know how he knew how to make fake cum, and I definitely won't be asking.

He wears himself out for well over a minute, freaking out and screaming, which is probably the most humorous minute of my entire life, before Cruz walks through the bedroom door and breaks the silence.

"Hey, Goose." I can hear his smile without seeing it, but when I look up at him, he's wearing a thoroughly fucked look like a pro. He's shirtless, the top button of his jeans is splayed open, and he's got a hand towel draped around his shoulders, using the ends to dry off his hands. His hair looks like it just battled a windstorm and lost. And he has what appears to be a mystery hickey forming at the base of his throat.

I've never met sexual Cruz before, but he's pretty damn hot.

In that moment, Matt completely freaks out. I've never seen a grown man have a total conniption fit, and it looks like a toddler temper tantrum on steroids.

Jake tosses his phone over to Cruz, who saunters over to the bed. Sitting down, he swipes and presses the middle of the screen, playing what sounds like a porn video. Sounds of begging, moaning, and pleas for more stop Matt from flailing around as Cruz lifts the screen to him. Matt's eyes bulge with visible pain and sorrow as he sees himself and Cruz in their own homemade porn.

This was all very strategic, of course. Every angle we recorded makes it look like Matt is taking it upside down and sideways in every possible position, and with Jake's software skills and a few AI overlays, it really looks and sounds like Matt is living his best life. Jake was even able to plug in some Top Gun references, including Matt begging, "Oh, God, Maverick," and, "Mav, don't stop."

Cruz swipes the screen, the sound pauses, and another video loads showing Matt just how many different positions we have.

"I knew you'd like calling me Maverick. Thanks for the good time, lover." Cruz blows him a kiss before standing up and tossing the phone back at Jake.

He kisses me on the cheek.

"Ciao, friends." He waves as he exits the room.

I look back at Matt, and his shoulders are completely deflated. His body has completely given up any fight, which matches the look in this face. It's blanketed with shame and guilt over the videos he just saw, and not guilt for what he did to me.

It makes threatening him so much easier.

Jake walks over and tears the duct tape off his face, his scream so high pitched it pierces my ear drums. The tape leaves his face a dark shade of pink with tiny pricks of blood where the hair has been ripped off.

I palm my neck, touching the tender bruises, reminding myself to not feel bad for him.

"You'll never get away with this." Matt stares straight at Jake, then turns to me. "You fucking whor—"

Jake smashes his fist straight into the middle of Matt's face, forbidding him to finish that sentence.

"THAT IS MY WIFE!" he roars in Matt's face. He places his palm at the base of Matt's throat and pushes him hard against the headboard. Matt's hands are still restricted over his head so he has no ability to protect himself. I gasp, questioning to myself if Jake can make himself stop.

I've never seen him so angry. Jake is never violent. Ever.

I'm only a little ashamed of how turned on that makes me.

"You will never touch my wife again. You will never look at her or even glance in her direction. Do you fucking understand?"

Unable to breath, Matt somehow nods in agreement, and Jake lets go as he wheezes, then gasps for air.

"How's it feel, asshole?" Christian asks him, as he moves my hair to expose my neck.

Matt, still gasping, looks my way, but says nothing.

"Here's what is going to happen, Mr. Randall." *Hello, business Christian.*

"We're going to untie you. You're going to leave and immediately send your resignation to your boss. We've already deleted the videos and pictures from your phone..."

"How did you get in my phone?" Matt questions, and Christian just cocks his head at him.

"What kind of dumb fucking question is that?" Jake verbalizes what Christian's face is showing.

"So the videos and pictures are gone, but if you saved them to your cloud and these show up anywhere, at any time, we will release the videos of you and Cruz to every social media platform, and I guarantee you, they will be viral."

Matt grits his teeth so hard I can hear them grind together from across the room.

"And for additional insurance, these, too." Christian brings out a manilla envelope, pulling a few 8x10 photos and throwing them on the bed in front of Matt.

I steel my spine and lift my chin to see what they are pictures of. They are grainy and pixelated, but I can see the distinct outline of the artwork from Christian's building lobby.

"You know, Mr. Randall, arson is a felony. It's usually only a few years of jail time, but aggravated arson to an occupied building..." Christian tsks, "that's some real prison time."

My jaw drops.

Matt started the fire.

I am both shocked and elated that this is just one more thing we have on Matt, and just a little pissed off that Christian didn't tell us. I say 'us' because the look on Jake's face is a reflection of my own, so I know he had no idea either.

Christian knows he's won and begins cutting off the rope that binds Matt's arms and legs together. He pulls them into himself, rubbing the area on his wrists that were confined.

"You'll forget about this. All of this. And keep these. I have plenty of copies." Christian presses the envelope of pictures into his chest, and Matt hugs them to himself. "Get the fuck out of here". Christian walks away, dropping an invisible mic, and leans up against the wall, crossing his arms and legs like he's patiently waiting for absolutely nothing.

Matt exhales loudly, on purpose, then clears his throat and throws in the white flag. Dropping his head, saying nothing to anyone, he shuffles out of the room, and Jake follows.

I hear the front door open and close, and then finally turn to Christian.

"Were you gonna share any of that with us?" I hold my arm out to the bed, even though it's empty.

"That call I received late last night was from Dietrich, giving me all these details. He found out about the fire, as well as the photos that were taken of us at my office." He reaches behind his neck and rubs at his nape before ruffling his own hair in frustration. "It was Jenny. I guess she's been in some financial trouble and Matt propositioned her. Out of everyone, I just never expected her."

My lips part is a quiet gasp.

"I'm so sorry." I couldn't imagine if Cruz did something like that to me. I would be devastated.

"It's okay. We found out, and that's what's important." He comforts me instead of himself.

"Well, we could have just ran with the whole arson thing instead of doing all of this." Motioning my hands to the whole room.

I don't miss his chuckle, and it's adorable. He's proud, yet shy, contradicting his powerful demeanor.

"We needed him weak. If I would have approached him with just the arson thing, it wouldn't have been enough. This was exactly what we needed to do." He steps up to me, tucking my hair behind my ear and checking on the light purple bruise that is already showing up on the side of my throat.

"I never expected him to do this, though. Are you okay?"

"Oddly, I've never felt better," I reply, not being able to hold back a genuine smile.

"Good, because I don't think I can hold back any longer." Christian steps forward, making me step back. He grips my chin with his thumb and forefinger and leans in, making me shuffle back a couple more steps until the back of my knees hit the edge of the bench.

Brushing his lips against mine, he grabs my arms and places them around his neck.

"Wrap your legs around me, Ellie."

So I do.

He pulls me into him, gripping my ass and kissing me hard. Just as my husband's shadow appears in the doorway.

30

CHRISTIAN

It's been over a week since I've had any taste of Ellie, which isn't that long, but now that her legs are wrapped around me, it feels like an eternity. There is a deeper connection and something stronger that draws me to her, which I've been fighting since the moment she told me she was married. After last night, it became clear to me how much all of this just makes sense.

In all honesty, it makes absolutely no sense in a general state of things. But after spending time with both of them, I realize it's the kind of relationship that makes sense for *me*.

I'm open and more of an exhibitionist in ways.

He's open and more of a voyeur.

And Ellie. Ellie is the connection. The spark. The knot.

I don't know if this is some poly relationship in the making or a friend with benefits situation or something more. All I know is I want to see where it goes, and I'm willing to take the risk.

I squeeze her ass and pull her into me. Running my tongue along her jawline, wanting to do anything to make her sensitive bruised skin better. I hate that he touched her, that he hurt her like he did. When I came into the room and saw her on the floor, my heart throbbed harder than it should have. I felt weak and powerless and needed to get to her.

Then, seeing Jake standing over Matt in the literal stance of a butcher at a slaughterhouse, the fear of what could happen to him took over all other emotions. Without any thought, I ran into him like I did in football training, tackling him to the floor. It's an absolute fucking miracle he didn't slice me open with that goddamn kitchen knife.

I push all that aside and focus on the gorgeous woman tangled in my arms. And her husband, who I'm certain will find a spot in the corner to watch once he finds his way back to the room.

A part of me is hoping he'll join us so we can please Ellie in more ways than she could ever dream, but we haven't broached that topic yet.

I gently place her back down on the bed and trail my hands over her body. I tuck my fingers in her waistband and pull her pants down slowly. Lifting her legs, she pulls her knees in to help me remove the fabric from her ankles, then lowers her feet to the edge of the bed.

She looks like a fucking goddess.

I take my time undoing each of the buttons on the shirt she put on after Matt ripped the first one off. I can't say I'm not tempted to do the same, but teasing her slowly, as I outline the shape of her breasts with my fingertips, is tantalizing for us both.

Leaning down, I flatten my tongue over the thin fabric covering her nipple and suck softly. A guttural moan comes from deep in her throat, and *fuck,* that does everything to me.

Reaching down, I unlatch my buckle and pull the leather belt through the loopholes of my pants, throwing it on the floor. This impatient little minx yanks open my fly and pulls down the waistband of my boxer briefs with one hand.

My cock springs free, bouncing just inches from Ellie's gorgeous lips. I can't wait to have them wrapped around my cock while I pump in and out of her mouth, but right now, I want nothing more than for her to be screaming my name while she comes.

She pushes her neck forward with her lips parted, attempting to take me in her mouth. It takes all my willpower to move back, but somehow I do, and lean down, crashing my mouth onto hers. Swiping my tongue over hers, we catch each other's needy moans while my hands roam all over her body. Caressing her stomach and hips with one hand, pinching her nipple with the other.

One of my hands, I'm not even sure which one, strays, reaching down between her thighs. The pads of my fingertips trail her smooth skin before getting soaked in her arousal, and my cock twitches at the feeling of how wet she is. My mouth follows the same path of my fingers until I'm on my knees in front of her. Breathing heavily on her skin, I run my lips gently over her inner thighs, placing kisses all around the apex of her legs. Everywhere except where she really wants it. She's moaning and moving her hips to try to meet my mouth, but like a professional dodgeball player, I juke her movements.

She's writhing and bucking, and now unable to control her groaning, which is turning into an adorable whine moan.

"Please. Please, Christian." She lifts her neck to look at me, and I'm unable to hide my lopsided grin. Our eyes meet and she's begging me with every part of her body. The desperate look in her eyes matches the neediness of her voice, and her trembling legs shake with anguish.

I flick the tip of my tongue at her clit before wrapping my mouth around it, sucking and flicking, no longer having any restraint. Her sounds vibrate the walls, and like an earthquake, it rolls straight through me. Her moans and pleas are like my own personal natural disaster, kicking me off axis, making me dizzy under her spell.

I throw one of her legs over my shoulder, opening her up wider for me, then press two fingers into her soaked pussy. The rhythm of my thrusts are in perfect alignment with the flicking of my tongue.

A shadow from the light in the hallway flashes on the ground, catching my attention. Without stopping my tempo, I glance in that direction to see Jake, shirtless, with the front of his pants pulled down over his impressively hard cock.

I didn't really get to see or watch him when we video fucked. *Is that a thing?* And, although I know we had his full attention then, seeing him stand here in the flesh, as I eat his wife like she's my last meal before death row, is making my cock crave so much more.

"You have the most beautiful pussy," I say between licking and sucking.

"You're so fucking wet." I suck on the bud, then flatten my tongue, putting pressure over the top.

She screams and jerks her body. "I'm so close," she whimpers.

I crook my fingers inside her pussy and thrust a couple more times, making her scream louder. Then, like the tease I am tonight, I withdraw.

There's that needy fucking whimper.

Her sounds will be the literal death of me.

My fingers are layered in her arousal, and I coat myself with it. Wrapping my hand around my swollen cock, I fuck my hand, desperately needing to be touched. I keep lapping at her clit and she starts to tremble. Everywhere. Her legs, which are wrapped around my shoulders, are shaking uncontrollably. Her hands that are reaching for my hair, her bucking hips and pouting bottom lip, all quivering.

Her voice is the most telling.

She's begging for me to keep going.

"Are you going to come for him, baby?" Jake asks, making me groan, sending vibrations through her clit that make her scream.

"Fuck. Oh, God." She manages to grit out.

"Do you want him to make you come?" he asks again, as patient and controlled as the first time.

She doesn't answer him, instead she grips my hair harder, keeping me in the space that she knows will do just that. I keep still and flick my tongue up and down, over and over, against her sensitive clit.

"Fuck, I'm... I'm coming." She looks between my eyes and his, then she throws her head back, saying other curse words and groans that make my cock ache.

She's still coming down from her high when Jake strides into the room, flipping her over onto her hands and knees. I move to sit in front of her, leaning my back against the headboard.

Jake's dominant side is showing, and I sit back, reversing roles with him. His eyes peer at me, then back down to Elena, as he caresses her hips, staring straight at her glistening pussy.

"Now she's ready for me."

31

JAKE

I've been turned on before and *turned on*.

This is the latter.

After the stress from the night, the last thing I was expecting was for us to end up in bed together, but the idea hasn't been far from my mind since meeting Christian in person.

I never expected my vision to turn into this, but I can't say I'm upset about it.

It's ideal actually.

A steady partner who I trust, that I can share my wife with, that she also clearly has an attraction to. Fucking jackpot.

I do love seeing her flirt with different men, but I don't need to see her fuck a variety of them. It's not like that old bachelor mentality of needing something new or different. This is about pleasure. Her pleasure. Mine. And seeing the man she's with fall apart for her is decidedly one of the best parts.

My cock is painfully hard as I run the pre-cum laced tip through her slit. She's fucking drenched. Her juices, mixed with his saliva, is the perfect lubricant for my cock.

I push into her without warning, knowing how primed she

is. She gasps and moans, pressing her face into the top of Christian's thigh, gripping the other with her hands. He's seated in front of her, with his back against the headboard, a front row view of her yearning face.

His jaw is slacked as he pushes back the hair that has fallen over her face like a veil.

"Oh, God, Jake. That feels so good," she mumbles into his leg, but it's still clearly audible because both of us moan in perfect unison. The sounds of us both must remind her that she has two men to please because she lifts her head, taking Christian's cock in her mouth, then lowers her head down to the base, taking everything. Christian throws his arms to the top of the headboard, needing something to keep him fucking grounded.

"Fuck. Fuck. Oh, fuck," he belts out, his eyes squeezing shut, probably trying to envision anything but the beautiful blonde with her lips wrapped around his cock.

"That's it baby, show us how much you love being filled by us." My words make them both moan in unison, as she bobs her head up and down with the same rhythm in which I'm pounding into her.

She knows how close he is and gives him a reprieve, releasing him from the literal chokehold her throat had on him. She's facing him, but I don't need to see her face to know the look that she is giving him. The one bathed in desire, saturated with lust. The one that turns me into a frail and puny excuse of a man.

She dips her chin, pressing the surface of her tongue at the base of his cock, and swipes it all the way to the tip.

Not sure that is much of a reprieve.

He grunts from some organ in the middle of his torso, and his body involuntarily pushes further back towards the backboard, which his fingers look permanently embedded into. His knuckles are blending into the whitewash of the wall.

She moans, knowing exactly what she's doing to him, and I have to hide my smirk. I have no idea how either one of us is going to last another minute.

"Ellie, you look..." She wraps her lips around his dick, pushing herself down so it easily slides to the back of her throat, interrupting his compliment. "Ahhhh, fuck!" he bellows through the room.

I reach down and wrap my hand around the base of her neck as she bobs her head up and down, and I can feel the full length of his cock tunneling inside the column of her throat.

Jesus, take the wheel because I'm about to lose all fucking control.

I release my soft grip and she pulls her mouth from him, tilting her head to the side, granting me a profile view and a lopsided grin.

Okay, she's Satan.

And she's really pleased with herself.

"Jake." I'm surprised when my name isn't coming from her, but from him. I glance up to see him with begging eyes, telling me he's ready.

Me too, man, me too.

I reach around, gaining access to her clit, knowing how I can easily throw her over the edge. She's held out well, but the little bundle of nerves at the apex of her thighs is always her undoing.

I stroke back and forth easily with how wet she is, and she responds instantly. Her forehead presses into the top of Christian's thigh, squirming and trembling, then even more when Christian reaches down and begins pinching and pulling on her nipples.

She clenches around me, moaning, losing the battle she was trying to uphold.

Her screaming echoes throughout the room and ping pongs off the walls. Her moans sound like heaven but feel like the heat of hell, singeing every layer of skin, melting my resolve.

She's barely coming down from her high when Christian starts bucking his hips softly, her hand still wrapped around his cock.

"Please, suck my cock, Ellie." His voice is weak, desperate, demanding. He somehow manages to be submissive and dominate cohesively in the same moment. Her eyes shoot up towards him and she immediately wraps her lips around him, taking him to the hilt.

Shocked how his begging affected me as much as hers, all the blood rushes to my cock and I piston into her harder, throwing my head back, chasing my own release.

"Goddammit. Your pussy feels so fucking good."

"You're going to make me come."

Our words and moans are mixed with slapping and slurping.

"Fuck, fuck!"

"Oh, fuck, I'm coming."

"I'm gonna come."

I don't know who says what, but we are all panting and screaming. A blend of the sounds of sex and profanities.

That must set off something inside Elena, because she clenches so hard around my dick I can feel my release dripping from her already. Her moans mix with ours, fading into heavy breathing.

I fall on top of her and roll over onto the bed. I feel like one of those Looney Tunes characters. You know, the ones that get hit over the head with an Acme weight, then just falls face first into the hardwood floor. Yup, that's me right now. I should be dead.

That was absolutely the best sexual experience I've ever had, and when I glance up at Christian, then over to Elena, it's written all over their faces as well.

There is no way I want any of this to end.

She reaches her hands out, grabbing mine in her left and

his in her right. Ironically, we both pull her hand to our lips to kiss it. Her eyes remain closed but she smiles, releasing a relaxed breath.

I look up at Christian, and he returns my knowing look.

Our fun is just beginning.

32

ELENA

Walking into the office on Monday is an anxiety-filled chore. We spent the weekend with Christian in our house, and it all came so naturally to both Jake and me, it was almost frightening. I'm reminded of it with each step I take as the tenderness between my legs overwhelms my senses. But the memories of our pleasure-filled weekend override the soreness residing in every crevice of my body.

We were animals. Ravenous, unhinged animals that couldn't get enough of each other. Like we were meant for this. Like this is where we are all supposed to end up.

As the elevator ascends towards my floor, I recall last Friday's events, which now seem like a lifetime ago. I didn't see Matt's car in the parking lot, but I'm still not putting anything past him. We have enough ammunition on him to not only ruin his reputation, but potentially put him in jail. He is aware he can't ruin my marriage and that both my husband and Christian were in on everything, so the only devastating thing that could happen would be me needing to find a new job.

At this point I don't even care if anyone knows about my

relationship status. I'm beyond happy. Jake has always fulfilled me, and I love him more than I could ever say, but having two sexy-as-hell men worship me? Well, that's another level of satisfaction I can't begin to explain.

I did keep a close eye on Jake this weekend, especially after I withheld everything that was happening from him. The guilt I felt about that was staggering. I wouldn't have blamed him if he wanted to separate or leave me after the stunt I pulled. Not sharing with him the details of everything that was going on, *then* leaning on Christian for everything.

If the roles were reversed, I would have probably killed him. Divorced him first, then killed him for good measure.

Although relying on Christian was unintentional because, for Matt, it was all about Christian in the first place. But a large part of his elaborate plan rolled over to whatever sexual favors he was going to bribe out of me, and I should have gone to Jake in the very beginning so I could have talked through it with him.

Still, he took everything in stride. As he always does. Supported me. Loved me. And did whatever needed to be done to make it right.

I have already been researching a therapist to talk to, who will help me open up and communicate. If whatever Jake, Christian, and I are doing is going to continue, I am going to need to work on that. Oddly enough, this relationship is already helping me do that. But I want to continue to make it work. So much.

It's unusual. In most cases, the more people there are in any given situation, the more that makes me want to retreat. But with the two of them, I want to do nothing but talk and explore. They open me up in ways I never knew I needed or wanted.

I look around the elevator that I have ridden hundreds of times in my career, and for the first time, I see walls. Restricting walls. Not only are they a really putrid color of fertilizer brown, but it feels small. I've been happy here for a long time, but for the first time, a change doesn't sound all that bad. I have enjoyed working for Bryan. He's a good guy. His ideals might be a little old school, but I do feel like he respects me.

There were a couple of instances that I was passed up for a promotion, but I felt like they were justified. In one way or another. At least I justified it in my head.

Jake did not. He was pissed, actually.

Maybe I'm just more understanding. Regardless, I'll be happier knowing that Matt will not only not be working here any longer, there is zero chance he'll ever be a director here.

And speak of the devil. As the elevator doors spread open with slow, calculated effort, Matt stands waiting, peering down at his shoes.

Every inch of my body tenses. I reach to the hem of my skirt to pull it down as a reaction to him. Like I need to hide myself, and I realize I'm still tormented by him. I get a whiff of that musk that is so familiar to him, and it's even more potent with the stale scent of alcohol. Whiskey, vodka, tequila, who the hell knows, but he looks like shit and I don't care.

He lifts his head up and realization hits as his jaw tightens when he sees me standing in the middle of the elevator. I'm fucking alone in the middle of this goddamn vault, and my heart beats out of my chest at the chance that he's going to lock me in here.

I quickly step through the doorway of the elevator and he matches my urgency by stepping in front of me, blocking my exit. The elevator door attempts to close, but it taps my shoulder and reopens.

We are level. Our eyes like razor blades tearing into each other.

I will not back down.

The sound of Bryan's voice tears our gazes away from each other as he approaches us with an envelope in his hand.

"Matt, this is for you." Handing it over to him. "A letter of recommendation for you. If you need anything, you have them call me." His smile is ear to ear.

"Thank you," Matt says simply, while side-eyeing me with a glare.

"Are you sure there isn't anything I can do to convince you to stay?" Bryan asks, making my stomach jump to my throat.

Matt now turns his full attention to me. His stare like the devil. His eyes burning with rage, but there is something else there. Shame. Regret.

He hangs his head, then turns back to Bryan. "No, sir." He holds out his hand. Bryan shakes it with a nod, then he steps around both of us into the elevator.

A part of me feels bad.

A very small part.

Then I remember he sexually abused me, blackmailed Christian, and oh, don't forget, choked me half to death.

And I smile and finger wave as the elevator doors close.

Good riddance, asshole.

"Elena, good morning," Bryan chants, a little too loudly. "Do you have a moment? Can you come to my office?"

"Definitely." I smile and follow him to his office, a little uneasy and curious as to what he's going to want first thing on Monday morning, when we already have our team meeting planned in an hour. More than likely it's Matt related, which makes me nauseous thinking about it. I hope he doesn't ask me anything about his swift departure because I'm a terrible liar.

I've walked through Bryan's office many times over the course of my career, and it has remained unchanged over the course of my tenure. The same day in and day out, which mirrors his personality in that nothing much changes around here. Today is an exception.

Today, there is a very tall, very new gentleman standing in front of Bryan's desk. He's peering down at his phone, his thumbs flying over the keyboard, as we walk through the doorway, and Bryan belts a random comment to take center stage, in usual form.

The new guy looks up as he lowers his phone into his pocket and smiles in my direction.

"Elena, this is Jonathan Jones. I've just hired him as our new Executive Vice President and Director of Marketing and Development."

My eyeballs are the only thing that are not frozen as they bounce between the two men, my jaw tight as I swallow thickly.

After all these years, I thought the best of Bryan, in that I would earn my shot at an opportunity like *that* one. But it's clear he will never see me in that light. Jake would comment about his short-sightedness and overlooking me before, but I have defended Bryan, knowing that he had my best interest in mind, but I see now it's always been about his company.

And it always will be.

"It's nice to meet you, Elena." Jonathan steps towards me, his hand jutting out towards me. I reach out to shake it with a more than fake smile, and since I'm still speechless, I just give him a firm nod. Unable to verbally agree with it being nice to meet him.

"I wanted you two to meet before the team meeting since you guys will be leading the team." Bryan fist pumps to himself like a jerk, and I wish he'd accidentally punch himself in the face.

So he wants to give Jonathan here the title, but have me *partner* to lead our teams.

What a great deal for them.

"I've heard great things about Elena. Both she and I together, sir, we are going to take this company to the next level." Jonathan smiles over at me like a freaking snake, and this is like déjà vu. Just like when Bryan hired Matt. Except Matt wasn't qualified in the least, so Bryan hired Matt as my peer, not reporting director.

"If you'll both excuse me, I have to get a few things ready for the meeting. See you later." Jonathan excuses himself with a polite bow as he passes by me, and I have the urge to trip him, but I don't. Unfortunately, for my ego.

"He's going to be so great. I've been gunning for him for a while. You are going to love working with him, Elena!" Bryan is excited. He's practically skipping around his office. He continues to talk about Jonathan and all his accolades, and although I'm never in the room when he would speak about me, I highly doubt he speaks about me with such passion and vigor.

I don't ask for a lot. But what I do want, and what I've realized I want, it's not this. I deserve so much more.

No. I've fucking earned it.

"Bryan," I abruptly interrupt him talking about his new golden boy. That's not my usual style, so he's taken aback and looks up at me, a furrow in his brow.

"Thank you for the amazing opportunity you have provided to me, but please accept this as my official resignation." I step forward, placing my keycard on the top of Bryan's desk before looking up at him, his jaw slacked, and I've never in my life seen the man so dumbfounded.

"You can't quit, Elena. You're the best I have!"

"If you truly thought that, you wouldn't have needed to hire Jonathan, sir." My tight-lipped sarcastic smile says more than enough as I take a few steps back, silently high-fiving myself for actually saying what I want to say and being so damn proud of myself for it.

"I'll have my portfolios delivered to you so you can hand them out at the meeting this morning. We have plenty of qualified account managers who can maintain those accounts without any issues."

"What about the Ford account?" Bryan's tone is frantic now. "Christian wrote a watertight clause in that contract that *you* were the one on the account or it's void."

Smart man.

"I'm certain Jonathan is qualified to renegotiate a contract." I shrug.

But he won't succeed.

I switch my purse from one shoulder to the other before making my final descent out of his office. As I grab the door handle, I stop and turn. Bryan is staring down at his desk, dazed and probably bothered, but he's still not stopping me. Because he doesn't care enough to. He cares about the image of whatever he thinks Jonathan brings to the company, and whatever Matt brought when he hired him.

Bryan has always wanted me to *help* on projects but never lead them. And it's time for me to take the lead.

"Goodbye, Bryan." I exit through his door one last time before going to my office, packing up my personal belongings, and taking one last ride down the elevator. The descent is slow, surreal, but powerful. Because for the first time, I took charge.

And it felt so good.

When I arrive home, I expect to see Jake, but not Christian, so I am surprised when both the guys are there. Apparently, Christian had a few video calls he could do remotely, so he decided to do that from our house while helping Jake fix some things in the house that he's been slacking on since he needed another pair of hands to help him.

They are both shocked to see me walk through the door so

early, and with a box in my hands. Needless to say, they both absolutely freak out.

"What did he do?!" Jake bellows out as he storms toward me, taking the box from my hand.

Christian's phone is in his hand, ready to dial whatever secret service assassin guy he has on call.

"No, nothing like that, you guys." I can't help but laugh, given the odd sequence of events from this morning. Well, quite frankly, this entire past week.

I summarize what happened, telling them about Matt resigning and Bryans excitement over *Jonathan*, unable to hide the nasally undertone when saying his name.

"Jonathan Jones?" Christian asks. "About six feet, platinum blonde hair, big teeth?" Christian shows all his teeth, squinting his face.

"That is definitely him." I giggle, because Christian couldn't have described him any better.

"What a mistake he made." Christian shakes his head.

It finally starts to settle in. I quit my job. Without anything lined up. I've never been without a job. Ever. I've worked since I was fifteen years old, sometimes multiple jobs. The job market isn't terrible, but it's not great, either.

I look over at Jake, and he doesn't seem to care at all or feel any stress. He smiles at me like he couldn't be prouder that I stuck it to Bryan like that. He strides towards me, wrapping his arm around my waist, and pulls me into him. Nuzzling into my neck, he kisses my pulse point and trails his lips up towards the shell of my ear, nibbling on the lobe, fuzzing all my thoughts.

"I'll start looking tomorrow and put some feelers out there," I whisper aloud as I close my eyes, trying to focus, but he's making it so very difficult.

Christian's neck snaps, almost in half, as he looks my way.

"No, you most certainly will not. You'll come run XConnect. Director of Operations. I already had the offer written up for you when our contract with Ashford and Stephens was complete."

"What?" I squeal.

"I can email it to you right now so you can stop annoying me with all that 'putting feelers out there' talk."

Jake looks at Christian and back at me with a *don't look at me* face, putting his hands up in surrender.

I open my mouth to push back, but Christian puts his hand up and starts to walk away.

"Do not fight me on this. You will not win."

Did he just use his professional voice on me?

Before I can speak again, the doorbell rings.

What the hell?

I stalk to the door, flustered, even though I shouldn't be. Christian is offering me a great opportunity, and I know that I earned it. It just feels too easy.

But, I also know how much I can bring to XConnect if it is my full focus, and now I'm starting to feel excited.

I can't show him that, though. I have to play a little hard-to-get.

As I open the front door, I gasp when Cruz stands there. His feet planted firmly into my "Hello There" welcome mat with a box of his own belongings in tow.

"Did Bryan fire you?"

He cocks his head to the side and looks at me like I'm the dumbest person in the entire United States.

"Are you kidding me?"

"Then why are you here with your personal belongings in a box?" I ask, popping my hip.

"I quit. The box I'm holding on your doorstep is for dramatics, because you left me behind and didn't fucking tell me you were quitting."

I hold the door open so he can pass through. As he passes by, I close the door and both Christian and Jake appear from the other room.

"Oh, good," Christian says as he looks at Cruz and his box. "I just hired her as my new Director, so welcome to Ford Enterprises, or more specifically, XConnect."

Cruz's jaw drops and looks at me, offended. "Were you going to say anything?"

I just shrug and smile because why not? I'm on a roll today.

His shoulders drop.

"Come here." Holding my arms out.

As he walks over, I can't help but smile as he circles his arms around me for a bear hug.

"Thank you, Cruz. You know, I don't deserve you."

"I know." His smug smile returns.

"Are we doing this?" I ask.

"Oh, we're doing this," he replies.

As he steps back, I leave one arm draped over his shoulder, keeping us locked together because we're partners through and through.

"We'll take your offer, Mr. Ford."

"It wasn't a question, but that's great." Christian's voice is as intense as the look he is beaming through me. Jake is in the corner of the room, leaning up against a wall with his arms crossed over his chest.

Cruz recognizes the lion's den he is currently stuck in and his lips purse as he glances at me.

"I believe I have somewhere to be." He kisses my cheek and darts directly for the front door as he gestures to his box. "You'll have these delivered to where they need to be, yes? Text me where I need to be and when and I'll be there. Ciao!"

The click of the door closing is like that starting pistol at the beginning of a race. Christian peels apart his button-up shirt, shrugging it off his shoulders as Jake one-handedly grabs his t-shirt from over his head, tearing it off. Both men stalk towards me in a synchronized step.

"She's mine," Jake calls.

"Mine first," Christian rebuttals.

I take a few cautious steps back before turning around and rushing up the stairs. I smile ear to ear as my two men chase me, court me, and worship me. Making me feel more wanted, more desired, and more alive than I ever knew I could.

EPILOGUE
CHRISTIAN

3 Months Later

I've run meetings with executives all over the country. I've met incredibly powerful people in entertainment and politics. I've had to present in front of thousands of people. But nothing, and I mean nothing, compares to the pressure and the high, of filling out sexual desires for our fantasy jars.

Jake's desire–*to watch his wife*–came out of Elena pulling that out of his fantasy jar, which led to the night she met me. It couldn't have worked out better for any of us, being that we have gotten into this working relationship that truly makes sense for all of us.

But now, I have my own jar to stuff full of desires. No holds barred.

They said they would consider any desire, they always do, but if anyone feels uncomfortable, we don't do it.

Seems simple enough.

There is a level of trust to get to, in order to confess to hidden desires that someone has wanted to try to experiment or explore. I think with any partner it would. There's judgment that could happen between partners if someone is stunned by some dark, deep desire that you fantasize about. But with them, I don't worry.

I trust both of them explicitly. Even with that trust, it was still difficult to share some of those and put them out in the open.

The first few I added were fairly basic. Elena and I, going to a sex club, with Jake watching in the crowd. They admitted to me that this happened at the bar the first night we met, unbeknownst to me. Although we never had sex, and since I didn't know Jake was watching at the time, that doesn't count in my eyes. This time I want to experience it with Elena, knowing he's watching us.

Elena might actually stab me with one of her unusually large high heels for this one, but I wrote it down, anyway. And all I wrote was, DP. Because Jake and I taking her at the same time, that is something that I have fantasized about for as long as I can remember.

Another one... Elena edging us both at the same time. I envision us tied up, restrained and at a complete loss of power. I've never been edged before, and as horrible as the idea sounds, it also sounds so goddamn sexy.

When I look back on all my desires, I realize they all have some semblance that allows us all some variation of control. Either having it or giving it up, and that appears to be the common denominator in my fantasies.

The balance of power between all of us.

So, here we are now. Nervous as hell as Elena reaches in my fantasy jar to pull one out.

The first one she's ever picked.

I can't remember the last time I felt so nervous.

Of course, I fake it well. I'm sitting on the couch, stoic as hell. One arm wrapped around my chest, using it as a base for my other arm as I cover my mouth with my hand, pulling on my upper lip.

Thinking about it, this is actually a tell of mine that no one is really aware of, showing a sign of my nerves. But, I like to pretend I'm just in deep thought.

Elena, painfully slow-like the goddamn tease that she is-pulls one out. It's folded over a couple times and my eyes trail it like it's an unpinned grenade, except it's my heart seconds away from combustion. She holds it up to the light, like she's trying to peek into something she shouldn't be, then looks at me with a smile.

"You're nervous." She calls me on my bullshit immediately.

There goes the whole 'no one is really aware of' thought.

"I am not nervous, Elena."

Jake's lips lift up in a smug as hell smirk, and I'd like to smack it off his face.

He probably knows exactly where I'm at, mentally with nerves.

"What does it say, baby?" Jake asks, his impatience showing.

She folds open the note at the pace of a goddamn sloth. The crinkle of the paper travels through the quiet room as it splays open, the sound drawn out by what feels like my impending demise. She silently reads the note and the corner of her lips turn up, smashing them together, thinning them to nothing.

Christ, the anxiety.

Her eyes lift from the note, to Jake, to me. She bites the corner of her lip, folds the note back up as she steps towards Jake. Kisses him on the cheek, then to me and does the same.

"I'll be right back." Unable to hide her amused tone.

"What?" I spit out.

"Where are you going?" Jake asks.

She scurries up the stairs quickly, ignoring our questions, and Jake backhands me in the middle of my chest.

"What is it? Lingerie? Sex toys? Is she bringing something down?" he asks.

"I... I don't know." I try to think of which fantasy it could be and what she would need from the room.

My mind flashes with all the fantasies, and I can't seem to figure out which one she pulled. It could be anything at this point, and the unknown is killing me.

I think Jake feels the same, due to the relentless bouncing of his leg next to mine.

Finally, after a goddamn century, she calls out, "I'm ready."

My neck swivels to Jake, his to mine.

"Whatever it is, it's happening in the bedroom," Jakes says, as he pushes himself off the couch.

He's always so calm, collected, and put together. He's one of the most easygoing and patient personalities I've ever met. But, I've found it's just another form of control for him, emotionally being able to manage any situation. That strength is showing now, as it usually does, but as I've gotten to know his tells, right now, he's anxious. Excited.

I follow behind him as we head up to the room. He turns into the doorway first, then stops dead in his tracks.

I step in behind him and glance around the room. The bedroom is lit only by the dimmest setting of the bedroom lighting and there is a chair–that is usually not there–placed in the corner of the room.

A noise grabs our attention, and we turn to see Elena stepping out of the closet. She looks like a fucking goddess wearing a black lace nightie, which is completely see-through. She's braless. Pantyless. Barefoot and fucking gorgeous.

Hanging off her pointer finger is a pair of handcuffs, as she elegantly swings them back and forth in a torturous rhythm.

"Oh, shit..." escapes my lips as I palm my face and pinch the bridge of my nose.

I now know which one she picked, and by the look on Jake's face. He thinks those cuffs are for her... not for him.

"Take off your clothes. Hands behind your back and cuff them to the chair," she instructs Jake as she steps toward him, placing the metal restraint in his hand.

His eyebrows furrowed together for the briefest of moments. He looks down at the cuffs, half hanging off the foundation of his palm, then peeks over to the chair sitting at the corner of the room, in perfect alignment with the bed, then back to Elena.

His face falls.

He gives himself a form of whiplash when he turns to look at me, putting everything together.

"You want me to get cucked?" His shock is obvious in his question. I reply with just a lopsided smile because, as much as I know he hates this idea, he fucking loves it just as much.

Elena told me she has had fantasies of tying Jake up, which she has shared with him too, that is what initially gave me the fantasy for myself. So, I know they both are in for this, as much as I am.

"You do like to watch." I respond back, giving him a pat on the back, as I strip off my shirt and walk towards the bed.

There's a brief pause and a slight shake of his head and he begins to undress, walking over to the chair. By the time he reaches it, he's left in only his underwear.

"You know, I can sit here... without the cuffs," he tries to negotiate and maintain some power.

"What would be the fun in that?" Elena replies as she follows right behind him. "These are sexy. Leave them on." He lets out a slight hiss as she pulls on the waistband of his black Calvin Klein boxer briefs, and it snaps back onto his skin.

She presses onto the top of his shoulder, guiding him down into the chair. He forms an X with his arms, placing them behind his back and around the open middle section of the back of the chair.

Elena leans down and reaches around his current torture device. The distinct sound of metal on metal zipping together echoes through the room, and just the sight of her restraining him has me hardening behind the denim of my jeans.

I lean back, pressing my hand into the comforter of the bed, as I use my other hand to unbutton my pants. Tugging on the corner, the zipper splays open easily, exposing the dark fabric of my own briefs.

Elena cups his jaw, pressing a soft kiss to his lips, then sits back on her heels as she kneels beside him. Jake peeks over his shoulder behind himself as he tugs into the cuffs, the metal clashes against the chair creating a loud clang throughout the room.

"You have to stay completely quiet." She caresses her finger over the top of his thigh. "Do you understand?"

He takes a commanding inhale, then releases his steady breath and nods.

As frustrated as he might be–being restrained like he is–his tight briefs do nothing to hide his arousal. His cock is engorged, the length jutting up to his abs, the black cotton hugging the crown, hiding nothing. He shifts his hips, lifting them slightly off the seat, a failed attempt at some kind of friction.

"Crawl to me, Ellie." My voice is gravelly and thick. My throat feels like a desert, dying for a thirst that only she can quench.

She listens, as she places one hand and knee in front of each other and slowly crawls towards me. I have a direct eye line to her stunning, lustful face, her black laced cleavage, and a restrained Jake in the backdrop of my view.

Jake's desperate eyes are on Elena, as she slithers further away from him and closer to me. Stopping in front of me, she sits back on her heels and places her hands over the top of my jeans.

Our eyes meet as she presents herself to me with a foxy smile and a sparkle in her eye.

"Take out my cock," I demand.

Tucking her hands underneath my thighs, she tugs slightly, silently guiding me to stand up. I push into my feet, to a standing position. My hips are now placed directly in front of her, as she peers up at me from her kneeled position.

Without taking her eyes off mine, she tucks her fingers into the waistband and pulls my jeans down, taking my boxers with them. I easily step out of them as she pulls the stonewash fabric from my feet, and now I'm completely bare in front of her.

The exhilarated chaos in her gorgeous eyes is a burning blue lava, and fucking undeniable.

Jesus Christ, she's so goddamn sexy.

My eyes glance over to check on Jake. His jaw is clenched, his breath is heavy and his eyes are pure pools of dark, desperate desire.

I gently run my fingers through her hair, tucking a rebel strand behind her ear. Which is pointless because the sexual craving takes over and I urgently grip a handful of the top of her hair, pulling her up so her lips align with my gloriously hard cock.

"Show me your tongue."

She opens her mouth, pushing her tongue out and over her bottom lip. Gripping the base of my cock with my other hand, I tap the crown on top of her flattened tongue, feeding her the uncontrolled precum that has inevitably leaked out of the tip.

She hmms as her tongue retracts back into her mouth, swallowing what I gave her.

"Jake probably needs some help with that, too." Tipping my chin towards him.

I keep the grip on my cock, rubbing back and forth, and the

friction feels like heaven as I witness her crawl back to Jake. Our view is now reversed and the lust in his eyes is more desperate than ever.

Using her delicate hands to pull his cock from the split in his boxer briefs, his distress is obvious. I feel as if his teeth will shatter into a million pieces, at least by the look of the strain in his jaw. He's shifting his body and his hips, as Elena touches him, silently begging for more. He attempts to tug on the restraints, but in a manner consistent with Jake's typical control.

And his cock. Christ. It's completely engorged. The crown thinned and pink, and screaming for attention.

His brows pinch together as she leans over his lap, wrapping her lips softly around the tip, cleaning it off with a pop before it bounces back towards his stomach.

I'm impressed with his resolve when his body flinches and his lips smash together to withhold a grunt.

"Mmmm, you both taste so good." Her voice is laced with pure sex and pleasure.

"Come back to me, Ellie."

This time she stands, taking the few steps she needs to place herself in front of me.

Releasing the hold I have on my cock, I replace it with hers. She tugs, rubs, and jerks me off as we stand facing each other, unobstructedly on display for Jake.

I trail my fingertip over her collarbone, then flick the thin strap of her lingerie to drape it over her shoulder, then do the same with the other. The fabric makes its last attempt to hug her body, but ultimately defies her, as it fails and falls down to her waist.

Her breasts are fully exposed, and I reach in to pinch her nipple. She gasps, gripping my cock tighter like she needs it to keep standing.

I glance over at Jake and as much as I'm sure he hates his

hands being imprisoned and the inability to touch himself, I've never seen a desire like he has now. His cock is so fucking hard and precum is actually dripping down the length of his cock. More than I've ever seen.

I reach down, slipping my fingers between her slit, and she's just as soaked.

Moaning floods the room as I rub small circles over her clit. She's still holding my cock, but forgets to continue stroking as I overwhelm her senses.

My finger continues a punishing tempo over her sensitive bud as my tongue trails over her skin. Leaning down, I alternate between flicking and sucking over the hardened peak of her perfect nipples.

Without moving my neck, my eyes spy over to Jake. His anguish is, admittedly, a turn on, and I'm unsure of my feelings on that. I love teasing Elena, but teasing Jake like this.

Well, it's definitely a new kink.

I'm ready to admit that to him out loud, but before I can say anything, Elena asks, "How badly do you want to tell him what to do to me right now?"

Showing his control, he just takes in a deep breath and releases, slowly. His eyes continue to laser into us, but he remains completely quiet as Elena instructed earlier.

The rise and fall of Elena's chest is evident as her breath heavies, her moans begin to mix with a few words and I can tell she's getting close.

Teasing her, I withdraw my fingers from her pussy and lick the arousal off my fingers. She tastes so fucking sweet, like a tropical paradise and I'm desperate for more.

Grabbing her waist, I turn her away from me, then pull her into my lap as I sit down on the edge of the bed.

Both her and I are full frontal, facing Jake. Our direct eye line to each other is like a death stare match as I spread Elena's legs open over mine. I feather my middle finger through her slit and she gasps, begging for more.

My impossibly hard cock is pressed up against the back of Elena as she rolls her hips, creating friction on both my cock and against my finger, as she begins to chase her orgasm.

"Oh god, Jake. He's going to make me come."

His eyes go to the back of his head as he looks up to the ceiling, taking another deep inhale. His hips buck in his chair and he's totally wretched.

I grab her hips, lifting her up. Her body floats above my legs as my cock juts out underneath her.

"Sit on my cock, Ellie." I demand.

She uses her hand to line herself up and inches down on top of me, removing all the space between us. Her arousal is the perfect lubricant as I slide into her, and her pussy chokes me instantly.

Unable to suppress my groaning, my sounds echo through the room and it affects Jake. A lot. He moans with me, squeezing his eyes shut as he tips his head forward, avoiding the view, to help his control.

"Watch me fuck your wife, Jake. Open your fucking eyes."

His eyes snap open, looking directly at me, then to where my cock is invading her pussy. He's just a few feet away from us, straight on, and can see everything I want him to see. I press my fingers on her clit and continue to piston my cock in and out of her throbbing pussy.

"Do you feel how hard my cock is for you, Ellie? Tell him. Tell him how hard my cock is and how badly you want to come all over it."

"Fuck, oh God," Elena screams.

The sight must be majestic.

Ellie naked, except for the black lace top that now hugs her waist, riding my cock that's dripping with her arousal as I drive in and out of her.

Her moans turn violent as her release barrels through her. As usual, she screams our names. His name, my name, God's. Her sounds have always done something to me and this is where I lose all my control.

She's still clenching around me as I look over to Jake. His jaw is slacked and his lips forming a dramatic "O". His abs are contracting as he presses his hips up and down in slow but frantic movements.

"Fuck," he whispers. Still trying to remain quiet, but losing the battle. "Please."

He begged.

He's fucking begging. Jesus, fuck. Shit.

My cock explodes. I roar something inaudible and my uncontrolled sounds are a side effect of the most intense orgasm I've ever had. Ellie takes advantage of my weakness as she rolls her hips vigorously over my cock, milking me dry.

"Oh fuck, someone please... Please, touch me," he begs further.

Elena and I both look at Jake, stunned by his desperate plea for anyone to touch him and beyond turned on by his begging.

And then Jake, Jake... fucking... comes.

Hands bound behind his back with nothing but air touching his pulsing cock. Cum sprays over his abs, and up like a spurting fountain, landing on his leg and dripping over his cock.

He moans and swears through the uninhibited, overwhelming eruption and his sound waves do just as much to me as hers does.

After what felt like an endless orgasm, he throws his head back, clearly exhausted. I withdraw from Elena and she stands up slowly, reaching for a hand towel she brilliantly placed on the nightstand earlier.

I fall back onto the bed, my cock still half hard, juts up to the ceiling and, holy fuck, I'm spent. I take a moment to catch my breath before grabbing my briefs and putting them on.

Elena has already cleaned off both herself and Jake. She keys the cuffs, releasing his wrists, and he rounds his fingers over them, giving them a tender rub.

"You fucker." His violent words don't match his satiated tone.

"You loved it," I reply.

Elena wraps herself around Jake, tucking herself into his chest. I lean in behind her, kissing the back of her head, in what is inevitably a moment of serenity for all of us, after we do anything sexual.

"I decided... I like the fantasy jars," I admit out loud to both of them.

"Your jar is going to be exiled, banished, voted off the island," Jake replies, but again, he can't hide his smirk.

"Nope. We are picking another one. A-SAP," Elena, our judge and jury decides.

"But not this weekend, since he's going to his bachelor party," I remind her.

"I don't have to go," Jake replies, trying to get out of his own belated bachelor party, like he's been since it's been planned.

"Yes, yes, you do. The guys are way too excited about this Vegas trip and he," she points at me, "is staying with me, like we all agreed. It's going to be a great weekend."

EXTENDED EPILOGUE
ELENA

"Hello," Jake's raspy voice barely comes through the phone.

"I've waited long enough. I need to hear what happened," I demand, speaking too fast and too loud for anyone's liking this morning.

That's what happens when your husband, of over three years, leaves for Vegas to attend his belated bachelor party and leaves you at home to wake up early on a Sunday with nothing but a too large pot of coffee and bad ideas.

At least Christian stayed over to keep me company, per my husband's request, of course. We teased him all night with half naked, and fully naked, pictures of us pretty much in every position that Christian decided to take me in last night.

Quite unusual for a groom in question, but there is nothing ordinary about our relationship, so there's that.

Over the past few months, we've navigated through learning how to have this type of *relationship,* and we're still figuring out things every day. There are still boundaries we mistakenly cross and desires we all have had a difficult time sharing, but all things considered, it's really been quite perfect.

Jake still loves to watch, and Christian loves to be watched, but based on what I've seen in Christian, his fantasies will pull all of us further out of our comfort zones. We tease Jake often, which is one of my favorite things, edging him for hours throughout the day until we see each other at night. It's not every night, but most nights, and although they both have fairly defined roles in our relationship, the guys have gotten more comfortable sharing me together. When that happens, the balance of power changes, and I see an alpha side in both of them that always sends me careening into another world.

I've also learned more about communicating in the last three months than I have my whole life, and it feels really good to be able to express myself. Both sexually and emotionally.

Physically, that comes naturally to all three of us. Almost like it was always meant to be this way.

"So, I'm waiting," I tell my husband impatiently as I look over at Christian, as he shakes his head swiping through the Sunday paper. I swear if he didn't have the sex drive of a rabbit, I would say he's the reincarnation of an eighty-year-old man who time traveled from the 1920s.

"Okay, okay. Hold on." Ruffled sounds and a painful groan distantly pull through the speaker. "I'm far too old for this shit anymore," Jake complains.

So I have two old men, apparently.

"We need to vote on who is the wildest. Tell us everything," I insist as I press the speaker button so Christian can listen in.

"I'm not sure voting is required on this one. I think we already have a winner." Jake's tone is unequivocal. Certain, yet something behind it is unsettled.

I turn to face Christian, both of us curious and confused, just waiting for him to continue. But he doesn't.

"Oookay... what does that mean?" A nervous giggle escapes me as to who could have unanimously won and how.

"Hudson got married."

THANK YOU FOR READING!!

I am a self-published author. If you loved this book, please consider taking the time to leave a review as it helps me tremendously!

www.berlinwick.com
Please sign up for my newsletter to keep up to date on my upcoming releases and receive exclusive content!

THE PROMISES WE BREAK
Hudson's Story

Ember

It was supposed to be one night with one incredibly handsome stranger. A night of giving into temptation and forgetting all my inhibitions. Instead, it ends with wedding vows and promises of "I do".

But it turns out, this is exactly what we need for the sake of both our blooming careers. Especially after my new boss tasks me with the opening of a hot new lifestyle club.

Hudson needs me to wear the title of *wife* for the benefit of his career, and I need him to teach me *the lifestyle* to solidify mine. Adding sex lessons to our agreement surely won't complicate things, right?

We're blurring the lines of business and pleasure, unable to avoid the contagious desire between us. But I need to keep this strictly professional and emotion-free; it's the only way I can get through it.

Forever is not what I signed up for, and there is no other way that this can end except with divorce papers and broken promises.

Hudson

I am never letting her go.
One year.
I have one year to convince her that our future *is* forever.

ABOUT THE AUTHOR

Berlin was raised in a tiny town in North Idaho who moved to the Bay Area, California, where she still resides with her husband and two boys. Her bucket list items include skydiving, attending the Oscars, becoming a New York Time best-selling author, and cruising the world for retirement. She loves writing and reading, ANY and ALL kinds of romance novels, and loves engaging in the booksta community. You can find her most active on Instagram!

www.ingramcontent.com/pod-product-compliance
Lightning Source LLC
Chambersburg PA
CBHW032256230625
28635CB00006B/160